History of Crime and Criminal Justice
David R. Johnson and Jeffrey S. Adler, Series Editors

PRISON WORK

A TALE OF THIRTY YEARS IN THE CALIFORNIA DEPARTMENT OF CORRECTIONS

William Richard Wilkinson

Edited by
John C. Burnham and Joseph F. Spillane

The Ohio State University Press
Columbus

Copyright © 2005 by The Ohio State University.
All rights reserved.

Library of Congress Cataloging-in-Publication Data

Wilkinson, William Richard.
    Prison work : a tale of thirty years in the California Department of
Corrections / William Richard Wilkinson ; edited by John C. Burnham
and Joseph F. Spillane.
        p. cm. — (History of crime and criminal justice)
    Includes index.
    ISBN 0-8142-1001-5 (cloth : alk. paper) — ISBN 0-8142-5143-9
(pbk. : alk. paper) — ISBN 0-8142-9079-5 (cd-rom)
    1. Prisons—California—History—20th century. 2. Corrections—
California—History—20th century. 3. Correctional personnel—
California—Attitudes. I. Burnham, John C. (John Chynoweth), 1929–
II. Spillane, Joseph F. III. Title. IV. History of crime and criminal justice
series.
    HV9475.C2W55 2005
    365'.92—dc22

                                        2005007147

Cover design by Dan O'Dair
Type set in Adobe Garamond
Printed by Thomson-Shore, Inc.

The paper used in this publication meets the minimum requirements
of the American National Standard for Information Sciences—
Permanence of Paper for Printed Library materials. ANSI Z39.48–1992.

9 8 7 6 5 4 3 2 1

CONTENTS

LIST OF ILLUSTRATIONS

Editors' Introduction

This is a unique work: an oral memoir describing how someone—William Richard Wilkinson—did the actual work of keeping custody of inmates in a large state prison system.

Dick Wilkinson served in the California Department of Corrections from 1951 to 1981, and it is his narrative that follows. He began as a correctional officer and then advanced to sergeant and lieutenant. Here, then, is the nuanced account of someone who had a sustained, successful career on the front lines in penal institutions.

His voice is of course the voice of a single individual. These are memories and impressions, and other witnesses to the same events may have differing memories and impressions. Much time has passed since the events described in this memoir occurred, and human recall is always flawed to some extent. Wilkinson's own evaluation is very modest:

> I have been out of the business for twenty years. So everything I am telling you is at least twenty years old, or more than twenty years. But you have to include the factor of my memory, and, also, I have nothing to compare with today—other than the few things I hear from the people I still know in the business. That is not very substantial. However, I am continuously told that I could not work in the business today. And I do not dispute that. I don't think I could work today, either.

These are, therefore, honest memories, presented as Dick Wilkinson presented them. He has been able to verify some basic details from his own personal records, and the editors have tried to verify others.

The Right Places, the Right Times

Dick Wilkinson's career spans one of the most important periods in American correctional history. Much has already been written on post–World War II corrections in America. A large and useful social science literature came of age during these decades.[1] Influential prison administrators, writing in the language of progressive reform, also left historians a substantial written record.[2] Finally, during the latter half of Wilkinson's tenure in the California Department of Corrections, there was a flourishing market in prison writing by prisoners, perhaps the most active and important period of inmate publication in the modern history of corrections.[3]

Rarely, though, was the voice of the correctional officer heard directly, especially that of the successful career correctional worker.

This memoir offers such a voice, and one is tempted to conclude that no historian could have invented a career in corrections that captures so many important developments.

Wilkinson's tenure began in 1951 at the height of the influence of what Francis Allen called "the rehabilitative ideal."[4] Although this ideal has no precise definition, the ideal generally emphasized the quasi-therapeutic role of the criminal justice system in identifying and treating the causes of criminal behavior.[5]

Few states embodied this ideal more fully than did California, where commitment to, and implementation of, progressive penology was rivaled

---

1. For a broad overview of the state of academic knowledge at the end of the twentieth century, see *Prisons,* ed. Michael Tonry and Joan Petersilia (Chicago: University of Chicago Press, 1999).

2. A brief listing of important works by prison administrators of the era would include: James Bennett, *I Chose Prison* (New York: Alfred A. Knopf, 1970); Clinton T. Duffy, *The San Quentin Story* (New York: Doubleday, 1950); James A. Johnston, *Alcatraz Island Prison and the Men Who Live There* (New York: Charles Scribner's Sons, 1949); Richard A. McGee, *Prisons and Politics* (Lexington, MA: Lexington Books, 1981); Tom Murton and Joe Hyams, *Accomplices to the Crime* (New York: Grove Press, 1970); Joseph E. Ragen, *Inside the World's Toughest Prison* (Springfield, IL: Charles C. Thomas, 1962); Walter M. Wallack, *The Training of Prison Guards in the State of New York* (New York: Teachers College, Columbia University, 1938).

3. A good introduction to this literature is H. Bruce Franklin, *The Victim as Criminal and Artist: Literature from the American Prison* (New York: Oxford University Press, 1978). In reviewing the literature, Franklin concludes (236) that *The Autobiography of Malcolm X* (1965) began the modern, politicized prisoner account. Franklin's *Prison Writing in 20th-Century America* (New York: Penguin Books, 1998) offers many more examples of the genre. California produced more than its fair share of prisoner-authors, counting Malcolm Braly, Edward Bunker, Caryl Chessman, and George Jackson among the best known. We have, however, not discovered any inmate accounts from any of the institutions in which Wilkinson served that covered the times while he was working in the particular institution.

4. See Francis A. Allen, *The Decline of the Rehabilitative Ideal* (New Haven, CT: Yale University Press, 1981).

5. For a more detailed treatment of what this ideal meant, see Michael Tonry, "Unthought Thoughts: The Influence of Changing Sensibilities on Penal Policies," in *Mass Imprisonment: Social Causes and Consequences,* ed. David Garland (Thousand Oaks, CA: Sage Publications, 2001). See also American Correctional Association, *Manual of Correctional Standards* (New York: ACA, 1954), and the subsequent 1959 revision.

Map of California showing locations of Department of Corrections institutions (1955)
Source: *Correctional Employees Training Manual No. 1: Introduction to State Correctional Service* (Sacramento: California Department of Corrections, 1955), 48

only by New York and the federal Bureau of Prisons. Although California had been the site of reform experiments since the nineteenth century, its modern "rehabilitative regime" was relatively new when Wilkinson began his career. Governor Culbert B. Olson had removed the old state prison board in 1940 and appointed Clinton Duffy as the reform warden of San Quentin Prison.[6] Olson's successor, Governor Earl Warren, completed the

6. See Kevin Starr, *Endangered Dreams: The Great Depression in California* (New York: Oxford University Press, 1996).

process in 1944 with the appointment of Richard A. McGee as the director of a new California Department of Corrections.[7]

The Prison Reorganization Act of 1944 also established the California Adult Authority.[8] The responsibility of the Adult Authority under the act highlights the characteristics of progressive corrections. It operated a Guidance Center to which all prisoners were sent for diagnosis and classification. After several weeks, they were assigned to a specific California prison that matched their security and rehabilitative needs. After an inmate had served six months, the Adult Authority was to fix the term of duration of imprisonment. Finally, the Adult Authority functioned as the California parole board, determining when inmates would be released. California's indeterminate sentencing structure gave the Adult Authority almost unlimited discretion in fixing terms of imprisonment and setting release dates.[9]

No individual institution embodied the spirit of reform better than the place where Wilkinson began his career, the California Institution for Men at Chino (usually referred to simply as Chino). Intended for younger, first-time offenders, or for those convicted of less serious criminal violations, Chino already boasted a nationally known program when Wilkinson came on staff in 1951. The institution featured a range of not-for-profit industrial shops, vocational training, basic education, and an institutional farm, and each inmate was expected to take on regular work and school assignments.

Wilkinson's first boss was Kenyon Scudder, superintendent of Chino since it opened in 1940. Often overlooked today, Scudder's 1952 book, *Prisoners Are People,* established him as one of most notable exponents of the rehabilitative orientation.[10] Sociologist Stanton Wheeler worked at Chino as a summer intern in the classification department in 1949, and he recalled the homely lessons in personal responsibility that constituted Scudder's vision. Wheeler described "the simple principles of Chino" as

7. On the work of McGee, see Daniel Glaser, *Preparing Convicts for Law-Abiding Lives: The Pioneering Penology of Richard A. McGee* (Albany: SUNY Press, 1995).

8. The special legislative session of 1944, called by Governor Earl Warren, was remarkable for its accomplishments. See John Aubrey Douglas, "Earl Warren's New Deal," *Journal of Policy History* 12 (2000): 473–512.

9. For a good early description, see California Adult Authority, *Philosophy, Principles, and Program of the California Adult Authority* (Sacramento: California Department of Corrections, 1945).

10. Kenyon J. Scudder, *Prisoners Are People* (Garden City, NY: Doubleday & Company, 1952). There was even a movie version of the book, *Unchained.* See also Kenyon J. Scudder and Kenneth S. Beam, *The Twenty-Billion Dollar Challenge: A National Program for Delinquency Prevention* (New York: G. P. Putnam's Sons, 1961), and Kenyon J. Scudder, *Between the Dark and the Daylight* (Berkeley: University of California, Bancroft Library, Regional Oral History Office, 1972).

"everyday, common sense decency."[11] Wilkinson's memoir offers the first glimpse of Scudder at work and evocatively highlights the extent to which the reform regime was the product of—and probably dependent on—the force of Scudder's own dynamic personality.[12]

In 1955, Wilkinson, now a sergeant, moved on to the California Medical Facility at Vacaville when it opened that year. Indeed, he helped open up the new facility and provides a fascinating glimpse of what that process meant.

The opening of CMF marks, in some respects, both the high-water mark for the rehabilitative ideal in California and a new direction for that ideal. Scudder's Chino focused on providing education and work for those young men "who seem to offer the best prospects."[13] In contrast, CMF was built on a medical rather than punishment model. It was a highly special-ized institution designed to treat and cure mentally disturbed inmates, and its programs focused on psychotherapy. Wilkinson shows the reader the day-to-day life of a penal institution more often described through assess-ments of specialized treatment programs, not the function of incarcera-tion.[14]

Wilkinson spent more of his career at CMF than anywhere, and his account reveals some of the virtues, and some of the limitations, of the medical model. Above all, this account reminds the reader that CMF was always a prison, whatever the loftier ambitions of its medical personnel. The contradictions between treatment and prison custody became fodder for an aggressive critique of the therapeutic prison that was already well developed when Wilkinson left in 1977.[15]

Wilkinson's final institution, Soledad Prison, brought him to the other

11. Stanton Wheeler, "Review Essay: Sentencing Matters," *Criminal Justice Ethics* 16 (Summer/Fall, 1997): 46–51.

12. The only extended treatment of Scudder's work may be found in sections of Joseph W. Eaton's *Stone Walls Not a Prison Make: The Anatomy of Planned Administrative Change* (Springfield, IL: C. C. Thomas, 1962).

13. California Adult Authority, *Philosophy, Principles, and Program.*

14. Glaser observes that the growing influence of Norman Fenton and J. Douglas Grant, leading advocates of group therapy and psychotherapy, in the Department of Corrections led to most of the research and evaluation efforts being devoted to psychotherapeutic pro-grams. The result is that we have a much better sense of how these programs functioned than of Chino's work and education programs, and our sense of what rehabilitation meant in California is similarly skewed in the psychotherapeutic direction. Glaser, *Preparing Convicts for Law-Abiding Lives,* 127. One recent reconsideration of the rehabilitative period in California corrections is Volker Janssen, "Democratic Visions behind Bars: California's Experiments in Therapeutic Penology, 1945 to 1968," paper presented to the 119th Annual Meeting, American Historical Association, Seattle, 2005.

15. The critique of the psychotherapeutic model played a large part in the attack on the "rehabilitative" prison. Representative examples include: American Friends Service Committee, *Struggle for Justice* (New York: Hill and Wang, 1971); Jessica Mitford, *Kind and*

end of the California postwar prison experience. Like Chino and CMF, Soledad started out as part of California's midcentury commitment to the rehabilitative ideal. Soledad was self-consciously designed to avoid the negative aspects of "Big House" prison architecture. Instead of a grim, castlelike design, Soledad featured a more modern design. Soledad Prison was actually three distinct institutions, reflecting the prevailing view in corrections that smaller institutions would create a more rehabilitative environment.

John Irwin remembers that, in its first years, Soledad "was a very peaceful and orderly institution . . . the general mood among prisoners was tolerance and relative friendliness."[16] By the time Wilkinson arrived at Soledad in 1977, any mood of enthusiasm or hope had long since dissipated. Instead, the prison and the entire Department of Corrections were still feeling the effects of the tumultuous previous decade. The year 1970 was Soledad's meltdown year, with the killings of a correctional officer and three inmates, prosecution of the "Soledad Brothers" for killing the officer, racial hostilities, an inmate strike, outside investigations, and the publication of George Jackson's *Soledad Brother.*[17]

The prison had been in crisis for some time before 1970, torn by racial strife and violence, and under ineffective leadership. Wilkinson's memoir makes clear that Soledad remained a troubled place in the late 1970s. Wilkinson recalls, "At Soledad we felt we had a riot a month and a stabbing a week." Indeed, official reports indicated that Soledad had an "incident" rate nearly three times that of a comparable security-level facility, the California Men's Colony.[18]

All American prisons experienced tremendous change between the

---

Unusual Punishment: The Prison Business (New York: Vintage Books, 1974); Eric Olin Wright, *The Politics of Punishment: A Critical Analysis of Prisons in America* (New York: Harper & Row, 1973).

16. John Irwin, *Prisons in Turmoil* (Boston: Little, Brown, 1980). Kenneth Lamott, on the other hand, visited Soledad just after it opened and "came away . . . in a state of profound depression. I had only to walk for 50 yards or so along the great central corridor, watching the faces of the passing prisoners, to know here was another failure of well-meaning men." Kenneth Lamott, "Cruel and Usual," *Washington Post, Book World,*18 November 1973, 3.

17. Min S. Yee, *The Melancholy History of Soledad Prison, in Which a Utopian Scheme Turns Bedlam* (New York: Harper's Magazine Press, 1973). Yee dates the decline of Soledad to at least 1960. John Irwin's earlier work, *The Felon* (Englewood Cliffs, NJ: Prentice-Hall, 1970), also provides a good deal of insight into the Soledad inmates of the mid- to late 1960s. Eric Cummins, *The Rise and Fall of California's Radical Prison Movement* (Stanford: Stanford University Press, 1994), does the same for the California system as a whole, with a strong focus on San Quentin. For a flavor of 1970–1971 national reporting, see also David Holmstrom, "Political Awareness Churns Prisons," *Christian Science Monitor,* 16 November 1970, 1; Steven V. Roberts, "California's Soledad Prison: A 'Pressure Cooker' for Rage among Inmates," *New York Times,* 7 February 1971, 64.

18. John J. DiIulio Jr., *Governing Prisons: A Comparative Study of Prison Management* (New York: Free Press, 1987), esp. chap. 2.

mid-1960s and the mid-1970s. The most enduring published works on prisons and prisoners from this period all highlight rapid change as their central theme.[19] So, too, with Wilkinson's account. Chapters 4 and 5 offer an officer's-eye view of some of the most important developments in corrections: growing politicization, inmate gangs, the presence of outside interest and advocacy groups, and the prisoner-rights revolution. A theme common to Wilkinson's account and many others is the sense that the formerly closed prison system was being overwhelmed by outside influences.[20]

Finally, Wilkinson's memoir takes the reader through the end of California's rehabilitative regime. This story has been told before, and the broad outlines are clear. Richard McGee stepped down as the director of the Department of Corrections in 1961 to take the helm of the California Youth and Adult Correctional Agency, a move that removed him from the practical governance of the prison system. His successors were unable to sustain the same kind of system that McGee ran, and Ronald Reagan's gubernatorial election victory in 1966 indicated a shift away from political support for the rehabilitative regime.

California prisons were in turmoil during Raymond Procunier's tenure (1966–1972) as director of the Department of Corrections—and for some years after. From all sides of the political spectrum, the foundations of the rehabilitative approach were under attack.[21] After sixty years, the

19. Along with Irwin, *Prisons in Turmoil,* two of the best examples from this period: Leo Carroll, *Hacks, Blacks, and Cons: Race Relations in a Maximum Security Prison* (Lexington, MA: Lexington Books, 1974), and James Jacobs, *Stateville: The Penitentiary in Mass Society* (Chicago: University of Chicago Press, 1977). A contemporary account of the debates in California is William Endicott, "Prisons: Are Convicts There for Punishment or Rehabilitation?" *Los Angeles Times,* 27 March 1972, II, 3, 18. A recent account of one California prison's experience before and after these changes emphasizes the continuity of inmate experience. Rosemary Gartner and Candace Kruttschnitt, "A Brief History of Doing Time: The California Institution for Women in the 1960s and 1990s," *Law and Society Review* 38 (June 2004): 267–304. Their study challenges historians to consider more carefully just how macro-level changes in ideology and policy influence the lived prison experience.

20. A typical summary is Harold E. Williamson, *The Corrections Profession* (Newbury Park: Sage Publications, 1990), 41: "For better or worse, the closed-system nature of corrections has changed forever. Correctional agencies could, prior to the 1960s, function largely as they desired with little or no influence from external sources. Politicians and the public were content to leave agency activity to the administrators. However, with the radical changes that began in the 1960s and which related to every area of society, that autonomy was lost. Social reformers, professionals from other areas, the courts, and the public became very concerned about what happened in America's correctional agencies. Inmates, once considered to have no rights, were granted many rights as a result of new laws, reinterpretation of old laws, and new policies and procedures specified by courts."

21. The most comprehensive introduction to the critique of rehabilitation is Francis T. Cullen and Karen E. Gilbert, *Reaffirming Rehabilitation* (Cincinnati, OH: Anderson

indeterminate sentence was eliminated in 1977. In its place, the legislature adopted a scheme of largely fixed sentences. The next year, the official mission of the Department of Corrections changed from rehabilitation to punishment.[22] This was perhaps a mostly symbolic move, but it marked the end of the era of optimism.

Prison Work

While many well-known figures appear in these pages, this is not their story. Likewise, although riots and other extraordinary events are documented here, this is not a history of the spectacular. Instead, the central actors in this account are the prison workers whose daily routines defined and continue to define the institutions in which they worked and work. These are people with no particular sense of making or having made history, but this history is theirs.

There is no attempt here to paint the work of the correctional officers and middle managers in glorious terms. Indeed, Wilkinson shows little patience for what he calls the "macho" posture of the California Correctional Peace Officers Association's (CCPOA) slogan, "We walk the toughest beat in the world." Instead, we see routine work interrupted by moments of grave danger (and some moments of humor).

We cannot pretend that Wilkinson is somehow representative of correctional officers and middle management generally, or even in California during his thirty years of service. The mere fact that his somewhat casual decision to take up prison work turned into a thirty-year career sets Wilkinson apart from many of his fellow officers. Wilkinson himself calls the reader's attention time and again to the ways in which he differed from his colleagues, such as the criticism—or at least wonderment—from fellow officers regarding his interactions with Black Muslims at CMF and Soledad.

The prison guard/correctional officer remains one of the least-understood figures in the literature on corrections.[23] Not until the 1970s was

---

Publishing, 1982). On the critique of the indeterminate sentence, see David Holmstrom, "California Convicts Charge 'Silent Beefs' Hold Up Paroles," *Christian Science Monitor,* 14 November 1970, 11; Douglas Kneeland, "Indeterminate Sentences, Once Urged as Reform, Now Attacked," *New York Times,* 27 September 1971, 39.

22. This shift began under the tenure of Procunier, who repeatedly emphasized that the primary goal of California prisons was not rehabilitation. See also Herman Schwartz, "Danger Ahead in Get-Tough Policy," *Los Angeles Times,* 25 May 1975, IV, 5, and Phillip D. Guthrie, "California Copes with Change," *Los Angeles Times,* 25 May 1975, IV, 5. Jonathan Simon, *Poor Discipline: Parole and the Social Control of the Underclass, 1890–1990* (Chicago: University of Chicago Press, 1993), maps this same terrain for parole in California.

23. To our knowledge, no comparable account by a career correctional officer from this

there any sustained effort to examine the correctional officer and sort out the reality of prison work from enduring cultural images and stereotypes.[24] These studies emphasized the variety in officer behavior and experience. Wilkinson's account reminds us once again of the truth in Ted Conover's recent observation about the correctional officer's job: "it took time (and confrontations) to decide (or to discover) what kind of person was going to be wearing your uniform."[25]

The history of prison work has, for the most part, tended to emphasize the prison more than the work. The correctional officer becomes for the social scientist just another device by which the prison may be usefully studied. But the story of prison work also belongs to labor history. To be sure, labor historians have not rushed to embrace this particular occupational category, perhaps because of the nature of the work.[26]

This "labor history" of prison work has many important elements, all of which appear frequently in Wilkinson's recollections. The correctional officers serve not simply as an extension of state authority and power, but as figures who can exercise their own judgment, set their own priorities, and negotiate their own understandings with inmates. These memoirs further remind us that while the officer-inmate relationship is important, the officer-supervisor relationship may be the more critical one in terms of work experience and job satisfaction.

---

period exists. The account that comes closest to this one is J. Michael Yates, *Line Screw: My Twelve Riotous Years Working behind Bars in Some of Canada's Toughest Jails, an Unrepentant Memoir* (Toronto: McClelland & Stewart, 1993). The one other exception might be the recent publication of George H. Gregory, *Alcatraz Screw: My Years as a Guard in America's Most Notorious Prison* (Columbia: University of Missouri Press, 2002), but this institution was self-consciously operated on a different model. Indeed, one of the points of the book is to highlight the Alcatraz-specific conditions. Other published "insider" accounts tend to take the form of somewhat sensationalistic journalism, with the tone, and sometimes the substance, of the exposé.

24. A good collection of early studies is *The Keepers: Prisons Guards and Contemporary Corrections*, ed. Ben M. Crouch (Springfield, IL: Charles C. Thomas, 1980). See also Gordon Hawkins, *The Prison: Policy and Practice* (Chicago: University of Chicago Press, 1977); Jacobs, *Stateville;* Kelsey Kauffman, *Prison Officers and Their World* (Cambridge, MA: Harvard University Press, 1988); and Lucien X. Lombardo, *Guards Imprisoned: Correctional Officers at Work* (New York: Elsevier, 1981). Two very early studies worth mentioning are Joseph Roucek, "Sociology of the Prison Guard," *Sociology and Social Research* 20 (1935): 145–51, and A. A. Evans, "Correctional Institution Personnel—Amateurs or Professionals?" *Annals of the American Academy of Political and Social Science* 293 (1954): 70–78.

25. Ted Conover, *Newjack: Guarding Sing Sing* (New York: Random House, 2000), 249. Conover's book, based on a year's work as a participant-observer, is the latest in a line of journalistic accounts that highlight the viewpoint of the correctional officer. See Roger Martin, *Pigs and Other Animals: A True and Thought-Provoking Story of Violence, Brutality and Perversion in Our Jails* (Arcadia, CA: Myco Publishing House, 1980), and Steven Herberts, *6–5: A Different Shade of Blue* (New York: Kroshka Books, 1996).

26. Among criminal justice system workers, only the police have received any attention from labor historians, and not much attention at that.

We also see Wilkinson's adjustment to one of the most important changes in the prison workplace in recent decades—the opening of prison employment to minorities and to women. When Wilkinson began at Chino, black correctional officers were rare, and no women worked in a custodial capacity in a men's prison.[27] The opening to minorities happened first, and by the time Wilkinson arrived at Soledad, minorities made up nearly 30 percent of correctional officers in the state. Wilkinson's long friendships with black officers and his relationship with Black Muslim inmates at times set his racial views apart from those of his fellow correctional officers. At the same time, he also voices the unease among older officers with the rapid expansion of minority recruitment, a tension reflected in many studies of prison work and in labor histories of this period.[28] Women entered men's prisons as officers somewhat later than minorities. Wilkinson's resistance to and discomfort with the idea of female officers in a male prison is similar to that described in many studies of male correctional officers, and, as in society in general, it is to some extent still prevalent today.[29]

One of the most important elements of this labor history is the comparatively recent organization of correctional officers. When Wilkinson began his career, most correctional officers worked as they always had—at the discretion of their warden or superintendent. Prison administrators might govern through fear or, like Kenyon Scudder, through loyalty, but their word was the final one.

The labor revolutions of the 1930s had no immediate impact on prison workers. Gradually, however, the system of authoritarian governance of individual prisons gave way to a more centralized, bureaucratized gover-

27. According to a national survey of correctional institutions conducted in 1968, 95 percent of all line workers in adult facilities were classified as white. John J. Galvin and Loren Karacki, *Manpower and Training in Correctional Institutions* (Washington, D.C.: Joint Commission on Correctional Manpower and Training, 1968), 12.

28. On race and prison work, there is a developing literature. One of the earliest studies (done in 1973–74) showed significant differences in work experience based on race, and the authors noted that new black officers experienced racial trouble with superior officers more than coworkers or inmates. James B. Jacobs and Mary P. Grear, "Dropouts and Rejects: An Analysis of the Prison Guard's Revolving Door," in *The Keepers,* ed. Crouch. On attitudinal difference between white and black officers, see John A. Arthur, "Correctional Ideology of Black Correctional Officers," *Federal Probation* 58 (1994): 57–65, and Dana M. Britton, "Perceptions of the Work Environment among Correctional Officers: Do Race and Sex Matter?" *Criminology* 35 (1997): 85–105. For considerations of these same issues in the larger labor field, see Barbara F. Reskin, *The Realities of Affirmative Action in Employment* (Washington, DC: American Sociological Association, 1998).

29. Dana M. Britton, *At Work in the Iron Cage: The Prison as Gendered Organization* (New York: NYU Press, 2003), is an important new study of the ways in which gender shapes prison work experiences. On male resistance to female officers, see Lynn E. Zimmer, *Women Guarding Men* (Chicago: University of Chicago Press, 1986).

nance. With this change came the opening for correctional officers to unionize. Even then, it was not until the 1970s that collective bargaining became commonplace in state correctional systems.[30]

When officers did finally organize, the impact was considerable. Leo Carroll referred to it as the "rebellion of the hacks" in his 1974 study.[31] Forms of organized activity, from sick-outs to political lobbying, became more commonplace. In general, these labor activities had the effect of pushing officers further from the rehabilitative regimes and stressed the primacy of controlling inmates.[32] Wilkinson's own account describes the new and aggressive posture of the CCPOA at the start of the 1980s. For better or worse, the reorganizations of prison workforces added one more nail in the coffin of the rehabilitative era.

Prison History, Prison Sociology

There is a remarkably constant theme in Dick Wilkinson's recollections: the power of people to make institutions. His experiences at three very different institutions—Chino, CMF, and Soledad—convinced him that each place had a distinct character stamped upon it by those who lived and worked there. As he commented reflectively, "You could not have found three institutions any different than the three where I worked."

Wilkinson compares institutional flaws to viruses, perpetuated by the staff over time. His account of Chino suggests that positive institutional qualities, not just the negative, were maintained in the same fashion. The variations from prison to prison, in Wilkinson's view, were not the products of general changes over time in all prisons, but of institution-specific characteristics.[33]

30. John M. Wynne, Jr., "Unions and Bargaining among Employees of State Prisons," *Monthly Labor Review* (March 1978): 10–16.

31. Carroll, *Hacks, Blacks, and Cons.* Carroll used the phrase "rebellion of the hacks" as a chapter title, and he tied the rebellion to long-simmering frustrations over inmate rights and administrative conflicts and the short-term issue of inmate disturbances.

32. James B. Jacobs and Norma Meacham Crotty, in "Implications of Collective Bargaining in Prisons," in *The Keepers,* ed. Crouch, 323–35, argued that collective bargaining did not necessarily imply one direction or another for penal policy. In the quarter-century since they made this argument, developments suggest that if there is not only one direction, officers' organizations have tended to support control models and the expansion of the prison system. A similar early conclusion can be found in Paul D. Staudohar, "Prison Guard Labor Relations in Ohio," *Industrial Relations* 15 (May 1976): 177–90.

33. To take one illustration from outside this memoir: E. J. Oberhauser, Scudder's assistant and successor at Chino, recalled the moment when group therapy came to Chino as part of a system-wide mandate. Custodial staff were supposed to help lead the sessions, and Oberhauser says that his officers quickly got used to the idea because "Scudder had trained them to chat with prisoners in a friendly manner." Officers at San Quentin and Folsom, on the other hand, strongly opposed group counseling. Glaser, *Preparing Convicts for Law-Abiding Lives,* 75.

This comparative dimension is important, for it challenges a historical literature that treats "the prison" as a singular phenomenon. The idea of a single prison with universal characteristics—independent of the keepers or the kept—was largely the brainchild of postwar American scholarship (although it arguably could also be drawn back somewhat further to the Marxist scholarship of Georg Rusche and Otto Kirchheimer).[34] Rooted in influential work by Donald Clemmer, Erving Goffman, and Gresham Sykes, the search for the universal prison involved exposing a single set of institutional imperatives and influences that shaped the behavior of inmates and officers.[35] Where advocates of the rehabilitative regime (and progressive penology generally) had celebrated the importance of individual weakness or virtue, postwar social scientists emphasized the structural limitations on individual agency. In *The Society of Captives,* Sykes acknowledged that some would point to the California Department of Corrections or the federal Bureau of Prisons as proof that some prisons could be better. Sykes discounted this possibility. He contended that whatever differences existed were superficial.

The gap between the universal prison and the progressive prison became the basis upon which the rehabilitative regime was attacked. The essays collected in Eric Olin Wright's *The Politics of Punishment: A Critical Analysis of Prisons in America* (1973) exemplify this critique. As Wright himself observed, "the 'correctional facility' is still a prison." Talk of rehabilitation was merely a façade, for custody and rehabilitation were, simply put, incompatible. The "totalitarian regime" described by Sykes meant that programs were of little value, and cooperation by inmates indicated only submission and docility.[36]

The sociology of the universal prison, in turn, gave birth to the history of the universal prison. Michel Foucault took this historical bent in one direction with his remarkable work, *Discipline and Punish.* Here Foucault laid out a vision of the prison as modern control technology, one part of a largely unidirectional expansion of disciplinary practices. Like the sociologists, but unlike the earlier Marxist history of Rusche and Kirchheimer,

34. Georg Rusche and Otto Kirchheimer, *Punishment and Social Structure* (New York: Columbia University Press, 1939).

35. Donald Clemmer, *The Prison Community* (New York: Rinehart and Co., 1940); Erving Goffman, *Asylums: Essays on the Social Situation of Mental Patients and Other Inmates* (Garden City, NY: Doubleday, 1961); Gresham M. Sykes, *The Society of Captives: A Study of a Maximum Security Prison* (Princeton, NJ: Princeton University Press, 1958). For more work in the same vein, see H. Adler, "Ideas toward a Sociology of the Concentration Camp," *American Journal of Sociology* 63 (1958): 513–22; and Richard Cloward et al., *Theoretical Studies in Social Organization of the Prison* (New York: Social Science Research Council, 1960).

36. Sykes, *The Society of Captives;* Wright, *The Politics of Punishment,* 132, 171.

Foucault was interested in actual mechanisms of control. These mechanisms, though, for him were mere dimensions of a singular "prison form."[37]

Historian David Rothman took the universal prison in a different direction with his 1980 book, *Conscience and Convenience*.[38] In this work, Rothman tried to document the fruits of progressive social control in the fields of criminal justice, juvenile justice, and mental health. In his synthesis, Rothman devoted a great deal of time to the sort of documentation irrelevant to Foucault. Rothman also decisively severed the history of prison ideas and ideologies from prison practices, just as the prison sociologists had done. To explain why prisons failed to turn out the way reformers hoped, Rothman also adopted the universal prison model. The demands of institutions, particularly custody, determined the fate of everything else.[39]

The idea of a pluralistic prison history, if that is the correct term, was no stranger to Progressive-era prison scholars and reformers. Their world was marked by very different visions of what the prison could be like. Progressive-era prisoner writings illustrate this point of view well. In the 1920s, Kate Richards O'Hare wrote of the vile and desperate conditions of her confinement—not to describe the universal prison experience, but to expose a corrupt regime.[40] In this sense, the term "rehabilitative ideal" is incomplete, for prison reform was more than reducing recidivism. Reform also meant treating people well, offering a measure of human dignity and respect, bringing order where there had been disorder.[41] These latter dimensions of reform, it must be emphasized, were very much dependent on individual agency and action.

37. Michel Foucault, *Discipline and Punish*, trans. Alan Sheridan (London: Allen Lane, 1977); for a sophisticated reading and critique, see David Garland, *Punishment and Modern Society: A Study in Social Theory* (Oxford: Clarendon Press, 1990).

38. David J. Rothman, *Conscience and Convenience: The Asylum and Its Alternatives in Progressive America* (Boston: Little, Brown, 1980).

39. The work of historians per se is summarized in *The Oxford History of the Prison: The Practice of Punishment in Western Society*, ed. Norval Morris and David J. Rothman (New York: Oxford University Press, 1995), and Scott Christianson, *With Liberty for Some: 500 Years of Imprisonment in America* (Boston: Northeastern University Press, 1998). A good general text is Thomas G. Blomberg and Karol Lucken, *American Penology: A History of Control* (New York: Aldine de Gruyter, 2000).

40. Kate Richards O'Hare, *In Prison* (New York: Alfred A. Knopf, 1923).

41. From the vantage point of 2005, a number of writers conclude that the collapse of the rehabilitative regime has brought a general worsening of confinement conditions. See Charles M. Terry, "Beyond Punishment: Perpetuating Difference from the Prison Experience," *Humanity & Society* 24 (2000): 108–35. Christian Parenti's polemical *Lockdown America: Police and Prisons in the Age of Crisis* (New York: Verso, 2000) uses Norman Fenton (director of the California Department of Corrections treatment programming in the post–World War II era) to offer a favorable contrast with 1990s punitive rhetoric.

Some scholars have returned to this essential progressive observation. Ann Chih Lin in her important recent work stresses what she calls "the day-to-day imposition of local ideals—order, professionalism, communication, self-respect—upon programs that must absorb or resist them."[42] For such an approach as Lin's, emphasizing that individual staff members' actions collectively constitute agency actions, Dick Wilkinson's reminiscences contain very rich resources indeed. The inmates who came to Chino from San Quentin, to take but one example, simply could not comprehend the differences between the two institutions.

His narrative renders the story of twentieth-century prison reform much more multidimensional then previously understood. The California Medical Facility was not merely a more fully realized or complicated version of Scudder's Chino. Rather, the two institutions differed in important ways—differences that reveal the important changes in the twentieth-century rehabilitative regime. Unlike Chino, CMF was born in the heat of postwar America's romance with psychology and psychiatry. Organizing CMF on a quasi-medical model marked a real departure from the Chino model, with its emphasis on education and dynamic/paternalistic leadership.

The third reform institution, Soledad, appears to have had its reform character entirely submerged by a hostile administration and fragmented officer corps. As Wilkinson himself observes: "At Soledad, I could never see the program—just keep them from hurting one another. That was about it." His clashes with both the administration and the officer culture at Soledad offer further evidence that prisons can develop a persisting identity that is the product of individual and collective action.

A History from Which to Learn

All of these theoretical and historical issues are presented here as a way of orienting the reader to the tale that will follow. These memoirs elucidate an individual life that was intersecting with historical change, and the general setting takes on greater meaning as the details and continuity of this career unfold. Indeed, a recurring theme is the shifts between generations in the second half of the twentieth century.

The careful reader will doubtless encounter many points at which

---

42. Ann Chih Lin, *Reform in the Making: The Implementation of Social Policy in Prison* (Princeton, NJ: Princeton University Press, 2000), 31. DiIulio's comparative study, *Governing Prisons*, made a similar argument about the varieties of prison functioning, and he used the Soledad Prison of Wilkinson's time as an example of a poorly operated institution.

Wilkinson's account raises questions that are not answered in the narrative or the annotations. Some questions will be general, about the broader patterns of the twentieth-century prison experience. His memoir implicitly and sometimes explicitly does speak to why we have penal institutions, as well as to how they developed the way they did. Many of the substantive questions that come out of his observations do not yet have good answers. Perhaps the policy questions never will. Regardless, we believe that this unique account and the many specific experiences described in it will stimulate further research and investigation.

It is only fair to add that, however important are the general issues that Wilkinson's tale raises, we have discovered that astonishingly few records are available (if they are in existence at all) to document what actually happened in the pacesetting correctional institutions in California from the 1950s to the 1980s.[43] Wilkinson's memoir therefore constitutes a major eyewitness source through which we can try to understand some very important history.

The witness who offers the candid observations below also passes on the wisdom that came from his decades doing the work of confinement. It is wisdom that is not necessarily limited to any period. Prisons are likely to be with us for a long time. For those who ordain and especially for those who implement and work with imprisonment, Wilkinson's is clearly an impressive "voice of experience."

Joseph F. Spillane
University of Florida

John C. Burnham
The Ohio State University

43. The holdings of the California State Archives and the individual penal institutions are particularly disappointing and surprising. Even published evidence is often episodic and fragmentary. The Department of Corrections did not issue regular annual or biennial reports such as were customary for many agencies in many states. We are nevertheless very grateful to officials of the three institutions, the California State Archives, the California State Library, and especially Eric Owens and Russ Heimerich of the California Department of Corrections Communications Office.

NOTE TO THE READER

The recollections and observations that follow are based on amended transcripts of recorded conversations held over a period of several days. *A substantial attempt has been made to preserve that conversational flavor.* Colloquial expression has often been preserved, along with informalities like use of the second person and interjected sentence fragments. Nevertheless the sense should be easy to follow even as the personal touches of the narrator come through.

Portrait of Wilkinson as a young man in his Navy uniform
Source: Viola Wilkinson.

INTRODUCING
DICK WILKINSON

William Richard Wilkinson served as a correctional employee in the California Department of Corrections from 1951 to 1981. He worked at three locations: California Institution for Men, Chino (1951 to 1955), the California Medical Facility in Vacaville (1955 to 1977), and Soledad State Prison (1977 to 1981).

Dick Wilkinson is a member of the World War II generation. He was born in 1925, and he entered the Navy in 1943 at the age of eighteen. The service experience was for him, as it was for millions in his generation, a formative experience. He served in the Pacific Theater, and he was one of the survivors of the sinking of the aircraft carrier *Bismarck Sea*. When he got back home, he married, held a couple of jobs, and went to school. He was twenty-five when he became a correctional officer. He and his wife, Viola Spencer Wilkinson, had two children, a boy and a girl, who now have their own children and even grandchildren.

But this book is about Wilkinson's experience as an employee. A brief personal chronology and work history provides a framework within which to understand his recollections of his service with the California Department of Corrections.

Chronology

8 August 1925 Born Grandfield, OK
Schools in Grandfield, OK
   in Oklahoma City
   in Silverton, TX
   in San Diego, CA
Pomona, CA, High School (graduated 1943)
April 1943–March 1946 U.S. Navy
   Aviation Radioman Second Class
1948–1951 Mt. San Antonio College (with an A.A. in Industrial Arts awarded in 1950)

April 1946–February 1947 Western Geophysical Company
 Surveyor's rod man
February 1947–April 1951 H. W. Loud Machine Works
 Turret Lathe Operator
1 May 1951 Joined California Department of Corrections
1951–1955 California Institution for Men, Chino, CA, Correctional
 Officer
 Housing Unit, Control, Farm, Engineering Crew
 April 1955 Promoted to Correctional Sergeant
1955–1962 California Medical Facility, Vacaville, CA, Correctional
 Sergeant
 Watch Sergeant, Control, Culinary, Mail and Visiting
1962–1977 California Medical Facility, Vacaville, CA, Correctional
 Lieutenant
 September 1961–April 1962 Second Watch Lieutenant and Captain
 Relief
 April 1962–October 1963 Watch Lieutenant—Third Watch
 October 1963–March 1967 Program Lieutenant, Psychiatric Unit
  Case work for 85–95 inmates
  General supervision, 225 psychotic patients
 March 1967–May 1969 Assignment Lieutenant
  Inmate classification and assignment
 May 1969–January 1971 Program Lieutenant, Psychotherapy Unit
  Supervision and casework
  Group co-therapist with unit psychiatrist
 January 1971–February 1972 Correctional Counselor
  Assistant Classification and Parole Representative
  Program Unit Counselor
 February 1972–November 1973 Inmate Activities Coordinator
 November 1973–September 1974 Program Lieutenant
  General supervision of 80 special housing inmates
 1974–1977 Watch Lieutenant and Program Lieutenant
1977–1981 Soledad State Prison, Soledad, CA
  Classification and Parole Representative
  Acting Associate Warden for Appeals
  Correctional Program Supervisor

Men's Prisons in California in 1953

The narrative refers frequently to several institutions that in 1953 were described as:

California State Prison at Folsom—
Older recidivists and habitual criminals. Serious problem cases including some younger men.

California State Prison at San Quentin—
More serious trainable cases. Industrial program; vocational training and academic education; religious and medical programs. Segregation unit for disturbed younger men.

California Institution for Men at Chino—
Younger first or less severe offenders trainable in agriculture and trades.

California State Prison at Soledad—
Inmates trainable in agriculture and trades. Unit for homosexuals.

Deuel Vocational Institution at Lancaster—
More serious and difficult younger offenders committed to the Director of Corrections or Youth Authority. (Temporary location at Lancaster. Permanent facilities now under construction near Tracy.)

California Medical Facility at Terminal Island—
Specialized treatment facility for psychotic, epileptic, low-grade feeble-minded, sex psychopaths, tubercular and other chronic illnesses. Unit for ambulant aged inmates. (Temporary location, Terminal Island, California. This facility will be located at Vacaville when the institution for 1,800 prisoner patients has been completed.)

(Abridged from Norman Fenton, *An Introduction to Classification and Treatment in State Correctional Service* [Sacramento: California Department of Corrections, 1953], 21.)

Aerial view of California Institution for Men, Chino (1951)
Source: *California Institution for Men, Chino, California, Orientation to Employment in State Correctional Service* (Sacramento: State of California, Department of Corrections, 1951).

CHAPTER ONE

CHINO—AN IDEAL BEGINNING

Getting Started in 1951

How did I get started? I had no interest in the prison business, but I was going to school, and I had the thought at that time that I could work the midnight shift at the prison and do my studying. However, it did not turn out that way. The requirements were that you could read the procedure manual and memos and things pertaining to the job—but nothing else.

I lived about a mile from the prison.[1] And a couple of my golfing buddies worked there. It was the leading industry for that rural area. And then the promotions came along so quickly that I was stuck. Not that I did not have an interest in it—it was like anything else, you get into it, and it becomes interesting.

But it was Kenyon Scudder who turned me on, his nontraditional philosophy.[2] Mr. Scudder had been probation officer of Los Angeles County until 1939, and there was gossip that he was related by marriage to one of the governors.[3] He was working in the federal prison system when he was appointed superintendent at Chino in 1940.[4] He got things going at the prison before the war slowed down. I did hear that the first thing he said

---

1. The Institution for Men was located in Chino, in eastern Los Angeles County. At that time, it was a fairly rural setting—quite different from today. The population of the town of Chino was about 5,800 in 1950. CIM held about 1,800 inmates.

2. Kenyon J. Scudder, *Prisoners Are People* (Garden City, NY: Doubleday & Company, 1952), presents his version of events and explains his thinking, especially in his conclusion, 273–82. Scudder had been superintendent of Whittier State School before 1931. California Whittier State Reform School was a pioneer reform institution for juvenile delinquents. Steven Schlossman, "Delinquent Children: The Juvenile Reform School," in *The Oxford History of the Prison,* ed. Norval Morris and David J. Rothman (New York: Oxford University Press, 1995), 340, concludes that no institution tried "more diligently and comprehensively" to "implement the individual treatment ideal."

3. This rumor cannot be verified.

4. Scudder, *Prisoners Are People,* 19: "Here was a rare opportunity, which seldom comes to a state more than once in a century, to start a new type of institution for the first offender. The brutal and impersonal treatment I had witnessed at the hands of ignorant and untrained guards in institutions where I had worked convinced me that there should be some better method of dealing with prisoners if they were to be restored to useful citizenship. Why

1

Kenyon Scudder with inmate in a field at CIM (1950s)
Source: Historical Albums, California Department of Corrections, Sacramento.

was, "Stop building that wall, and it is unnecessary to build those towers, because we are not going to put anybody in them."[5]

It wound up that the only part of the prison that looks like a prison, other than the ten-foot fence that runs around the Quadrangle, was the lower half of the south dorm. It had about twenty cells. The top floor was nothing but one big dorm.

I think that if I had started at San Quentin or Folsom, I would not have stayed in the business. They were just warehousing inmates at those two institutions. Chino, however, was productive. They had a good vocational setup there: welding, carpentry, cement work, the trades. Especially the welding. Scudder had no problem placing his people. He had immediate jobs for the welding people because the training was so good. And the carpenter shop was pretty much that way.

---

not weave into this new fabric the best we could find in the good prisons in America and develop a different pattern of care and treatment for men in trouble? Here emphasis could be placed on freedom of choice, acceptance of responsibility while in prison, and preparation for return to community life." See also Shelley Bookspan, *A Germ of Goodness: The California State Prison System, 1851–1944* (Lincoln: University of Nebraska Press, 1991).

5. The substance of this story is confirmed in *California Department of Corrections 1977* (Sacramento: The Department, 1977), 10. Walls with gun towers were routine security precautions in American prisons at that time.

This was the leadoff. The inmates do their time, they get their training, they go out to get a job. You could see that at Chino.

And there was the education for the inmates. If you did not have a high-school education, then you spent half your day in class and the other half of the day picking tomatoes or shucking corn or whatever you had to do. You have to work to survive, and you have to have an education to make it. At Chino, they made room for both.

Breaking In as a Correctional Officer

There were about a half dozen of us correctional officers who started out together. We had a two-day orientation. The first day was listening to Mr. Scudder. Then we went down and spent the rest of the day with the second watch, the day people.[6] Then we came in at four o'clock the next day and saw the four-to-midnight shift—what went on there. Then we saw the midnight shift, worked that, came back one more day, took a day off, and then started work at midnight on Saturday. And that was it.[7] (Currently the Department has a six-week academy that is quite extensive. The graduates are qualified peace officers under the California penal code.)

The midnight shift was listening to the inmates in the dormitory snore. And waking up the early calls, for the kitchen, for the green-field crews, all the people who had to get out at 4:30 or five o'clock in the morning. So you would just sit there and read the procedure manual and wait for the sergeant to come around and talk to you.

After being in the service and finding out how good you were, and how clever you were and how capable you were—the first night I worked, something interesting happened. There were seventy men in the barracks. I sat in the middle in a little open office right next to the toilet area so that I could watch everything. I could probably tell you every man who rolled over in bed, every man who passed gas, every man who snored. I had them all down pat.

About three o'clock in the morning, I went to eat my lunch. I opened up my lunch box, and it was empty. It had a note in it that said, "Thank you very much." Best break-in period I ever had. I knew I didn't know a damned thing. That lunch box was washed out, and there was no way they

6. The first watch, or shift, was midnight to 8 A.M., the second watch was 8 A.M. to 4 P.M., and the third watch was 4 P.M. to midnight.

7. California Institution for Men, Chino, California, *Orientation to Employment in State Correctional Service* ([Chino]: State of California, Department of Corrections, 1951), 2, stipulated a five-day orientation, including control procedures, classification, housing, patrol, farm operations and industrial training, meal supervision, mail handling and censoring, dormitory, and car patrol.

could get to that toilet without my seeing them and hearing the water running. And that lunch box was not out of my sight all night long. Anyway, that started me off right: they were clever, you had better keep your eyes open, and you don't know a thing about them.

In that day, on-the-job training did not really amount to much. I went out to take over the barracks. The guy was standing outside the barracks with the keys in his hand. He said, "You the new guy?" I said, "Yeah." He said, "Here," handed me the keys, and walked off. That was my on-the-job training. It was not unusual, it was typical. Some of them got a little more conversation: "The paperwork is here." I didn't even know where the count sheets[8] were. I had to run around and find out. I knew from orientation they were there someplace. I never will forget that guy I relieved that night. He set the tone. We never did talk after that. No need to talk to him. Smart-ass. He really wasn't very competent; he didn't understand where he was or what he was doing. You came to know that as you worked around him, saw him, heard about him. He was just putting in time. I don't know what kind of break-in he got. Maybe that was what happened to him, and he just passed it along and didn't know any better.

What the Work Was Like

Working in the barracks on first shift, you went to work at midnight, and then at three o'clock in the morning, you had to start waking people up for various crews. Dairy people had to go out—you'd wake them up at three o'clock, and they transported them at four. There were kitchen people who woke up at four, and they transported them at four-thirty. There was a whole raft of culinary workers to get up at five o'clock. That pretty much made up your routine. Then the inmates were getting up around six o'clock to shave and do whatever they were going to do to get ready for breakfast, so you were down only about three hours before things started happening. Then it started picking up at that point, all these little odd things you would have to do.

Before they put the cement floors in the barracks, as you walked along, it would rock the bunks, and they were double bunks. So you had to be kind of careful as you went down, or you would have inmates growling and complaining. There was some difficulty in waking some of the inmates up in the morning, and some of them would try to trick you, take a swing at you. They were awake, but they could say, "Oh, I'm sorry, but

8. The count sheets were the sheets on which the presence of each inmate was noted. They were the basic element in "control," making sure that every inmate was in the institution and in place—and had not escaped.

you startled me." I had a different way of handling them, a trick that worked very well on a difficult inmate. I would pull the covers back and take a rubber band and wind it just as tight as I could around his big toe and then go off and leave him. In about ten minutes, he was fully awake, trying to find what was the matter with his toe. He might have a cuss word or two, but then you would reach an agreement with him so that when you woke him up in the morning, he would not take a swing at you. I used to pass that along to the other housing officers.

I never did work the housing units after the first few months. My first job after that was to work in the Control Room, which amounted to doing four counts a day. The officers counted the inmates. They called it in to you, and you worked it out so that all the inmates were still there. It was just book work.

Doing the control was not all that easy. You had to keep track of everything from when you set it up to the end. The control room was where all the phone calls came in and where all the housing and bed files were. Inmate Joe Blow was in Barracks 2, bed 4. All of that was on a big sheet. You had to get a positive count and a negative count. The positive count was counting heads, the negative count was empty beds.

At Chino if you came up short, you could tell immediately who was not there. I took all the calls for the security check every half hour. I had a board up there with lights, and the lights would stay on to indicate that they had called in. If they didn't call in, then you got somebody out there to see why they hadn't called in. You didn't call back, you sent somebody out to see what was happening. That could get embarrassing after a while. If you were not making your calls every half hour, and somebody had to check on you, you weren't doing your job. Were you sleeping? Or what the hell were you doing?

There was another security feature. When the officer took the phone off the hook, the light would let you know what unit it was. You could hear the phone buzzing and an alarm would go off. So that way you knew exactly where the situation was, and you would get the watch sergeant or whoever was available, and you checked out the alarm. Then you would talk into the phone asking the officer if he was okay. "Oh, Jesus, I knocked the phone off the hook." But you couldn't stop with that. Once the phone was off the hook and the alarm had sounded, you would still have to go down to the unit and go through the whole process.

All the institutions had this kind of system. It was a safety device, and also it was a check on the officer to make sure he was alert on the first watch. He had to rouse himself every half-hour. And that is not so far-fetched. You can train yourself to sleep for twenty minutes and still make your rounds and call-ins.

Later, when I was sergeant on first watch, I would go around visiting guys. The first thing I would look for was that sheet of paper. It would have check marks every half-hour: twelve o'clock, twelve-thirty, one o'clock. . . . The guy may be dozing off between call-ins and have a silly grin on his face. I would just laugh and tell him to try and stay awake. It did not even have to be deliberate. It became just habit after a while. Dozing off is one thing, but being able to get conscious in order to make your call-in is something phenomenal. But you could be trained that way.

I worked control for several months and got sort of tired of it, and they had what they called the utility position.[9] You would relieve one of the utility men for two days. You would relieve both of the utility men, one of them for two days and the other for one day. Then another guy would pick up the second relief day. After doing that for a while, I got into running errands with the utility person. The officers would call in, and we would check out noises—what was this noise over here, or that noise over there—or some problem that was reported. Or I would simply refill a thermos jug with coffee from the canteen and take it back to them. It all helped. I really enjoyed that sort of work. When I later went on the engineering crew, it was the same kind of variable routine. That established my working pattern throughout the Department, really. As soon as I got the problems pretty well taken care of, then I wanted to take care of something else. So I burned out very easily, even on the farm detail.

There was a lot of running around for the utility officer to do. You would cover the dorms when the officer was making the count. You had four separate units. In the barracks, you were right in the middle of the floor, and there was no way that you could cover this area or that area, and so you had to have someone cover you. Then there would be various things happening. You would have to go out to the dairy about something out there, or down to the sewage plant. And there was a lot of paperwork that had to be done—things for parole and so on.

The guy I worked with, John Collins, was a sharp kid. We had this system: I would dictate, and he would take it right on the typewriter. Man, we were good. We would turn that stuff out. When they first put us on it, there was a backlog. We decided that, hey, we were not going to be tied up by this paperwork, and we were going to work something out. John was not all that proficient to begin with. There were quite a few typing errors. But I said, "That doesn't make any difference. We've got the information, and somebody else can correct the spelling errors." They wanted to know how we were getting the paperwork out. In the period of a couple of weeks, we had cleaned up the backlog and had our routine going.

---

9. The utility officers did not have fixed duties. They were to help where needed—assisting with the counts, running errands, escorting inmates, filling in for an absent officer.

It would take us maybe fifteen minutes a night. The rest of the time we would sit around and use the time to our own advantage—searching common areas, whatever, just being available until somebody needed us. I really enjoyed all that, and that was why I did not want to leave the first watch.

But we weren't tied to paperwork. We were doing what we wanted to do. Go out to the barracks and talk to the guys, the officers, just for the hell of it. It was lonesome there, so if we were in the area, we would just stop and say hi. Bring some coffee. We would step over to the guidance center and help them out. Jack-of-all-trades, and that was what I enjoyed.

Another Change in Responsibility

You worked your way up on the shifts. You started out on first watch. You worked that for a year. Then you worked the third watch for eighteen months. Then you worked days as long as you could stay there. It's eleven to seven now, which makes a whole lot more sense.[10]

I did not want to leave first watch. It came as a shock when I was told I was changing shifts. I did not even know the captain knew I was there. I never saw him. He was generally holed up in his office. He saw me one day and said, "It's time you got off first watch." I didn't think he knew I was alive, which was just fine with me.

But on this one day when I was walking to breakfast, the captain came by and says, "You're going on days Monday." So I skipped the third watch and never did work four to midnight at Chino. I don't have any idea why. I told the captain I was happy where I was, but he told me I was going on days. So at that point I went on the farm crew. That lasted for three or four months.

It wasn't all bad; it was just making the shift change. It made it easier at home. I was driving my wife crazy. We had two kids. My son, Denny, was too young to understand the night work routine. He would come in to my bed and say, "Dad, are you asleep?" I would say no, and he would ask me why.

Skipping the third watch did not do my reputation any good. The rest of the officers grumbled. They wanted to know why I didn't do the third watch. I told them I didn't know, and that they should ask the captain. Which was the wrong thing to say. They were alluding to that to begin with.

And there I was on the farm crew. I didn't know anything about farming. As a matter of fact, we used to have an old joke. Down in Arkansas

10. See below.

they had a prison called Tucker's Farm, after a character named Captain Tucker. And they ran their prisons much differently. When it came time to work the cotton fields, they would tell the inmates, "That is my cotton. And those are your weeds. Get your weeds out of my cotton."[11] So we used: "These are my tomato fields. Get your weeds out of my tomato fields." We had a farm advisor, Wes Coblentz, a great guy, and he supervised the farm, furnished the information.

For one thing, we found out the hard way that you don't put smokers in the field transplanting tomato plants, because the nicotine on their fingers kills the plants. After we killed a field—you could see it: here was one guy, who did not smoke, and he planted a row, and they all grew, and the rows planted by smokers all died. That was the only thing we could come up with. We were just all standing around, there were three or four inmates there, and somebody came up with the idea that maybe it was the nicotine that was killing the plants. It was really strange. But after that, when you went out to transplant the tomatoes, normally you do your work and then wash up. But now you got off the truck, and we had these ten-gallon milk cans full of water, and they washed their hands before they planted the tomatoes.[12]

They had night irrigators down there, which was unheard of. You put an inmate out there in the middle of the night to irrigate the fields, and there were no guards or guard towers. You put him out there and hoped you would find him in the morning. Inmates were very clever. Give a man a pair of pliers and a tin can, and he could make anything for you. They were always figuring out ways to do things, and one of the things that really impressed me was: the irrigator would start his water, and then he would go down to the end of the field, and about five or ten feet from the end of the row, he would take his shoes off and lie down and go to sleep, and when the water hit his feet, he would know that it was time to get up and start shutting the water off. They could get a full night's sleep out there and still do their job. They could do anything.

The Engineering Crew

After three months working in the tomato patch, I ended up with the engineering crew. I died and went to heaven on that day. It was a great job.

11. Tucker Farm, which was touted as being self-supporting, eventually became notorious and was the site of scandals, the occasion of a famous lawsuit, and the object of reform; among other accounts, see the contemporary description, Robert Pearman, "The Whip Pays Off," *Nation* 203 (1966): 701–4.

12. The observation had been made by others. The cause was, however, not the nicotine but tobacco mosaic virus disease, which spread from the tobacco to the tomato plants.

I was getting back to utility work. Which seems to be what I do best. Or at least that is what people think I do best. That is the kind of job I've had. That is why I did so much "acting" time as I worked for the Department. They don't give you the position, but they put you in there to do the job. So they make you "acting" this or that.

I really got to express myself when I got on the engineering crew at Chino. It was a six-man crew, and we just went around tidying up things—cleaning out storm drains, hauling materials for crews who were pouring cement, and so on. I just felt that I was free, floating around, doing what needed to be done. And on a rainy day, I would lay four of them in and take two of them with me and go around and check all of the storm drains to make sure things did not get flooded out. We kept right on top of everything. We were good.

We had a filling station down there. We had to dig the hole for the tanks. We ran into a stratum of blue clay, which you could not get off your shovel. It was just terrible. So we were digging these holes, and we had a dump truck, a three-yard dump truck. It was hard to get all the crew around so they could get their shovels in, and there just wasn't much work space. So we worked up a contest to see who could load up that three-yard dump truck the fastest by himself. And I'll tell you, it was a wonder there weren't some heart attacks. These were young kids, and I was a young kid myself, yapping back and forth, "I can do it better than you can." I can remember that there was one guy who loaded that thing in forty-five minutes. So everybody else says, "Hey, man, you've got it, I ain't even gonna try." I got criticism for that: when you have one guy working, what are the other four or five going to do? You were supposed to keep them all busy so you would know what they were doing. That was standard. They just said something; it was not a common thing for people to get written up. It was not that kind of workforce, and it was not that kind of philosophy. People just kind of looked out for one another, and there was competition. There was the put-down and indirect comment from supervisors and other staff, but nobody was out to hurt anybody as they did in the other institutions I worked in. That is not too surprising, since we did not have the physical means of control at Chino that the traditional prisons had. We had to depend on one another.

The Institution

Chino was the only facility in Southern California. There were about two thousand inmates in Chino, I think.[13] The number changed later on due to population pressure. They were triple-bunked and sleeping in tents.

13. The official count while Wilkinson was at Chino ranged from 1,790 to 2,104, but this latter number may have included inmates in the Guidance Center; the statistical reporting varied.

They even did away with vocational training and housed inmates in there. This is now. While I was there, it was the same number all the time. The number varied a little of course. You would receive some, fifteen or twenty one day, and lose six or eight the next day to San Quentin or what have you. But basically the number was somewhere between eighteen hundred and two thousand, if I'm not mistaken.

The percentage of minority inmates was not as high then as it later became. At Chino, it was mostly the young white offender. The minority was definitely the minority at Chino.[14] It did not have anything to do with the selection process. Again, the criterion was very narrow: the young first offender. And we just did not have that many minorities as first offenders. As I said, later on, it changed.

What minority inmates there were all slept in the same barracks as the other inmates, and they did the same work.[15] In general, there was not any friction at all, at least on my crews. You would have a fight, but there was a place to have a fight without getting in trouble—behind the barracks or in the gym.

Inmates did not go directly from court to Chino. They were all picked out of the system. When Chino was first put into operation, what they called the Guidance Center was at San Quentin.[16] All new arrivals went there for processing and were sent to various prisons according to their background or circumstances. This was the place to which we came to help them see what we wanted: the young first offenders. Then they opened a Guidance Center in Chino in 1951, and after that, we didn't go to San Quentin. We had enough to go around. Of course we had them going both ways. We shipped inmates out about three times a week.

14. In 1951, of the 1,790 inmates at CIM, 64.5% were classified as white, 15.2% as Mexican American, and 19.9% as black; *Characteristics of Felon Population in California State Prisons by Institution,* mimeographed copy in California State Library. All felons in California institutions at that time broke down into white, 64.5%, 13.2% Mexican, and 19.9% black, which meant that CIM in fact had a slightly higher representation of minorities than the state prison system as a whole. In 1955, when Wilkinson left, CIM still had 57.6% white, 17.3% Mexican, and 23.5% black. At that time, the average age of CIM inmates was 29.2 years, as opposed to the statewide male prison population of 32.1 years. California Department of Corrections, *Introduction to State Correctional Service* (Sacramento: California Department of Corrections, 1949), 59, noted that 36% of the prisoners were born in Southern states, 20% in California, and only 6% in other countries.

15. Daniel Glaser, in *Preparing Convicts for Law-Abiding Lives: The Pioneering Penology of Richard A. McGee* (Albany: SUNY Press, 1995), 36–37, recounts that Chino was the first integrated correctional facility in California. Scudder had insisted on integration from the very beginning. San Quentin and Folsom resisted integration into the 1960s.

16. The original Guidance Center opened in 1940 at San Quentin. Guidance Center staff prepared case material on each inmate they received. Inmates were also given a series of medical, psychiatric, and psychological examinations. Finally, staff conducted vocational, recreational, and educational tests and interviews before assigning a convict to an institution.

Of course we had guys down there who didn't want to go to San Quentin—they wanted to go to Chino—and we had a little trouble getting them on the bus. One of the best ways we found of cooling a guy down was to strip him down stark naked and march him up the main hall of the institution naked. He may have been a bearcat in the housing unit, but you get him out in the hallway naked and he would be as mild as could be. Never say a word. Just to get some clothes on was all that he was after. Worked like a charm. First, of course, we had to hold him down and tear the clothes off him (they were state property).

The buses left about four o'clock in the morning, and people on the night shift would get calls to come to the Guidance Center to beef them up in getting a couple of recalcitrants on the bus. So we just discovered this technique by accident. This one guy did not want to go. There was quite a tussle down there, and that was how his clothes got torn, and he was talking about "You gotta get me some more clothes" to go, and the sergeant told him he could just walk down the hall like that. "We'll get you coveralls when you get to the receiving room." And then he turned just as docile as he could be. We got him down there and put the coveralls on him, and he started mouthing off. We had to iron him up.[17] He was not the only one who went to San Quentin in irons. But this procedure just changed the difficult ones. These were big tough guys. I don't know what happens to a man's mind when you strip him down. They had no trouble being naked to take a shower, and women were not introduced into the prisons until the 1970s. The shock on the guy's face when you tell him take his clothes off wasn't all that great, but when you walked him out the door, some of them would almost weep. And this would be a guy who was going to cut your throat. They didn't know if they should cover their privates with their hands, they didn't know what to do with their hands, they didn't know how to walk. Some of them would strut, but they couldn't make it all the way to the receiving room. Before that, with some of them, you would have to grab them by the collar and drag them down the corridor.

Working with the Regular Inmates at Chino

The regular inmates on their first day at Chino had an orientation. It was a set piece. The officers would gather them up and get the truck, and the truck would pull up to the barracks, and they would load them all on there. Some of these guys had been in the service, so it wasn't all that strange. It might be crazy, but they would put up with it. And you would

17. Convicts who went out of control were put in restraining devices such as handcuffs, and it was this process for which the term "ironed up" was used.

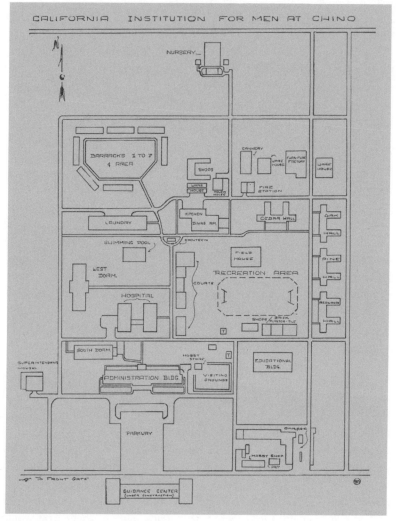

Diagrammatic map of CIM (1951)
Source: California Institute for Men, Chino, California, *Orientation to Employment in State Correctional Service* (Sacramento: State of California, Department of Corrections, 1951).

see that truck driving around the institution, across the fields, to the cannery. The inmate tour guide knew what to do: take them around the quadrangle, then drive out the east gate and take them down to the dairy and the piggery and the slaughterhouse and the cannery and everything else and then make a big loop back to the permanent pasture behind Scudder's house. There the truck would stop. And then you would see this kindly old man walking across the alfalfa fields to meet that truck. It stopped out by the fence, by the road. The first thing he'd do—he wouldn't introduce himself or anything—he would walk up to an inmate and say, "May I have your jacket?" and he would take the jacket and throw it over the barbed wire at the top of the fence, and he would tell them, "That way if you escape, you won't get hurt, the barbed wire won't tear you up. But just remember: you can never come back." Then he would introduce himself and give his orientation talk, telling them what his expectations were. And he told them, "If you have any questions, just ask a correctional officer." (I just loved the way that man did business.) Some of the inmates thought the performance was a little tacky, and they would he-he a bit and make comments. But then you would tell them: "Hey, listen to that man. He means every word he says."

Chino provided a thoroughly enjoyable way to break into the business. Of course I was enthusiastic. Everything was new. So I probably paid closer attention to that and not to any disappointments. But all in all, it was a really pleasant situation.

There were disappointing inmates. You would put in time and energy on an individual, and then he would not take care of himself and would go down the drain. And he would get shipped out for homosexual activity, for refusal to work, for theft, or for some other violation. A guy could escape. He could commit suicide. One fellow—we could not keep him from sniffing paint thinner and that sort of thing. He finally fried his brain. He was a good kid, too. But he just could not keep from sniffing, and finally it got him to the point that he was standing on his bunk and diving into his toilet, he was so far gone. I had him in the kitchen at CMF [the California Medical Facility].[18] He drew weird pictures, but he was quite an artist. A hardworking kid, too. So he was just one of those guys you get interested in, and try to get him going, but he just won't leave that particular thing alone. They just poop out on you. If you don't get personal, you won't be bothered by that stuff. But in this case I got personal. I hated to see it happen. I suppose the effort you put into it was not the issue. But sometimes you cut corners for them, and it makes you wonder why you did it.

At Chino, at one point I had problems with my half-day people. I had to balance out my crew. I would have so many at work in the morning and so many in school, and vice versa in the afternoon. And then there would be some who did not want to go to school but wanted to work all day. They preferred to work, and so they would let school slide. And then we had a stroke of genius. I don't know who thought of this, but my hand was in it a little bit, because I had an inmate who was just not going to go to school.

18. The California Medical Facility in Vacaville (CMF), which is taken up in the next chapter.

Anyway, among a bunch of us, it wound up, "Why don't we have night school for some of these people?" And they worked it out budgetwise and personnelwise to have a night school. This one inmate in particular who did not want to work just half a day, he worked all day and then went to night school. Explain that to me. Even though the education was remedial, for some reason it made sense to him not to give up half a day of work to go to school. That was what had happened to him before. He had to go to work because of family or whatever, but it was okay to go to school at night. I believe he was Mexican. He was typical on the street. He worked, and he had a beer. I don't remember why he was in there—probably burglary or something of that nature. But it was ingrained: you work all day. And all we were doing at that time was hoeing weeds along the fence line.

Some of the others, too. I thought they ought to go to school. I got interested in them. And then they would goof around and get shipped out. They were about my age, in their mid-twenties. Of course I had it all down pat. I knew what was happening and how you were supposed to do it. Even though we were about the same age, I had all this wealth of experience so I could tell them what to do! It disappointed me that they did not listen to me. (I have a tendency to get impressed with my own importance, and after a while when you tell people what to do so many times, you begin to believe it.)

The age factor was a big thing, the age of the inmates and my age. We just weren't that far apart. In fact, there were three people there I had gone to high school with who were convicts. (You would have to report this, get it out front. And they saw that they weren't on your crew.)

The Special Institution at Chino

The institution at Chino was different. It was a new concept. All the traditional prison people put it down, in terms of prisons. But Chino dominated the promotional lists. They just weren't promoting people anyplace else in the state. At that time, promotion was by statewide examination, and it was pretty comprehensive, too.

There wasn't a dime's worth of difference in any of us whom they hired down there after the war. The service experience, a couple of years of college, about the same age, in the early twenties.[19] And so they just hired very heavily, and this group moved through the Department together over the years.

---

19. With respect to college experience, the California experience may have been unusual. A 1968 survey of line personnel in adult correctional institutions indicated that 75% had no college experience at all. John J. Galvin and Loren Karacki, *Manpower and Training in Correctional Institutions* (Washington, D.C.: Joint Commission on Correctional Manpower and Training, 1968), 12.

When you hire somebody out of the service who has spent years in the military, you are getting an instant correctional officer. He knows how to talk to people; he knows how to handle groups. All he really needs is just a little emphasis on locking doors and some of the tricks that convicts had and maybe the troops he was handling in the service did not.

I found it strange that ex-officers were pretty good at adjusting right now. I did not think they would make the adjustment as quickly as, say, a master sergeant. The noncoms were dealing with the troops, and the officers were dealing with different things. But the officers understood the system; they understood how to go and what to do. They were used to not having to succumb to enlisted men. They conformed, and that is the way the officer approached the inmate. It was not "How dare you ask me that?" Their attitude was: "Don't ask, because I am not going to say yes."

But the ex-service personnel served us well. We had some really great people. Some of them went on to become lieutenant and beyond and had a second career. They were just good people. Particularly as correctional officers, great people. You did not have to spend time getting used to being around people or being in a housing unit, because they were used to that. The only thing they were not used to was the homosexuality. They just did not see it; it was kept out of sight in the service. But you might stumble on it anytime if you were working what we used to call K Wing at CMF, when it was the lockup for homosexuals. You just might stumble on it anytime. But in the service, and in places like Chino, you did not see it.

Even though they were a bonus, we were missing some good people because of the age limit. We increased that later on. We could take forty-year-olds. The age limit was based on the retirement picture. At that time you could retire at fifty-five with twenty years. Even at forty, they could work until they were sixty and retire. The ones who stayed with it did well. Retired as lieutenants, and one of them was a captain. We got good mileage out of them. However, even though Vietnam was over in 1973, I do not recall any Vietnam veterans in my time. There were one or two exceptions; one of my very good friends who is a captain at Soledad now, he was a Vietnam veteran. I am sure there were others.

The salaries were not very high. When I took the exam to get a position with the Department, the salary was $255 a month. By the time I was hired, it was $325 a month. In the late 1940s, I had a job with Western Geophysical, with an oil exploration crew, on the survey crew, and they paid about $400 a month, which was an excellent salary at that time. The prison business had traditionally always been low paid, but then right after that, within the first year after I was there, I was making almost $400 a month. We just got raise after raise after raise, which we kind of knew was going to happen. They had to meet the competition, and they had the tidelands oil money.[20]

Scudder had another principle. He would not hire anybody who had worked in a prison before. He wanted people who didn't have any prison backgrounds. He did not want to have a bunch of ideas to get rid of.

He gave us his philosophy on Day One.[21] We had not been there fifteen minutes before we knew exactly what he wanted, how he wanted to do it, and how we were going to help him do it. At orientation he explained it all.

Since these were young first offenders, "We don't have any locks on the doors." And correctional officers, he said, are expected to be Superman and able to do anything that needed to be done. And he had another theory. "We don't wear evidences of rank. We want the inmate to understand that a staff member is the same, whether he is talking to me or a correctional officer. He talks to us all the same way." We all wore the same uniform, khakis—khakis and boots. And the official hat was the Stetson, appropriate for working out in the fields. But I never did have one. In fact I used to get in trouble for wearing a baseball cap. If you were going to wear a hat, you would wear the official hat, the Stetson. Any supervisor who would drive by and find you with the wrong hat . . . but it was a minor thing.

So here was this man with ideas that were not traditional, and this would appeal to twentysomethings who had just saved the world. You find out in the service that at the age of eighteen or nineteen, you can do things that you just didn't dream of. So you just carried that over into your career—accept new things, do new things of which you were perfectly capable. You had to get along with people. And you had to get along with authority. But—again—if I had started out at a traditional prison, I don't think I would have stayed.

Contrasts with Other Institutions

I met people from the other prisons. And when it came time for promo-

20. In 1953, Congress granted California and other coastal states rights to the royalties from oil production in the tidelands adjacent to each state.

21. California Institution for Men, *Orientation to Employment,* 1, spelled out the Department mission in these words [probably Scudder's]: "The protection of society, both immediate and ultimate, is conceived to be the primary purpose of a correctional system. The basic concepts upon which our correctional program is built must be those of Democracy and Christianity. Within this framework, objectivity and realism shall be the keynotes of our correctional program. . . . Each inmate is to be regarded as an individual, in need of varying degrees of restraint, treatment, and supervision . . . so that he may eventually assume the responsibilities of citizenship."

tion to sergeant, I was interviewed at both Folsom and San Quentin.[22] I just did not want any part of those warehousing operations. Nothing was happening there, just traditional warehousing. The facilities were not conducive to making any real changes. You've got those stone walls, and you're not going to change them a whole lot. At Folsom, they built the cell blocks out of the native granite, and then they built a building over the cell blocks. The inmates never got to see the stars or the moon. They locked them up at 4:30 in the afternoon and let them out at eight o'clock in the morning, so there was no way they could ever see the stars or the moon. They have since changed that, due to population pressures and other factors; they now call the institution "New Folsom."

Scudder used to get a lot of heat because he did not take personnel transfers from the other institutions. Just before I left, they had a "compassionate transfer"—someone with family problems, and they transferred him down to Chino. The poor man was absolutely lost. He almost could not function. No locks. No walls. No guns. He did not have any way of working. At Folsom, you would walk out in the yard and have the guard tower covering you as you walked. At Chino, when you walked across the yard, the only difference between you and the convicts was that they had on blue clothes, and you had on khaki clothes. He did not know whether he was talking to a sergeant or a captain or a lieutenant, because they did not have any insignia. It just took his whole world away from him. He was a nice guy, and eventually he adjusted.

While I was at Chino, they started sending convicts from San Quentin and Folsom who were six months to parole to prepare them for release, get them used to some freedom, and these inmates just hated Chino. With the lack of insignia, the lack of regimentation, nobody bothering you, not locking you up at night, living in the dorm, being able to step out of the dorm at midnight into the compound. All of this just dumbfounded them: "You can't do that." They would say, "I hate this place. Send me back to Folsom." Over a period of time, they would relax and learn to enjoy it. And then they would get paroled. But before, it was all regimented for them. You would eat your dinner, go to your cell, and they would let you out in the morning. Jobs were at a premium in San Quentin and Folsom, and inmates held on to them, even using violence to protect their jobs: "I've got a job in the kitchen, and you're not going to take it from me, and I'll cut your throat if you try!" But at Chino, everybody had a job, a job every day.

---

22. San Quentin and Folsom were California's two oldest prisons. San Quentin was opened in 1852 and housed both male and female inmates until 1933. Folsom State Prison was opened in 1880, originally designed to hold the state's most difficult convicts. Both prisons quickly acquired reputations as tough institutions and functioned as what today would be known as maximum-security.

Chino had visiting only on weekends. That was so that the program would not be interrupted during the week—had to get those tomatoes picked and so on. They had picnic tables, and the families could bring a picnic lunch, and the kids could run around. It was a rare thing to have a visitor during the week.

The inmates worked seven and a half hours, which is unusual for a prison, because of the count, the feeding, and so on. But we worked it out so that they worked seven and a half hours. It was a big operation, with the farm and cannery. We grew everything down there. Produce—corn and what have you—was distributed throughout the state by Prison Industries. And then we had the slaughterhouse and the dairy. In fact, we produced so much milk that Knudson's Dairy used to buy our milk. And when convicts came from other institutions, they could not get over the big jugs of milk sitting there with all they wanted to drink. None of the food was like Mama used to make, but there was plenty of it, and it was all good food. When we would be in the field and get the corn in the truck, it would be in the can twenty minutes later. That's fresh, good stuff. There were people like Wes Coblentz there to oversee the operations. I don't know what their backgrounds were, whether they had previous training or got their training there. These were the guys we did business with

That was a great place. Probably for my own benefit, I should have stayed there. The program at Chino was ideal: education, vocational training. Learn how to carry that lunch box, do the job.

The fact that we had special inmates at Chino weighed heavily in our success rate. We had a tendency to overlook the fact that we had a screening system in place for our inmates. At the time I did not realize that. I saw it as a break for the inmate, not for myself.

Old-Timers Had Trouble Adapting to Chino

Even with Scudder's great leadership, my attitude about Chino would have been entirely different if we had been forced to take any inmate who came down the line. But we did not have the bad apples to deal with. Every one of the inmates was pretty much the same except for the old-timers from Folsom. And our biggest problem with them was to keep them from having a heart attack. "You mean I have to walk all the way across that quadrangle by myself?"

The old-timers had a real dependence on the officers and the setup. I felt sorry for some of them. One guy on my crew was in his late forties. I remember we were hoeing weeds at the time. Every morning, he had the same routine. He would say, "I hate this goddamned place." He would say he wanted a transfer back to Folsom. We would be near the fence, picking weeds. I told him if he wanted to go to Folsom to get out on the road, which was right by the fence area, and walk there. I told him he might have some extra time to stop by home first before we would pick him up and take him to Folsom.

I told him he could not get transferred back to Folsom; that he was there for a purpose. "What purpose, choppin' weeds?" "You're out here by the fence, two steps from the highway. Now you can either handle that, or you can't. That's what you're here for."

But was it awful for some of them. They would get them off of the bus and put them in a dormitory! It was generally late at night because of the long bus trip down. Go in there when it was dark and there is your bunk. You do not know who is sleeping around you. Then the officer goes away. The inmates could tell some real stories about that and how they felt coming down there.

It was tough for the old-timers because they did not have to think at Folsom. It was taken care of for them. I could see where Chino would scare them to death. At Chino you had to make decisions for yourself. You had to be at the place where they were going to count. Nobody was herding you around to make sure you got there. It was up to you to deal with that.

One time an inmate who had been with me for a week (he also was in his forties, a burnout period) said, "I'm sick." I told him to go to the clinic. He said, "What?" I said, "If you're ill, go to the clinic." He thought he needed an escort or a note or something. It took three tries to convince him that all he needed to do to get into the clinic was walk over to the clinic. We were working in the quadrangle; I could watch him go to the clinic from where we were working, and everything was fine.

The other part of that thing was that the correctional officer could make that kind of decision, outside of the regular routine. So the inmate went to the clinic, and they gave him some cold pills, and he came back, and that was the last I heard from him. Then he stopped standing right next to me. Some of them were like leeches; I could not get away from them for their first couple of days.

It did not seem to mean a thing to them when you would talk to them about why they were there at Chino, to prepare them for parole. They would say all they needed was to be released. I would tell them that here they were, standing in my hip pocket, moaning and groaning because there are no locks on the door, no gun towers to protect them, and they wanted to tell me they were ready for parole? They would just say that they did not need Chino. "Then quit moaning and groaning and get out of my hip pocket, will you? If you are able to stand on your own two feet and are ready for parole, act like it."

They just did not get the connection. They stood around like whipped dogs and three-year-olds. Then they would say they were ready for parole. Yeah, right, for a period of about five days until they would get drunk and commit another burglary and be right back in here. They had just squandered all of their money and did not have a place to sleep.

We had a lot more inmates who were inadequate when I first started to work than we had later. Or maybe the misfits and incompetents just manifested their character in different ways. The ones I am talking about were the old drunks.

Special Inmates and a Generation of Officers

I still continue to be impressed with Chino and with Scudder. He had an idea. He had the means and the opportunity to put it into effect. I think it worked. I think it worked well. The recidivism rate for Chino was considerably lower than for anyplace else in the Department. Of course, as I have commented, that may have been the type of inmate as much as the program. [23]

The staff at Chino chose the inmates. They would send us up to San Quentin to review the records and take a look at the inmates, and they could end up at Chino a couple or three weeks later. I went a few times. It was not part of my regular job, but it was part of training to get everybody involved. My part was very minor. But you were part of the process. I had worked there for probably eight months, was still on the midnight watch, and I was walking down to eat breakfast when the captain came up and said, "Oh, next week you're going up to Quentin and Folsom with the crew," and I said, "But I don't know . . . ," and he was saying, "Well, just be ready."

The one time, there were four of us. We went to San Quentin, did our job, stayed overnight, then went to Folsom and did our job again. The next time, there were six or seven, and one crew went to San Quentin, and one crew went to Folsom. Then we all met back at the institution. But I had not been there long enough or have the background to make that kind of decision. It was strictly training, exposure. But Scudder had the theory that you could do whatever needs doing. A correctional officer had just as much power as a captain. You could make those kinds of decisions. That was what got me in trouble with the rest of the Department, because that was not the way it worked at San Quentin or Folsom. There were people

---

23. Recidivism is the rate at which released convicts committed another offense and were recommitted to the prison system. Independent data for this period are not available.

who were trained in those areas. So in their minds, I was always making decisions that it was not my decision to make. But at Chino, it was my decision to make. The institution was centered on the correctional officer, and the supervisors were supportive staff. That was the way it worked. You were the workman, you were the guy who made it go. You were where the rubber met the road. If you couldn't handle it, then you would talk to your supervisor, and then he would lend his tools to make it work. And my first four years were that way. I never got it out of my head, and I never made the adjustment to the old style.

Due to our age, if nothing else, most of the correctional officers at Chino had much in common. We socialized after hours. There was a golf course right there. I had known a couple of them before. Probably three of us lived near the institution. Then there were the two guys with whom I had gone to high school who were working out there. Other than that, I did not have too much background with the others.

There were some old-timers who had worked in the institution during the war and were just phasing out. So the institution was hiring pretty heavily when I came aboard. They were picking from my group because it was there.

And it carried on through. Later, at the Medical Facility, all of us lieutenants had a couple of years of college. We were in our early forties. I mean all of the lieutenants—after the first two years that CMF was open, the older lieutenants went out, and that is not good. Because we all thought the same, our kids were the same age, the whole works. So we pretty much had control of the institution. As in any case, you have oddballs. But our instinctive way of doing business was pretty much the same. Our background was the same, our family life was the same. So there was not a lot of variety after we settled in, after four or five years.

When I first transferred to CMF, it was all old-time lieutenants from Folsom and San Quentin, and I could not wait for them to leave. Eventually they just retired and faded away. What happened at Chino was that during the war, all the able-bodied and the young were gone. All the officers who stayed were old. The younger people did not come back to the prison system after they had gotten their feet wet and "seen Paris," because wages were so low, they had better training, and they knew they could do better. So they just did not come back.

What you had at Chino, then, were the wartime people who had filled the gap while everybody was gone. It did not take them long to retire when everybody got back, because they were so old when they were retreaded.[24]

It was like a feeding frenzy, hiring guys who just came out of the service.

---

24. Retreaded is a metaphor, using the retreading of worn tires, for older workers who were enlisted into a new type of employment.

Some of them hired on before I did because they did not go to school. I think I was twenty-five when I hired on. So some of the guys in my age group had been working there a couple of years before I got there.

We started having people retire every day. I was new there, and so I got to know only a few of the older officers. Most of them were local. They had not worked at Folsom or San Quentin. They had just hired on at Chino as local talent.

My first extensive experience with people from San Quentin and Folsom was at the California Medical Facility. That was a whole different world.

The first time I saw San Quentin, there it was, just a pile of rock out there. I was rather amused by the guy at the gate. It was just like Folsom. The staff there were peas in a pod. They just moved back and forth between San Quentin and Folsom. They didn't have anybody new in the place. They had an image to maintain: the deadpan, the silence. I can't really describe it. Just like a robot, as far as I was concerned. No recognition that we were fellow correctional officers or anything. "This is San Quentin. I'm on the gate, and you are just something I have to deal with." And it was no better inside, pretty much the same. That was the way they were trained.

How the Inmates Were Treated at Chino

But things changed very rapidly in the prisons. Prewar, the old system was: lock them up, don't deal with them unless you have to deal with them. If an inmate attacked an officer, when they got him subdued, they would drag him to a corner and whip the crap out of him. Everybody who walked by was offered a piece of this. That was the old style. It prevailed for quite a while at San Quentin and Folsom.[25] At Chino, we did not see any of that. The guards never were attacked at Chino. I don't remember a case.

I do remember one time one of the officers was having a little trouble with one of the inmates on his crew. So they went behind the vineyards and duked it out. When they came back, it was all settled. That was not the thing to do, but it solved the problem. The officer never had any more trouble with anybody after that. It worked.

That was the difference with Chino. It was just an entirely different

---

25. George Gregory, *Alcatraz Screw: My Years as a Guard in America's Most Notorious Prison* (Columbia: University of Missouri Press, 2002), describes correctional officers' operating under this kind of system, but in that case in a federal prison, and perhaps an institution idiosyncratic in the federal system.

philosophy. In that day and age, if an inmate attacked an officer and drew blood, he was sent to death row. Which made it kind of easy. That was what was in the convict's mind: "Hey, I don't need to do this, because I am going to get myself in some real trouble." It was not just two guys doing their thing. That all changed. That was part of it; but on the other hand, as I commented, you had guards dragging an inmate off in a corner and kicking the shit out of him for raising his hand to an officer. So it was a balancing act. The officer who took the guy behind the vineyard and thumped the guy's head was in between. But that guy says, "I don't want any more of this."

So we were encouraged to be friendly with inmates at Chino. Be firm, but be fair. Make damn sure that they do meet the requirements; but you did so in a friendly manner. If you got friendlier with one than with another, if somebody picked up on it, then you were talked to about it. It was explained how to maintain the equilibrium. In my time at Chino, I don't think anybody got into trouble for "dealing"[26] with the inmates. I am sure it happened before and after me, but I do not recall, during my time, anyone bringing stuff in for the inmates or getting overly familiar. As far as being friendly, you did not talk down to them: the "I am an officer, you are the convict" type thing did not exist. It was kind of with a smile, get your weeds out of my cotton. Except in a friendly manner. The message was: Do what I tell you to do, but I am not going to abuse you while I am telling you to do it.

Of course an inmate might have a bad day. You just did the same thing that happened when an officer had a bad day, you just tolerated it. Unless it was really bad. Or you might take the guy and give him some extra duty.

Working Conditions

That is another thing. I did not write a disciplinary report all the time I was at Chino. But I disciplined a lot of inmates because I had that prerogative as a correctional officer. I did not have to buck my problem up to somebody else; because I could take care of it at the time. If an inmate was not doing what I needed him to do, then I could tell him to do this until you learn to do what I want you to do. And I was backed up. That is what Scudder meant with "You are next to Superman." That was what the supervisor was for, to back you up. Not to make the decision for you or take the problem off of your hands. He was there to back up your decision.

26. That is, bringing in contraband goods in exchange for money or some consideration. This subject comes up repeatedly below.

He would do that. If that was not the proper decision that you made for that convict, then they would tell you why it was not, and not to do it again. That was about all it ever amounted to.

The strength of the thing, and what Scudder tried to accomplish, and it was subtle, was that you keep constant pressure on, and the inmate soon understands that "Hey, that correctional officer is the guy I have to deal with. That is the guy who is going to manage my life. And it is not going to change. The rest of the people are there to help him do that."

At the other institutions, you wrote your 115, your disciplinary report. You sent it up to the sergeant. The sergeant took a look at it, maybe handled it if that was his philosophy. Some sergeants at some institutions handled it, but mostly lieutenants handled it.

In that arrangement, in the inmate's mind, the correctional officer can't do anything to him. He can just write the report. Then they can bullshit the lieutenant who was not there out of whatever the hell it is. But it was not that way at Chino. They had to deal with the correctional officer. It was not going anyplace else.

It made your job so much easier. There wasn't any question about "Hey, I'm going to go see the sergeant." They knew that they were eventually going to have to deal with the correctional officer. And the sergeant or the supervisor had a twofold job. That was, make sure the inmate had it clear in his mind that he had to deal with the correctional officer, and, also, he had to make sure that the correctional officer knew that he had to be fair with what he was doing. It was positive.

This is another comment I would make about Scudder. A brand-new correctional officer who had a wife and a couple of kids had preference on the summer months for vacation because he had kids in school. The old-timers' seniority did not count a bean for that. You talk about pumping a guy up and making him feel welcome . . .

Down at the end of the property, there was a low spot they could not do anything with, and so they made a lake out of it, and they stocked it with fish. You could take your kids out there and fish, but you could not go out there as an adult and fish. Only adults accompanied by kids could fish. Again, how could you have it any better as a new employee?

At the end of the growing season (corn, tomatoes, etc.), the fields were gleaned. On that part of the property, there was just a four-strand barbed-wire fence. So Tony, the farm supervisor, would put out a memo that on Thursday afternoon from 1:00 to 4:00 we are going to glean the field, and you come on down and get your vegetables for your family.

Thursday afternoon he had some inmates out there gleaning corn or whatever. You would go home with a big box of fresh-cut stuff. The inmates were volunteers. They wanted to see the women and talk to the kids. They would pick all that stuff and hand it over the fence to you, and away you would go. Just a regular roadside stand.

Another thing that was kind of unusual. I mentioned the green-field crew that would go out and cut alfalfa for the cows every morning at five o'clock. The pheasants would be nesting, and they would not leave their nests. The mower would come across and clip their legs off or damage them. The inmates tried to raise them without their legs, but they just would not make it. So they would give the pheasants to us, and occasionally we would have pheasant dinner. It was a hell of a place. They were good fringes.

All rolled into a package, it made a guy like me feel pretty good about work. There were not any put-downs, and they let you in on things, treated you as if you knew something.

My First Experience with Escapes

They had a correctional officer designated to follow up on escapes and coordinate with the police. He had been around for ten years or more. So, again as a training thing, he would grab one of us brand-new correctional officers to go to El Monte[27] to visit this inmate's parents and tell them that if he gets hold of them, they have to contact us and everything. So you are working with this outfit for six months, and they have you chasing an escapee. Great learning process.

Chino was scattered out over 2,600 acres. If you couldn't locate an inmate in fifteen minutes, they blew the whistle for an escape. Then you brought them all in and counted everybody, and you would know if somebody was gone. At other institutions I've worked in, the attitude was, "As long as they are inside the fence, we don't care where they are." But at Chino, everybody was accounted for. Fifteen minutes was enough time to get anybody. It did not matter if he was out at the end of the 2,600 acres. Radio cars would go out and pick up inmate Joe Blow, who was assigned to your crew.

We had inmates just walk off. Like the night irrigator, who would just get tired, put his shovel over his shoulder, and walk down the road, and some farmer would pick him up. And we'd find him later on someplace, perhaps in Mexico or Los Angeles. One guy took off midweek, maybe Thursday, just walked off down the street, left the shovel leaning up against the fence. Somebody must have come along and picked him up, which would not be uncommon in that area, where you had farmers doing irrigating. He got clear to Mexico, but his folks came to visit him—and he

27. A nearby town.

wasn't there! They must have passed on the road someplace. He was an old-timer, too. You did not get that kind of night work unless you were pretty well seasoned. He later said, "I don't know. I just got out there and got to thinking about my family. And so I just walked off down the road, and this guy picked me up." He had to come back and do another two or three years, but he had to do that in San Quentin or Folsom. As a group, these were impulsive people, and it is not too surprising that something like that would happen.

None of the staff got in trouble. You just put the inmates out there at night and gathered them up in the morning. There was a check—a two o'clock count, and a four o'clock count. But he was there both times.

Problems We Did Not Have at Chino

Gangs did not come along until the Mexican Mafia. Then La Familia formed to protect themselves from the Mexican Mafia. But that was all considerably after I left Chino. We did not have any real gang trouble until the sixties.[28]

We also did not have the problems with things coming in at Chino, visitors bringing in knives, or items like that. Until they got educated, or banned, we used to have problems, troubles with the picnic tables and stuff they would bring in. For example, supposedly there was a jar of olives, but there was gin instead of olive juice, that kind of thing. There were some weapons brought in, knives and such. But we did do an inspection, which is something I never liked—pawing through their picnic baskets. But they were basically inspected. That doesn't mean a pill couldn't get in or something. We just didn't really worry about it. We paid attention and gave it a good effort, but we didn't worry about it. Having visiting on the weekends and having the picnic tables was convenient and best for the institution as a whole.

A visiting room in a prison—that's no way to do it. I'm not talking about the phones though the glass. I'm talking about sitting in a big room with your kids. Nothing for them really to do, and you're sitting around a table, going to the Coke machine every now and then. Down at Chino, with the picnic area, and lawn area, the kids would run around all over the place. Mom and Dad could sit at the table and see them, call them back, what have you. We had a canteen-type thing there, where our employee organization sold some stuff almost at cost, but not quite, because we used the profits for our activities. But the inmates got a good break on what was sold.

---

28. The subject of gangs comes up later, in chapter 4.

Visitors and inmates picnicking in the Chino visiting area (1953)
Source: Norman Fenton, *Correctional Employees Training Manual III: An Introduction in Classification and Treatment in State Correctional Service* (Sacramento: Department of Corrections, 1953).

It was an excellent visiting center. There wasn't any problem with wandering from table to table. This was your area, this was your visit, and you do it the way you want to do it. Just don't get outside the perimeter. We just turned it over to them, and they either messed it up or they did it right. If they messed up, you just took care of it, and you go on down the row.

I have no idea why they would have brought knives in. With all the stuff they had around there, there was no reason to bring a weapon in. My God. All the farm implements, the shovels, the welding shop, the grinders out there. I have no idea except that the people outside would bring the prisoners a cake with a file in it: "I brought the file." "Yeah, I've got a dozen in my locker."[29]

Narcotics I understood, but narcotics were not that big a problem at the time. It would have been alcohol mostly. But there again, it didn't take long for word to spread: one drink would get you back in San Quentin. "So cool it, man." He had a good deal. Mom is coming down, the kids are coming down. And he'd take that one drink, and you'd smell it on his

29. Contraband is discussed again below.

breath, and he'd be off to San Quentin Monday. So it didn't take long for the word to spread.

Scudder gave them something to protect, and that was all new to them. And it was so subtle that nobody knew that that was happening. I'm speaking of staff, really. I don't know what made me so perceptive at that time, but it was like having a map on the wall: "Hey, this guy is good. People are doing things they didn't even know they're doing." Most of it was by design, some of it was just by accident. You've got that visiting situation, and the rest of the prison people are complaining about the freedom and saying, "You guys are going to have trouble," and all that, or "We don't let them do that here." Well, okay, the convict sitting up there doesn't have anything to protect. He can bitch or get dope in or have his girl visit as his sister or whatever. The guy on the visiting grounds at Chino had to make a decision: protect what he had. And that's the big difference. A lot of staff at other institutions did not seem to understand that.

Another correctional officer asked me one day, "How about that visiting deal there, you know," and I said, "I think it's great." He asked me why I thought it was great. I told him what I just told you. He looked at me like I was crazy. He was uncomfortable with it, or he thought they were getting too good of a deal, or whatever his process was. And he was taken aback that "Oh, there is a purpose here?" or "There is something good coming out of this?" I don't know why it struck me that way, but those were the lessons I learned down there, and I learned to look for them, and those are the lessons that got me in trouble when I got out into the real prison world.

I was at Chino from 1951 to 1955. American society was an entirely different society then. The emphasis in running prisons, as I have tried to indicate, was entirely different, too. The giveaway program did not come until the mid-1960s.[30] We cut our own throat by anticipating instead of maintaining what we were doing and how we were doing it. The Department director decided that the trend was going this way and loosened up on some things, which was a definite mistake. But that is the way it went.

In the prison business, you do not give up anything that you don't have to give up. That is the wisest course. If you absolutely have to give it up, then you give it up and make it work the way it is supposed to, but you do not volunteer to give up the farm. And we did in the sixties. Some very good tools we needed at the time were taken away.

---

30. This subject is taken up below, especially in chapter 4.

Scudder's Special Style

I don't think there is any way that I can really make the contrast between the Chino philosophy and the philosophy of the rest of the Department. There were so many subtle things going on at Chino. Perhaps I am reading things into some of this. Maybe the emphasis on the correctional officer was not that great. But I thought it was that way. I thought that was what they were trying to do. So I lived my life as a correctional officer that way. If I had been too far wrong, I would not have been promoted.

One of the things, just to show you how things worked: when I had this construction crew, some of us had an hour and fifteen minutes off during the middle of the day because of the count and the inmates' eating. Out front we had a lawn area that Scudder was kind of concerned with. It just did not look right to him. One day he came around when we were fixing something, and I said, "I think I am going to put some horseshoe pits in that patch of ground in front of the administration building." And he said, "That sounds like a good idea."

I put in two horseshoe pits. It was so popular, I had to put in three more for the counselors from the Guidance Center, for the captain—everybody but Scudder shot horseshoes. That was the kind of thing it was. They were for staff only. The inmates were eating and being counted. Later on in the day, the inmates who swept out the administration building or had duties as gardeners or whatever would go over and throw the horseshoes—until their supervisor came and got them and put them on something else. That was the way staff was. Some people would not eat so that they would be first at the horseshoe pits. I can remember one guy saying, "Jeez, I wish I would lose. I want to eat before I go back to work." He was one of the counselors from the Guidance Center.

In the staff dining room, there were no distinctions. You just sat down. That was Scudder all the way. You walked into the dining room and took the next available seat at a four-man table. It did not matter who was sitting there. If it was the director of Corrections and Scudder, and you walked in there and there was an empty seat at his table, you sat down at his table. That was a requirement.

It was a staff dining room. But you don't gather up in little cliques. Administrators don't sit over here and correctional officers over there. You fill up the seats as you go. You would have people down giving the oral exams. It might be an associate warden at Folsom or someone like that. So the oral board comes down to eat, and there were only three of them. If there was an empty seat, you would go and sit down. Sometimes they could hardly handle it. It did not happen that way in their institutions. Maybe you just got finished talking to them upstairs. You sit down and eat and just carry on a conversation as if you were a real person. It was tough for them to take. Scudder was adamant about that, however. Everybody is treated the same! Don't care what your position is.

I really did not know the man that well. But I have to say he was the best I ever saw. His wife died right before I got out there, just a matter of weeks, and he had this big superintendent's house out there. In that day and age, when they built a superintendent's house, they built a superintendent's house. Chino was kind of isolated because everything was up north. So we had to have a place to entertain whenever people did condescend to come from northern California to southern California. He was kind of a lonesome old guy at that time. But I understand he wandered all over the institution even before she passed away. It was just his style, to go out and see what was happening, what was going on.

How I Got Hired at Chino and How I Left

We had a captain who was office-bound. He could not get away from that paperwork. He could not get out of that office. I could watch Scudder work on him gently about getting out of the office. Scudder would go so far as to stop by the captain's office and say, "Let's go over to the so-and-so. . . ." And then you could hear bits of the conversation: "I find that this works well for me, to get out of the office." So finally it came down to the point that Scudder told him that he had to spend a half a day out of the office. "Now, you choose, do you want to spend the mornings in the office and the afternoon out, or the other way around? And starting tomorrow." I happened to be in the hallway when he stuck his head in the captain's office and said that. When I walked by his office, the captain was just stricken. "Jesus, what I am going to do?" He did not want to get away from the telephones and the security of the paperwork.

And damned if that captain did not wind up to be the associate warden at CMF. He had not changed a bit; he learned nothing. He had his way of doing business, and that was the way he was going to do it. He learned his way as a police officer in Ontario [California] when he got hired as correctional officer. Don't ask me about that. He was well thought of down there, other than this thing of being office-bound.

He insisted that I was going to go to work there at Chino in the first place. I was working at the machine shop and was real happy with the salary, and I went down for an interview. He extolled the virtues of the place, and I told him I could not do it at that time because of a project at the shop, and I wanted to give them notice. This was one o'clock in the afternoon, and I had to go to work at four at the machine shop.

By the time I got to the machine shop, he had already called my boss. My boss was out there fuming, wanting to know what was going on. And after that captain had finished talking to my boss, he phoned my wife. He insisted that I come to work. So that ended it for my boss at the machine shop. He said, "Well, you're going to work down there, go now, if you want to, or go later, it doesn't matter to me." That kind of hurt my feelings, because I liked that job. He was an old-timer who grew up in the machine shop business. He really had his employees' interest at heart. Anyway, it just kind of died on the vine. So I went to work at Chino. It still irritated the hell out of me that the captain would call my boss and also call my wife. And I guess our relationship did not improve over the years.

While I was at Chino, I went to CMF and interviewed for a sergeant's job, along with a friend who interviewed for a lieutenant's position. Okay, there was not anything for me at CMF at that time. I went back to Chino. We were having plumbing problems at home, so I had a crew come out and dig a great big cesspool, a septic tank–type thing. Dirt was everywhere, and the plumbing was all messed up. I had been back one day, and this captain (now associate warden) at CMF phoned me and said, "Come up here. I want to talk to you." He said, "We're going to hire you, and we want you here Monday morning." And just two days before, he had said there was no position at this time.

So there it was. I had to leave my wife with all that mess. Then I get up to Vacaville on Monday morning, and the first thing they asked me was, "Do you want to take some time off? You have a lot on the books." So I did. That is just how vague that man was. Very poor administrator.

You never saw him at Chino. You never had to deal with him at Chino. Up at CMF, you had to deal with him—mainly because of his outlook and that of the rest of the staff. They mostly came from San Quentin. The captain we had at that time had never taken a civil service exam in his life. Back in the thirties he was running a poultry shop in San Francisco. One of the administrators at San Quentin found out that he had clerical skills, so he hired him at the institution, at San Quentin, as a captain's clerk. He stayed there and never got into a housing unit, never got any place except what they call the captain's porch. He went right from a correctional officer clerk to sergeant, to lieutenant. Then they blanketed him in[31] as a captain and sent him to CMF.

There was a man who was totally unequipped. You put him with this other guy who thought he knew the business. The associate warden at CMF thought that the captain knew all about how to run the prison. But

31. That is, promoted him as part of a general change, without individual review.

the captain did not know shit about running a prison. So that made a hell of a combination.

How Chino Seemed So Ideal

At Chino, I was not aware that people from Sacramento were coming around except for the ones who conducted examinations. If there were people from Sacramento down there, they did not come to my area. And I don't remember hearing anything about constant visits. But I'm sure there were people down from Sacramento. I couldn't say why. You did not have staff competition, since Scudder didn't hire people who worked in prisons before. So you didn't have that roadblock or distraction. The only thing you had was the guy who was hired before you who had been at Chino for a year. He had experience. But it was Chino experience. And Scudder told you what that was. And it wasn't something out of left field or some guy's personal opinion. Because the person who had been there for two years had the same philosophy that you did, being there for two months. And that made it great. Within reason of course. It wasn't set in concrete. Basically when it came down to the nitty-gritty, we all thought the same. And we all thought the same because that was the way Scudder trained us to think.

I don't remember any of the correctional officers' resigning or getting fired at Chino. You wouldn't come to work drunk or anything; you wouldn't do that to your fellow workers. I don't know, of course; I am just talking about what I felt. There may have been people fired, for whatever reason. I just don't remember missing anyone without an explanation—he is in the hospital, or he moved to Wisconsin, or something. It was pretty stable.

Chino made sense. So that made it a happy place, and that made it easy. Almost everybody shared that attitude. Most liked to work there. We didn't have too many complaints. We all complained from time to time about things, but nothing serious. People always complain about jobs. We would complain about who would get in the cribbage game. There was a running cribbage game every day at noon with the outside workers. So people would complain if it had been a week or so since they were in a cribbage game or if the horseshoe pits were full, that kind of stuff. If they served banana fritters too many times in the personnel dining room— important things.

There was quite a bit of gossip, as in any group. This guy is going to visit this guy's wife when he is out to camp or something of that nature. There was quite a bit of that. It was all minor stuff, nothing big, as I remember. I don't know, maybe I washed all of that off. Maybe there was an undercurrent there that I did not understand. But it never reached me. It was very comfortable, very comfortable.

Getting a Promotion

I was a correctional officer for four years. That was because the exam was not given except every four years. I think I had been there for two and a half or three years when they gave a combination exam for sergeant and lieutenant. They wanted to pick up some people who had transferred from Oregon and Ohio and so on. One guy had been associate warden in Wisconsin. Two guys who had worked in the California system before had gone to Oregon to run their prison. Now they were ready to come back. So they wanted to pick these people up because they were experienced. So they had a combination sergeant and lieutenant exam.

I took the exam for sergeant. These were statewide exams. At that time, the written counted 60 percent, the oral counted 40 percent. Sometimes they would need people at San Quentin or somewhere and schedule the exam early, but generally the list lasted four years. The length of the list would vary. They would anticipate they were going to need "x" number of people over "x" number of years, over the next four years. So they would make a two-hundred-man list. Or they might say, "We don't need that many, we are going to make a hundred-man list." So then it would run out before the four years was up, that type of thing. Or they would have more promotions due to more people's retiring, resigning for health reasons, or whatever. The mistake they made in the long lists was they were denying the new people a shot—so that, for instance, for me it was almost four years to take the exam. Making sergeant before that is not what I'm talking about. You had to take the exam to see what was there, to see what you had to do for the next time, to have the opportunity.

I came out tenth on the sergeant's exam and twenty-fifth on the lieutenant's exam. After I had worked there for only three and a half years. And it is all due to what they gave me at Chino. I just had a better opportunity than my competition, really.

Let me see if I can describe the exam. One of the big kickers was a comprehensive essay. There were generally ten or fifteen of those. I do fairly well with exams as far as speed goes. These were three-hour exams. I had perhaps fifteen or twenty minutes left over. So it took a while to do these exams. It was steady work. Not just tapping your head trying to figure out what they were talking about. Especially steady effort was needed on the combination exam.

I was really impressed with the scope of the written exam. Then I was really impressed when I placed as high as I did on the lists. That was partly due to the oral, of course. They finally did away with the written exam altogether and went with 100 percent oral. That is where we got into real trouble. But that is another story.

I have mentioned the combination exam for lieutenant and sergeant. I had no intention of making lieutenant right from correctional officer. But it was very encouraging to come up number twenty-five on the list. That is an indication that you can handle what you have to handle. Whether it was fruitful at that particular time, or within the next year. Or if you were on the other end of the stick, hey, I did not do this, I had better jack myself up or find a new job or learn how to do this one. So that is why, to me, the value of having the exams more often was to let a guy know what he was doing and how he was doing it and where he was doing it.

I did not talk to people who did not do very well on the exams; I let them talk to me. I didn't pursue it; I didn't ask them about it. Oddly enough, I had four or five people talk to me. They didn't want to talk to anyone else about it. But they wanted to talk to me. I have no idea why. On the other hand, I had people talk to me like, "You lucky dog, I've been here six years," that type of thing. That is just people.

In later years, it came to the point where I was not promoted, and I was doing the same thing two or three times. Then I really got frustrated. Too soon to get out, and too painful to stay. And I really did not do too much career-wise, as far as compensation goes.

But at Chino, we were one big happy family. That is an overstatement. But the climate was that we were all staff. Scudder worked at making you feel welcome, making you feel important. Breaking down barriers between officer, sergeant, captain, and lieutenant helped the whole climate. You talked the same to everybody. There was not any class distinction. So it was easy at Chino.[32]

32. Elsewhere in these same years of the early 1950s, riots or rebellions were appearing in prisons all over the country; see, for example, the summary in Scott Christianson, *With Liberty for Some: 500 Years of Imprisonment in America* (Boston: Northeastern University Press, 1998), 266–67, who counted at least forty-seven events from 1951 to 1953.

Aerial view of CMF shortly after opening in Vacaville (1956)
Source: State of California, Department of Corrections, 1955–56 *Biennial Report.*

CHAPTER TWO

THE CALIFORNIA MEDICAL FACILITY

STARTING IT, AND GETTING IT TO WORK

At the time that I started with the Department, we had four institutions: San Quentin, Folsom, the women's prison, and Chino. Now they have thirty-one. But already in my day when I quit, they had thirteen institutions. So in that thirty-year period, the system had grown to thirteen. But earlier, it was kind of ingrown. There were not that many places to go.

The prisons became like the old missions: they are just a day's travel apart. Just go down the Central Valley. You drive sixty-odd miles, and you hit Tracy. You drive another sixty-odd miles, and you hit Corcoran. You drive another, and you hit Chowchilla. Then all the way down to the Mexican border, there is one every day's travel. Today, you are never out of sight of a prison in California. As a matter of fact, if you want to get along in California, become a prison guard or an inmate. Because that is the leading industry. We have more locked up than anybody in the nation.[1]

Arriving at the New California Medical Facility

I really did get in on the beginning of the expansion. When I left Chino, I transferred to a new special prison, the California Medical Facility in Vacaville.[2] When I arrived in Vacaville, there were no inmates. As a matter of fact, they were still building the prison. I slept in the firehouse, and

1. In 2001, California had 159,444 inmates in state prisons, out of a population of 33,872,000. The number incarcerated in other levels of institution, such as county jails, both in California and in other states, makes a precise comparison impossible. For more on the growth of prison populations in the state, see Franklin Zimring and Gordon Hawkins, "The Growth of Imprisonment in California," *British Journal of Criminology* 34 (1994): 83–95.

2. During Wilkinson's work at CMF, the institution had a steady population of about 1,350 inmates. State of California, Department of Corrections, *1955–56 Biennial Report*, 38:

some of the other people slept in the cells down at the end of the building. They had a temporary wooden wall up there while they were still constructing the last two units. The wall was to block the corridor off and keep the construction people from wandering into the institution rather than staying on the job. On one occasion, a couple of workers were out sleeping when it came quitting time, and they were locked in. We were standing there about four or five in the afternoon, and we heard *Wham! Wham! Wham!* They were kicking down the barriers. So we put on quite a show for those two idiots. "Well, goddammit, I'm gonna get outta here." But we ran them right into a cell and told them they would get out when we were ready, when they got the wall fixed. "You aren't going to tear up this institution." We put them both in the same cell. Of course nothing really happened to them.

But they complained to their boss. They claimed we did not treat them right, so when he found out why we did not treat them right, the boss fired them, because they were off sleeping when they were supposed to be working. Real thinkers, you know. But they were not prepared for the institution—they did not know anything about prisons. They were not prepared for that kind of attitude. They were big-time construction workers who thought they owned the world.

The town was not prepared for us, either.[3] In early 1956, shortly after we got there, they were having an election for city council. The local veterinarian was in it, and we kind of adopted him as a candidate. When I

A unique institution, the California Medical Facility has the custodial and legal features of a prison, but the staff and climate of a hospital. The Medical Facility, a special unit for handicapped male offenders, particularly the mentally disabled, was authorized by the Legislature during 1945. A site of some 900 acres near Vacaville, Solano County, was purchased. . . . The complement of patients includes approximately 200 tuberculars, 200 psychotics, 150 homosexuals, 100 drug addicts, 400 sex deviates, and a variety of others who are physically or mentally handicapped plus a group of about 100 workers. . . . [T]he method of choice is group psychotherapy, which has been expanded to such an extent as to embrace almost all of the patients. The group program is conducted by highly trained therapists. An average of about 10 patients is assigned to each group. All patients attend two group meetings a week.

M. R. King, "Psychiatric Program of the California Medical Facility," *Journal of Social Therapy* 2 (1956): 243–56, offered a detailed description and rationale for the program. A journalist, Charles Raudebaugh, offered an eyewitness account of the program in "A Jail That Tries to Cure Criminals," *San Francisco Chronicle,* 4 May 1958, 1, 6, and Vacaville Convicts Talk It Out," ibid., 5 May 1958, 1, 12. Morrie Camhi, *The Prison Experience* (Rutland, VT: Charles E. Tuttle Company, 1989), contains photos of CMF a number of years after the events described in these memoirs.

3. Vacaville had a population of 3,169 in 1950. In 1960, there were 10,898 inhabitants, and in 1970, 21,690. Between February 1955 and May 1956, when 300 CMF employees arrived, the population of Vacaville increased by 1,699 people. "New Population Figures Reveal Vacaville Has 7349 Residents, [Vacaville] *Reporter,* 1 June 1956.

Guard tower under construction at CMF (1955)
Source: Historical Albums, California Department of
Corrections, Sacramento.

first got to Vacaville, the kids got the measles, and the family couldn't come
up, so I didn't have anything to clean the house with. I went down to buy
a broom. I commented on how much the broom cost—not because I was
in Vacaville or in that store, but simply because I did not have that much
experience with buying brooms. I thought it was pretty expensive. This
guy tells me, "Hey, you got to get used to the price we charge." I said, "I
have a little story to tell you if you are going to be a businessman here.
These people who came up from the Los Angeles area, some of them drove
twenty-five, thirty, forty miles to work each day. You think they are not
going to Vallejo or Sacramento to shop? You'd better get used to what's
happening." And I padded it a little bit, telling him we were bringing a

three-million-dollar payroll to town: "If you want part of it, you'd better change your attitude."[4]

At any rate, a local election came, and we decided to vote in uniform. I voted at about five-thirty. The registrar said, "I have never seen so many green uniforms in my life." In the townspeople's minds, we were like the airmen at Travis: just somebody else to prey on.[5] We had a bunch of Air Force people living in temporary shacks where the Vacaville city hall is now. We hadn't had any leverage, we didn't do anything. Except that we had brought all this money into town. But we became a presence, and we elected our man to the city council. We became viable people after that. They certainly knew we were there.

Open Houses

At the beginning, and again later, the institution held open houses, one of which was for the community. That was to acquaint the townspeople with what a prison looked like before the inmates came. It was mostly so townspeople could see it firsthand and not hear about it secondhand—how a lock works and that sort of thing, and how we treat this type of inmate. They had no idea what a prison was. We gave them an overview of the procedures with the inmates.

Members of the public still startle me with their attitude about the prisons. Some people do not understand that inmates are not locked in their cells twenty-four hours a day. "You mean they are out running around?" They don't realize that we do not carry guns. I would tell them to think about it this way: "I'm capable and I can handle a gun. But if you're in there, and the prisoners take your gun away, they'll shoot you." They do not understand that you cannot take out 150 guys with six bullets, if the situation ever arose.

The two open houses I was involved in were for the officers' families. Get them out to the institution so they could see where we worked. The wife had heard about Q Wing forever, so now she knew where Q Wing was. By this time, it was hard to do because we were full of inmates, and in order to be able to do the open house, we had to lock them all down.

---

4. The initial operating budget was in fact well over two million dollars. An editorial, "Considerable Criticism Manifested Over Escapes from Medical Facility," [Vacaville] *Reporter,* 20 January 1956, read: "It is our belief that the people of the Vacaville area generally have accepted the institution as a necessary one and have voiced very little protest in its establishment here. . . ."

5. Travis Air Force Base was located just a few miles down the highway from Vacaville, and a number of the personnel lived in Vacaville.

Or set aside a housing unit so they could tour it. So we would set up a movie for those inmates. We showed the families all of the facilities from the laundry room to the hospital so they knew what the old man was talking about when he came home.

Most of us did not want particularly to do the open house, really. Frank O'Brien, the program administrator for whom I was working at the time, made it mandatory to attend. No excuses. Part of your job. Frank's wife and my wife were well acquainted, PTA and stuff. So we went out there and had cake and coffee and mingled. So Officer Joe Blow's wife would come up and say, "Are you Lt. Wilkinson? Are you Mr. O'Brien?" For the most part they were pretty polite. Some of them were pretty disappointed, so obviously the old man was not too happy working for us! This was down in the psych unit. That was the job I was working at the time.

Both open houses were to get people acquainted with the facility. The first time was to see the actual physical plant. Then when we got full of inmates and we could not interrupt the flow of inmates, we had the open house in the visiting room. You could come and go as you pleased. They had games set up for the kids. One old-timer convict dressed up like a clown. He said, "How far can I go?" We said, "You'd better leave some of your blue jeans showing"—that is, we had to remind him not to walk out the front gate with the visitors. We had a good rapport with that guy. It kept the kids busy. They put on a little skit. This guy could do something with puppets, if I remember correctly.

Another convict used to work at Disneyland, and he put on a stocking cap and put on a tumbling act for the kids. He was pretty short. Disney rehired him when he made parole. I didn't think they would, but they did.

At the Beginning at CMF

As I said, I lived in the firehouse for a couple of months before the place really opened. The firehouse was on the prison grounds. It was out back in the maintenance area behind the institution. It was a perfect dormitory. The other people who came up later had to sleep in the cells and make up their own beds and get their own linen and everything. We had one inmate out there. After the first month, we got thirty inmates up from some place, I don't remember where. One of them took care of the firehouse. He got us our clean linen, made coffee. He was such an old-timer that he put eggshells in the coffee to settle the grounds, that kind of thing. I won't forget that first pot of coffee he made. I don't see why it didn't eat the bottom of the pot out. He had probably been in and out of prison three or four times. He was just an old, burned-out, alcoholic burglar. He was on the end of his string. He was in his late fifties at the time, maybe older. You can hardly tell with inmates. I have seen them in their seventies and look like they were in their forties because they have been in prison for thirty years and have had regular hours and good meals. An inmate like that comes out looking as if he's found the fountain of youth. So it was kind of hard to tell the age of some old-timers. But we had been taking care of our own needs up till then. I got the coffeepot. It was a dripulator, but he didn't use it that way. He just put the grounds in the bottom, threw the eggshells in, and—*WHEW!* So when I taught him how to make the coffee, he did pretty well. He thought it was pretty good, too. "It tastes good," he said. All those years he had been drinking it out of an oil can. He kept care of us like an old hen. He was a typical old con. Starts out getting drunk and writing bad checks. At that time we were putting them in jail for bad checks, forgery in particular. So he would get out, and nobody would take his checks anymore, and so he went to burglary, and over the years he was just in and out on burglary.

A burned-out convict made the best kind. That's how we used to run the institution, with those people: check writers and embezzlers. You had two strata for a long time, up until the late sixties. The embezzlers and the check writers—people like that—they were the upper stratum. They were the clerks down in the kitchen, working for accounting, working in the warehouse. The other guys worked in the kitchen, the laundry, and so on. These guys would get out on parole, come back in three weeks or a month, and come through the Guidance Center and take back the same job they had when they left. Well, you get a good, experienced man, what the hell. You need a vacation every now and then. Why not go get him again? You don't have to break in another guy.

Finding Inmates for Work Assignments

We did have an advantage out there because we could go over to the Guidance Center and get what we wanted.[6] Later, I was assignment lieutenant for a long time at CMF. It was our job to see that the institution had the workforce. So I would go to the Guidance Center and pick these guys up if they had any skills—and the ones who were coming back a second or third time had prison skills. They knew how to be a clerk in the kitchen or the warehouse. They knew where the good jobs were and where the bad jobs were. And what they were trained for. So I had to match them up and make sure we had enough to run the place.

6. The Guidance Center for initial evaluation and assignment of convicts opened in 1957, soon after the main Vacaville facilities began functioning.

As a matter of fact, in that day and age I had about a sixty-thousand-dollar budget. They had pay numbers at that time, like thirty-five or fifty cents a day. This was an incentive for an inmate to work or not. It was a nominal amount, but it would buy a carton of cigarettes or a candy bar or what have you. But the most important part was that they had a paying job. A lot of them were interested in not the pay, but in having a paying job: "I'm not a complete loss. I'm not a complete failure." For the old-timers at San Quentin or Folsom, having a job was a status symbol, so they carried that with them if they came to CMF. So it was status for their own self-respect, not for the other convicts. They could cry to mamma and get more money sent to them than they could make on their own. There were some who were really honest about it: "I want to take care of myself, I don't want to drain my family." Damn few of them, but they were sincere about it.

There were a whole bunch of inmates who did not want to work. You know, "I'm here, now it's your problem. Do something with me." We had ways of dealing with that. Like putting them to work in the kitchen, assigning them to school, whether they wanted to go or not—then disciplining them because they did not act properly in school. You make them vulnerable. It would dumbfound them when you would tell them that. "You dummy, you played right into my hands. You would not conform on the job that I put you on, that you could handle. So then I put you in school, knowing that if you screwed up, I could jump down your throat." "Aw, well, you know . . ." "Yeah, that is something you need to think about. Why make yourself vulnerable? I have the tools, and I have the control. You can't beat it. You can mess with it, but you can't beat it. So be good to yourself. Go take that job in the kitchen, and settle down, or do your thing."

The inmates could work a number of hours. In the kitchen, for example, they came down in the morning, served the morning meal, served the noon meal, and served the evening meal. In the meantime they went to school or had free time in between.

What did they do in their free time? Mostly they would go to the yard or lie in their bunks, shoot the breeze with other people, or whatever. It kind of varied with what period you are talking about.

Managing the Inmates

It was a whole new world, whole new prison when the day shift left. Everything was new after four o'clock. You were on inmate time then. Work was over, the institution was closed down. This is when they watched television, this is when they went to the show, this is when they visited with their friends, this is when they were "friggin in the riggin." This is when they got into trouble, and this is when you had fewer staff to handle them. And they were all loose. Again, this progressed as things changed in the institution. In the early days, they did not have that much freedom. Of course always by ten o'clock you would lock them up. Everybody went to bed. But from four o'clock to ten o'clock, it was a busy place. And you were messing with inmates' time.

They did not have to stay in their own areas. There were areas they could not get into, but the housing units were open, and they could get up and down the hallways. It was up to the officer to cut down the visiting in the housing unit. You don't run from this housing unit to that housing unit; you meet out in the hallway. Or you meet somewhere, or you meet down at the activities in R Wing: night school and so on. The yard closed at three-thirty when we locked them down for the four o'clock count. But they were on the run for about five or six hours at night. And your [custodial] workforce was about one-third of what it was in the daytime.

When I first made lieutenant [1961], I had nine people on the first watch, beginning at midnight, for the two thousand convicts. The inmates were locked up most of the time, but come about five o'clock, about one-third of them were out and running. And I had nine people. That included my housing officers and my tower men. I had three people in the office with me. And we had to feed the inmates.

We campaigned to change the hours to 7:00 to 3:00 in the daytime, 3:00 to 11:00 in the nighttime, 11:00 to 7:00 in the morning. That way, when you fed them in the morning, you had a full workforce. All the second watch was there. Before, you had three people running two thousand convicts through the mess hall. Actually, it was more than that, because you had an officer on each serving line, but to handle the traffic, you had three people and the housing officer. So if you changed the hours, you had a full workforce there to feed them. You got it to where they could be handled. I say I campaigned for it. I don't think it was my idea, it was just in conversation that it came up, and it sounded good to me, and so I really pushed it. Other people said, "It sounds good to me, too, so you carry the ball and we will back you up." So by this time the old associate warden had retired, and we got a real guy in there who was open to suggestions. So he did it.

It was just like the count. I fought that count until I just wanted to scream. And so I talked the new guy into going to the old Chino system: beds and people. It worked just like that. Before, the count would be held up for sometimes thirty and forty minutes trying to find out where the error was. Worse yet, sometimes it was cleared on an over and under:

Wilkinson and colleagues working in the Control Room at CMF
Source: Viola Wilkinson.

"Well, there are too many inmates in this unit, and there are not enough here, so we will just clear it because we got them all." Since I had worked in control down at Chino, I said, "This is not going to work, this is not going to get it." They had this one sergeant who understood this system, and nobody else understood it, and I could see why. I said, "Greg, the first escape we have, it is going to take us hours to find the guy." And the first escape we had, Greg said, "It only took us five hours to find him." He felt it was an accomplishment that it did not take all day or something. It was just a really idiotic system. You could not get anything through the captain, because he had absolutely no understanding of the count system. This was the guy who was blanketed in as a captain. He was the one who used to pluck chickens, and he was still plucking chickens as far as I was concerned. They would have to call Greg in when they had an escape. They had to call him from home to come in and do the count. That did not set well with me at all. If I was going to be control officer, I was going to be control officer, and you stay out of here. So I never had an escape while I was control officer, but I had some screwed-up counts. You had all this pressure. They were waiting to feed, and you could not clear the count. The food was getting cold. The convicts were getting bad treatment because they were locked in their cells, and the whole works.

Well, we changed the count system, and the whole thing was cleared up in ten minutes. If you had a bobble, it would take you maybe another ten minutes to straighten out the correctional officer who made the mistake. If the mistake was not made in the control room, then it was made by the correctional officer. They forgot to out-count an inmate [who was on assignment elsewhere in the institution], or what have you. It would take you just five or ten minutes to clear it up. People got used to that, and they wondered, "How in hell did we survive under that old system?"

Beginning with a Bad Administration

There were a lot of changes at CMF over a period of time. But first we had to get some new administrators in. We had a twenty-five-million-dollar building and the finest medical setup of any place in the state. And the way we used it was like hauling shit in a Cadillac. We were not using it for what it was supposed to be used for. It was a brand-new building, the latest in penology, and you have these two dump trucks—administrators—you can't get out of the 1930s.

The captain was using the old correctional system because that was all he knew. And the associate warden was paperbound in the office. So that's the way it was. "Don't change a thing because I only understand this much, and I don't want it changed, because then I won't understand anything." I could not keep my mouth shut. As a matter of fact, it got so bad that the captain put me on the first watch when I was a sergeant. We would meet in the hallway. He would be coming in, and he would say, "Haven't you transferred yet?" And I would tell him, "I'll be here when you are dead and gone." And that's exactly what happened. I was there when he died. He was just not up to it, and the associate warden did not want to get out of his little routine. Actually, the associate warden was not up to it, either.

Our philosophies were so different. As an example: one time I was complaining about something, and he called me in and said, "Hey, what you should be doing is—the way this works is a good employee will keep his mouth shut, and then if he leaves the organization, he can criticize it to the high heavens." And I said, "I'm sorry, but that is just backwards as far as I'm concerned. You talk about it when you are there, when you can be corrected, when you can be disciplined, when you can have an explanation. Then when you leave the organization, you shut your mouth because you are no longer there, and you don't have any connection with it." And that is just where we were, on opposite ends. Well, that just pissed him off no end, and things got worse. And all I was doing was telling him how I thought.

Well, the captain thought that putting me on first watch would be a punishment or an inconvenience or what have you, and it didn't work.

I was a watch sergeant. I did have a lieutenant, and I just took care of the troops and saw that we had enough to run the institution, general things. No particular responsibilities other than running the watch and taking care of the troops. Made the rounds.

At that time, if somebody got sick, you had to get somebody in to man that post. At that time, they did not pay for it as they do now. It was not overtime. So they just gave you comp time. It was hard to get people in. But after a while, you could work it out to where, "Hey, counting the relief people, there are fifteen of us on the first watch. We can make it easier on ourselves if we cooperate. I have a list here; and I will call you. Then you won't have to do this anymore for a month or two months. Then we will go down to the next guy, and I expect you to come in. That way the heat is off, you know what is happening. There will be exceptions, when you have had plans, this kind of thing, and we will acknowledge that. But basically we will go down this list, and we won't have this hassle that the rest of the watches are having to get someone to come in and cover a sick post. And you will think about it before you call in sick. Because you are imposing on one of your fellow workers. So make sure that you are sick before you call in." And it worked, and the hassle just died, and that was the kind of watch we had. It was painless, easy, and you did not have any trouble sleeping.

The second watch guy would have to convince forty people. So it was a difficult job for him, as compared to what I was doing. But hopefully these people on the first watch were new people. And after they did their first-watch time, they went to the second watch, and I hoped that they would take the idea with them. Then when I would go on the second watch, I already had them trained my way. That is what I used to tell them.

For myself, the kids were old enough that I could come home, eat breakfast, go to bed, and get up at two or three o'clock in the afternoon. I might doze a little bit after that, but that gave me the family thing with the kids. No different than being at work. First watch was not any problem to me, but they did not know that. They thought I was being punished. So I just let them think it was so.

More Trouble with the Captain

At one time I did not even have a job. I was a sergeant, and I was just coming to work. I had no assignment. But I found all kinds of things to do. I would go down and help the guy in Receiving and Release. I would do his paperwork that he could not get to. I would go out and visit the towers. I would go out and spend some time with the yard man, the guy at the back gate. I would be out there doing something for him. I would be out at the garage, talking to that guy about what his problems might be with his help. I just went everywhere. I saw everything I wanted to see and find out about. They had a wonderful library, and I spent hours in the library reading medical books and books on how to run a prison. Some of it was historical penitentiary information. I thoroughly enjoyed myself. And I got to know the institution intimately. They acted like "Hahaha, we've got you. You're suffering, I know you are." It was funny. That was the thing, you know: "What the hell do we do with this guy?" And that was their way of doing it.

So I don't know what sergeant's position I was occupying in the budget at the time. It did not make any difference to me. There was a lot to do around there. This all started because the captain ran three or four of us through as second-watch sergeant, and that was his key man. He ran that institution through the watch sergeant and six inmates. So he selected me to be his sergeant. I told him I did not think I could do it, because of the six-inmate arrangement and what went with it. Well, that irritated him no end.

The six inmates just informed. This inmate is doing this; the other inmate is doing that. This officer is doing that. They took it as gospel. In addition, the associate warden had two or three correctional officers who each day, at the end of the shift, would stop in and tell him what was going on in the institution. That is where a lot of trouble came from. Particularly with me. Sometimes they felt that they just had to tell him something, so sometimes they would manufacture something, or else put a slant on it. So those two individuals showed what it meant to be office-bound.

Another incident irritated the captain. It got hot out there in Vacaville.[7] He was in an air-conditioned office, but he had us wearing heavy wool green uniforms. The guys out in the yard, the guys in the housing units, were dying. I asked him, "Why don't we wear khakis?" His answer was, "Well, you go home and work on your car and then you wear them in to work the next day." So I had to get smart with him and said, "They do that in the greens, but we just don't see it." He said, "No, they don't do that in their greens," and I said, "Then why would they do it in khakis?" He said, "Get out of my office."

Anyhow, it came down to a big investigation about him. He was living on the grounds, but he was building a triplex in town. Somehow or other,

---

7. From July through September, the average temperature in Vacaville is above 80 degrees F, the average high is in the 90s, and readings over 110 are possible.

on the weekends, paint, lumber, and stuff would get over to the garage on the grounds, and then it would be transported up to his house. So when they had the big investigation, they thought I would be the star witness. The captain had his buddy on the back gate. But they got crosswise. The captain did not give his buddy what he thought he should have, and so the buddy blew the whistle. And he kept a book. I was very prominent in that book because of being put on the first watch, and "Haven't you transferred yet?" and other things. So they had the investigation. I told them I did not make any complaint, and I did not want to be there. And they told me it was an official investigation, and I was going to participate or I might not even be in the Department. So I said I just wanted to make it clear, and I didn't know what I could tell them.

The guy who blew the whistle thought I was eager for revenge and made sure that I was a star witness. So after they settled that I had to testify, they asked if I was put on the first watch for punishment. I told them that I did not consider it that way. It may have been that way in his mind, but I did not consider it that way because I was told that I would have to work all three shifts when I came to work here, including the first watch. But what was in his mind, I don't know. That got kind of a chuckle out of one of the parties.

They finally settled the thing. The captain agreed to an early retirement, and they agreed not to file charges. So he retired.

My situation improved when he left. The associate warden was still there, but not for long. At the end, the captain went down to the lockup and said good-bye to an old-time convict, Bob Wells.[8] Wells was pretty notorious and was on death row at one time. He coincided with the captain's career at San Quentin. So he said good-bye to Bob Wells, and then he called me into his office. He said it was too bad that we did not get

8. Wesley Robert Wells appears again incidentally in the narrative below. Wilkinson recalled, "He ran a joyriding beef into death row. He was one of the original nonconformists. He had probably been in the joint twenty years when I got there. He was a character, all that time in the joint. We used to have these ceramic pots for them to urinate in over at San Quentin in the old building. He threw one of those and hit one of the staff members and turned his head into mush. He never was right after that. That put Wells up on death row." Theodore Hamm, *Rebel and a Cause: Caryl Chessman and the Politics of the Death Penalty in Postwar California, 1948–1974* (Berkeley: University of California Press, 2001), esp. chap. 4, tells how Wells went to San Quentin at the age of nineteen, in 1928, on a stolen property charge. He killed another prisoner in a fight and was transferred to Folsom until a brief release in 1941. Committed again for larceny, first to Folsom and then San Quentin, Wells finally did throw a vessel at a guard in 1947 and was sent to death row for assaulting an officer. Wells was a constant troublemaker, and he quite plausibly believed that he suffered additionally because he was an African American. He was not afraid to speak out on his own behalf, and with the help of Communist and then civil rights organizations, he became a *cause célèbre*, to the point that the governor in 1954 commuted his death sentence to life without parole, and he in fact was released in 1974.

along any better than we did. He said, "I guess I just kind of misunderstood you." This was his apology for my not blowing the whistle on him,
I guess. So he went on his way, and I went on mine.

Other Personnel Who Needed to Leave

But the guy who really messed things up was the associate warden. He
should have been smarter and taken control to make sure things did not
happen that way. His mind was always someplace else. As long as he could
shuffle paper, he did not care. I could not believe what that man took out
of that institution: a truckload of memos. Every memo he had ever written, from day one, he saved. He had boxes and boxes of them. When he
went up to Vacaville from Chino, he sent all that stuff and put it in a
garage, the stuff he wasn't using. Then he sent for more boxes. By the time
he retired, he had a truckload full of memos. What he did with them, I'll
never know. They were not that important to begin with.

He was just absolutely paper-bound and office-bound. He hated to
make that trip from his office to the security area to the captain's office and
the watch office. He just hated that trip and very seldom made it. When
he left and the new associate warden came in and took over, the new man
knocked a hole in the wall and put a door in there so the inmates could
have access to his office, and we could have access back and forth, without his having to walk all the way around and be isolated the way his pred-
ecessor was.

Early on, one of the jobs I got was to do the Christmas packages. In the
beginning years of CMF, they decided to let Christmas packages in. It just
about devastated the local administrators that they were going to have to
do this. They couldn't make up their minds what they were going to let
in. So what I had to do was take a room in the basement, go through
everything, list it, label it, and put it up on the shelf. They never did get
around to deciding what could come in. In the absence of instructions, we
had stuff from City of Paris [department store] and everything in the
world coming in. We pulled out the obvious, of course. So because the
associate warden would not make up his mind what he was going to let
in, you had a double job to do there. He just looked at the list. I had a
double set of books. Some of that stuff you obviously had to pull out, had
to keep track of it and send it back to somebody. Finally some of it we just
donated to the Irene Larson charity, the kids' charity—chocolate Santa
Clauses and that sort of thing. For some reason, inmates were not allowed
to have those. We would get this Middle Eastern bread, baklava, in. "Well,
what do we do with this, boss?" "Well, I'll let you know."

But it went well. We didn't have any complaints. We did have a lot of stuff we had to get rid of. But how much easier it would have been if he had decided what he wanted so we could just go by that. He just could not make up his mind.

And it bothered me, as I have said, how they used that building. It bothered me no end to see that waste of space and resources and talent. Day to day, just keep it down. Don't make any suggestions. Don't change anything. Just come to work, and get the hell out of here before something happens.

The very first riot, and the only riot we ever had in California prisons up until that time, occurred when the man who later became the first captain at CMF had gone to open up Soledad.[9] He just did not have control. Then they shipped him up to CMF to a nice quiet place where there would not be any trouble. His lieutenants were all in their sixties and had been in the system for a time. Some of them, however, were in the expansion program and had been in the system for only seven or eight years, but they had experience and got promoted. Normally it would have been fifteen years. So there were a lot of hangovers from the war, and some people had come in right after the war: "This looks like a good job that I can handle at my age, and I don't have to learn anything new." They would put in ten or twelve years and retire.

When they went to revamp the retirement system, those old guys would retire at 107 dollars a month. They were under the old system. Their wages were so low. I am talking about 1955–1956. So they wanted to go under Social Security. We fought that battle, and they gave us a grandfather clause: we could opt in or opt out of Social Security. I did not want any part of Social Security. I opted out, as did a lot of other guys. The older officers opted for Social Security and retired at around $400 to $500 a month, which was a good deal for them. I was happy to see that, because 107 dollars was an insult.

The new guys coming in were paying Social Security and state retirement both. They were paying more into theirs than I was into mine, since I was under the old system. And those kids were just getting crucified. At their age, paying that percentage, compared to my age and what we were paying in, was just plain backwards. Theirs should have been cheaper than mine. They will cash in only because of the wage increase. A four-year

9. "Prison Riot Quelled," *New York Times,* 1 July 1952, 13, reported three hours of vandalism by "more than fifty rioting prisoners," who were controlled with tear gas. Vernon Fox, *Violence behind Bars: An Explosive Report on Prison Riots in the United States* (New York: Vantage Press, 1956), 4–13, 41, confirmed that after a 1927 Folsom incident, the Soledad riot in 1952 was unique among California prisons and was, moreover, one of those occurring in an institution that had "satisfactory" conditions.

correctional officer now is getting paid what I got after almost thirty years—what is now entry level.

Working into the Institution

The thing that decided me to come to CMF was that it was a specialized situation. As I said, I could have gone to San Luis Obispo,[10] I could have gone to San Quentin, I could have gone to Folsom. But I chose CMF because of the size of the town and the nature of the institution.

The medical part of the institution, the psychiatric part, appealed to me. Something was happening at CMF, as it was at Chino. There was a purpose, a direction. Little did I know that when I got there, there was a burned-out public health guy as superintendent [Marion R. King].[11] The other two administrators, as I have indicated, were burned out, too. They were just sitting on things, hatching eggs, hoping the whole thing did not blow up before they retired. However, by law you had to have a medical person as superintendent at CMF. That put the security burden on the associate warden and the captain. Neither one of them participated in their jobs.

The superintendent was so petty. There was a bulletin board outside of his office. I was going out one morning, and he called me over to his office as I was walking by. "Sergeant, come here a minute. Look at that bulletin board." It was blank, except for a little box drawn in the corner. "Does that look like 12 by 12 inches to you?" I told him no, that it looked a little bigger, 14 or 18 by 12 inches. "Well, I thought so. I told the Employees Association[12] that they could have a 12-by-12-inch spot for their messages, and look what they've done." That was our superintendent.

That was the extent of it, though. That place was like a morgue out there in the early days. You would have maybe one visitor in the visiting room, all by him/herself. Nobody came up. It was like that for the first few years. Not because of low inmate population but because of the isolated location. It was hard to get there. Most of these people were from Los Angeles. It took a long time to get visiting built up. We had a full staff, but you'd have maybe one visitor the entire day.

10. California Men's Colony, San Luis Obispo, opened in 1954.

11. Marion R. King, born in 1889, was founding superintendent and medical director of the California Medical Facility in 1950, when it began operation at Terminal Island. After taking an M.D. from Stanford and serving in World War I, he joined the U.S. Public Health Service. In 1935, he was assigned to be chief medical officer at the federal prison at Leavenworth, and he spent most of the rest of his public heath career as a prison physician. He was board certified in psychiatry in 1941. He retired in 1960 from the California Medical Facility. Information from "Dr. King Appointed Superintendent of Department Medical Facility," *Correctional Review,* February 1950, and professional directories.

12. The local chapter of the California State Employees Association. See chapter 6.

Dr. Marion King (second from left) and some other staff at
Terminal Island before moving to Vacaville
Source: Historic photograph, California Medical Facility,
Vacaville.

As for the administration, they set it up so there would not be any overcrowding. After two hours, the visit was over. So there was a room built to
handle fifty or sixty visitors, and only one inmate had a visitor, and that
visitor would still have to leave after two hours. Then the visiting room
would sit empty the rest of the day. Real thinkers.

Receiving the First Prisoners

I don't know how they determined which inmates would go to CMF when
the prison opened.[13] I am not sure if it was the regular classification or if

13. Surviving public records do not make it possible to show exactly through what changing processes the inmates were assigned to CMF. Both psychiatric and custodial considerations weighed differently at different times. In the 1950s, as noted above, all convicts passed
through one of the reception centers, and CMF was one of the options for them. By 1971,

there were medical personnel involved or not. First off, of course, we needed a workforce. Then they had a classification for therapy patients—I
don't know how they evolved that, but that was done locally at the other
institutions. In the beginning, we would typically get a therapy patient
who had done three or four years at another institution. The Adult
Authority[14] or someone would want this kind of inmate to have a year of
therapy before they paroled him. That was where we got the majority of
the therapy patients. The psychiatric patients just got shipped to us.

I was, however, there when they opened the place and started to bring in
the workforce. They shipped in thirty homosexuals from Soledad to do the
laundry and set it up. They were not in the general population.[15] When we
moved them within the institution, we had to shut everything down to get
them from place to place. That was a pain in the butt, but that was the way
we were handling it at the time. Then they brought in inmates to serve as
painters and stationary firemen. Over a period of time, they slowly built the
workforce on a maintenance basis. After a year or two, we had a basic workforce to run the institution: cooks, welders, general maintenance.

The homosexuals were sent to get them out of the other institutions. It
was believed that there might be some change in behavior and that the
work was therapeutic. So they were both work and therapy inmates, sent
up primarily for their own good. They were excellent workers. Then we let
them out into the general population, and it became hard to handle.

The lieutenant I was working for at that time did not want anything to
do with the homosexuals. When they came in, I went to bring the bus in,
bring the thirty of them in. Of course when I got on the bus, they were
hooting and hollering at me—"Hot dog!" "Look at this guy!" "Hoo, boy!"
The bus driver rolled his eyes and said, "I've had six hours of this shit."

So we brought them in, and they had all kinds of questions, wanting
to know this and that. I looked around, and the lieutenant had disappeared. So I'm getting them settled, answering all their questions. And he
just told me later, "They're yours." So they had a lot of questions, "Am I
going to be put on the Main Line?"[16] and all the things that they were told
were going to be different up here. I had to tell them, "I don't really know,
but I'll ask and find out, give you what information I've got."

---

it was "usually on the recommendation of the local prison psychiatrists" at various institutions in the system. Luke I. C. Kim and T. L. Clanon, "Psychiatric Services Integrated into
the California Correction System," *International Journal of Offender Therapy* 15 (1971): 169.

14. The Adult Authority, as noted in the introduction, determined when an inmate
might be released.

15. At this time, and reflecting conditions in American society, the homosexuals were a
distinct, labeled group. Working with this labeled population was different from the problem of homosexual behavior among inmates, a subject taken up in chapter 6.

16. In one of the regular units holding the general prison population.

They were by themselves for about a month. They thoroughly enjoyed themselves, with all that freedom, and we did not have to shut everything down when we moved them from their housing unit to their work area. Of course when the institution got full, we got back into keeping them separate. We were constantly looking for a way out of that. But they stayed isolated for the next couple of years. The policy remained that way until a change in administration came along. Somebody came in who would take chances and make decisions.

Integrating the Homosexuals

We slowly progressed until the old administrators got out. We held on to Dr. King, the superintendent, for quite a while. Then we got a new associate warden who was a worker, and he did his part to help straighten things out. That was fine with Dr. King. He did not want to be bothered with the small details. So there were some issues and policies that needed to be worked out. The new captain was pretty tractable, even though he came from Folsom. The thinking of the new associate warden was, we need to get this thing settled. "We can't go on this way all the time." So he was thinking can we do this, can we not do this, can we petition so we can do something different? He did not believe that we should have been treating the homosexuals as we were, that is, shutting everything down while we transferred them.

At the time, the thinking was that if the homosexuals were put out on the Main Line, they would be abused. To an extent that was true—it did happen. But over a period of time, there was an adjustment, and they could stand on their own two feet and take care of themselves. But that took time. During the adjustment period, they were subject to rape, got beat up, sold, whatever. There were casualties, but it had to be done, and someone had to make the decision to make it happen.[17]

The significance of the integration is this: it signified the beginning of change in the correctional system. Before that, we were, as I have said, not able to use our resources. We were not doing what we [were] supposed to do. We were not doing anything. Then you break the logjam. The old captain went. The new associate warden I have mentioned came a little later. The new people who came in were not eager to turn everything upside down, but they saw the wisdom of making some changes. They could see the wisdom of using the resources and the staff for what [they were] intended. They did not do it overnight. So we were gradually inching into

17. No available records show exactly when CMF integrated or when, later, the rest of the Department followed or who made any of these decisions.

this in the late 1950s and into the 1960s, just a piece at a time, a little progress.

Working the Psych Unit

During this particular time, I worked in the psychiatric unit as a sergeant. In the early days, the psych ward was used as a place to hide people and get the unruly inmates out of the general population. Staffing was very thin. We were required to use inmate attendants. These were inmates who did not get along on the Main Line and were by nature aggressive. So they were locked up in the psych ward as attendants, where they were under constant supervision. This way they were not out messing around. But it took constant supervision to keep them from abusing the psych patients.

So we had that situation. We had no MTAs [medical technical assistants] to hand out medication (such as it was at that time—this was before tranquilizers).[18] The psychiatrist came down once a week, on Friday. All of his information about the patients came from me and my officers. "This guy did this last week. This guy needs that. This guy cut his wrists." And so on. Some of the information he had been alerted to ahead of time.

In those early days of the CMF, electroconvulsive therapy was used a little on a strictly voluntary basis, with positive effect in one case I remember—but never later that I know of.[19] I emphasize that at the time we did not have tranquilizers, only Sparine,[20] I think, and paraldehyde. They were useless. Paraldehyde just gave them a drunk feeling, but they could still function, they could still hurt themselves. Furthermore, it was hard to administer (they had to drink it) and hard on the inmate's system. It was, as I understood it, an old-time treatment in the mental health area.[21] So the MTAs developed what we called "kickapoo joy juice." That was the name that the MTA who recommended its use called it.[22] It was Sparine

18. We have been unable to find records of when psychoactive drugs first came into CMF or the prison system; they were generally introduced in hospital psychiatry in the last half of the 1950s. They were clearly being used by 1956, the time of M. R. King, "Psychiatric Program," 251.

19. This comports with King, "Psychiatric Program," who reported that some selective use was disappearing as the psychoactive drugs came in.

20. Sparine was the trade name for promazine, a weak phenothiazine antipsychotic drug introduced in the mid-1950s. Further comments on the administration of psychoactive medications are found below, in the next chapter.

21. Paraldehyde was a common sedative in use since the 1890s.

22. The name was obviously taken from the special moonshine featured in the comic strip *L'il Abner*.

and something similar, and when the two were mixed, it really quieted them down. It kept the violent ones from hurting themselves too badly.

So it was like a zoo in the psych ward. And they can say what they want, but before tranquilizers, the day before a full moon or the day after, look out. If someone does not believe that, then let him or her take away the tranquilizers and other medications from the patients and spend the full-moon period with them.[23]

Taking Charge of the Intensive Treatment Center

As I mentioned before, things began to change with the new administration, and up the line they began to have new attitudes about how to manage and how to treat. Along about 1962, I made lieutenant. They were planning an Intensive Treatment Center.[24] It came after I became lieutenant. I took it over from another lieutenant. I had to go to the Senate Select Committee, and all I had was a rough chart as to what this was all about. I did not have a clear concept about what they were after.

We had twelve million dollars available to build this place and staff it, and the Senate Select Committee told us to just go do it. So they built the thing. I turned up with an embarrassment of riches. I had two officers to each floor. You should understand that before this, I had three officers in S Wing for 90 inmates, and one officer in Q Wing for post-psychotics, a total of four officers for 180 inmates. Then we put in the Intensive Treatment Center. I still had S Wing with 120 post-psychotics. But over in the ITC I had 120 inmates with two officers per floor, three nurses, two psychiatrists, and two counselors—to run those 120 inmates. Talk about an embarrassment of riches. . . .

One of the things that always struck me about the mentally ill patients was hygiene. So when we started the ITC, I said okay, all that the third watch was going to do was to keep those guys clean. They are going to get clean clothes every day, and they are going to take a shower every day on the night watch. And after that's done, they could go watch TV or whatever the heck they were going to do.

The first thing I ran into was the warehouse man. He told me that he did not have that kind of clothes. I told him, "Yes, you do. You have that kind of clothes if you just stop and think about it. They are wearing a set,

23. In the pretranquilizer era, others believed that they had seen this phenomenon, although most experts were skeptical; see William Harris Stahl, "Moon Madness," *Annals of Medical History* 9 (1937): 248–63.

24. This was a medical unit at CMF completely unrelated to the so-called Intensive Treatment Program in other California institutions.

and you have a set in the warehouse. If we start this thing, you just have to move a set from the warehouse up here, and a set to the warehouse from here. You still have the same amount." So I ran into that.

Now when they gave me the unit, the associate warden told me, "If you need any help, come see me." So I told him this was my first problem. The warehouse guy was under the impression that the clothes belonged to him. I said I wanted clean clothes every day so they could take a shower every day. I had two nurses on nights on the third watch. Two nurses!

After a couple of weeks of hassling and everything, the inmates demanded clean clothes and that shower every day. I used to have trouble with them after they went out to the post-psychotic unit, because they went back on the regular routine of two sets of clean clothes a week. The daily shower was optional for the post-psychotic ward, but the clean clothes were not, because they were out among the big boys now and had clean clothes only twice a week. They would say, "I want to go back, because I could take a shower and get clean clothes and talk to Mrs. So-and-so the nurse. I can't do that over here."

I also had some other problems, especially with a psychiatrist, Dr. John McNeil.[25] This doctor wanted to put in an aquarium. I was dead set against it for safety reasons: the convicts would break the windows and cut themselves or someone else. I was finally overruled by the new superintendent. He told me, "Let them have the thing, and if they bust it, we won't get another."

I was dead wrong, dead wrong. Damnedest thing I ever saw in all my life. We got this aquarium. We got these tropical fish. The inmates would take chairs and line them up as in a theater and watch the fish. The only problem we ever had was two guys got into a fight. One of them was sitting there, and he says, "Hey, look at my fish. He's doing it." And the other guy would say, "No, that's my fish. That's not yours." And they had a fight. But otherwise, it was just like watching TV. You'd have to use dynamite to get some of those people out of those chairs.

Contrasts in Administrations

So that was the contrast between my two experiences. My first time in the psych unit as a sergeant with no staff and with communication with the doctor only once a week to the exact opposite, this sublime situation. All kinds of staff and everything. Just get the right people in to use the

---

25. We have not succeeded in identifying McNeil, who shows up below in an important way.

resources you've got, and look what happens. The difference between day and night.

At CMF, when I first got there, I was upset, as I have said, because they were running the place like San Quentin. That was what the staff communicated to me, and there weren't even any inmates there at that time! So what I was dealing with [were] officers who came up from Terminal Island to be with the captain.[26]

Things that I picked up from my supervisors just did not work at CMF. So I had to do some things differently in order to establish myself. The correctional officers had already been broken in at Terminal Island and San Quentin, and a few from Folsom. Some staff came just to follow the old supervisors. "I got along with him there, and I'll just go along and do the same thing with him here that I did at San Quentin." But it was not the same type of institution or the same type of program or the same type of inmate or the same type of plant. We had an outstanding plant, as I have mentioned, that was not being used for what it was designed for. But that changed, and CMF got to be a very desirable institution for both inmates and staff.

We had one weight around our neck because, as I explained, the superintendent had to be a medical doctor, and then he had to be a psychiatrist, and then it changed back to medical doctor. That did not end until I left the Department. So what you had was a psychiatrist who could be just great in his field, and very perceptive, but I never saw one who understood a convict. They understood the mental patient, and to them it was just the same thing. They had the answers, but it just did not fit with the convict. Getting that through their thinking was difficult. I understand that later they put a nonmedical person in as superintendent of CMF, and I don't know specifically what the result of that was, but instead of hearing from the line staff, the uniformed staff, about how bad things were, I began to hear from the counselors and social workers about how bad things were. Their attitude was, "How can a nonmedical person understand this place?" So it was just a reverse of what we thought. They tried to do two things with one building. You took one building, and you staffed it twice—you staffed it psychiatrically, and you staffed it custodially, people in uniform. There was bound to be friction. There was bound to be misunderstanding. And there were bound to be different points of view.[27]

26. The state of California leased several hospital buildings from the U.S. Navy on Terminal Island in 1950, and those buildings served as the first Medical Facility while the Vacaville facility was being planned and built.

27. The clinical director in 1956, Nathaniel Showstack, "Preliminary Report on the Psychiatric Treatment of Prisoners at the California Medical Facility," *American Journal of Psychiatry* 112 (1956): 821–24, noted the natural conflict between medical and custodial

I had problems with it when I took over the Intensive Treatment Center at CMF. I wanted to start fresh, with a clean building. I instituted some things that we did not do in the old system, because those buildings were dirty from years before. But in this one—the search of the inmate: if they had to go out, they were under escort constantly. When they came back in, they were strip-searched. We did a thorough search before we put any inmate in there, and then we did continuing searches. So we never had a stabbing or a cutting or anyone hurt by a weapon there.

But that interfered with the psychiatrists and social workers. They tried every way in the world to get those regulations out of there. You are just harassing the inmates, and so on. "No, we're not harassing them. We are just protecting them." And in all the time that I was in there, almost three years, we never had an inmate hurt except for a black eye. There was a guy who got his parole date and punched out the window to the office because he was so happy. And that was all we had. I guess I thought it was the right thing because I had a hand in it.

Over in the other building, we were having cuttings and stabbings all the time because some of that stuff had been in there for years. That was when we had inmate attendants, and they could come and go and bring in whatever they wanted. The guy who was running the psych unit had his hands full, not only with the nuts but with the predators the captain had put down there.

Superintendent Keating was an unusual person.[28] By accident, I set this unit up from the beginning. The guy who had been slated for it fell ill. So they just put me into it. Keating was always extending us. So he suggested that I interview the medical staff. I was very uncomfortable interviewing the psychiatrist for his position. I thought the man was going to have a heart attack before the interview was over, just because he was so upset that a mere lieutenant would be interviewing him. Keating had almost certainly already hired him. I had no business doing that. But Keating told me, "If you are going to run this place, that is what you are going to do." It worked out, because in some minds I really did hire them. And they resented it until the day I left.

---

staff, but he believed that "Since the psychiatric staff works side by side with custody, there has come about a synthesis of divergent philosophies; thus the typical frictions between custodial and psychiatric staffs are reduced. . . . The usual tensions that exist in prisons are markedly lessened," in part because the staff become therapy-minded.

28. William C. Keating Jr., born in 1920 in Sacramento, with a 1947 M.D. from Tulane, was well trained as a psychiatrist, including work at the Menninger School in Topeka. He served as a state hospital physician in California before becoming assistant superintendent at the California Medical Facility in 1957 and, in 1958–1960, associate superintendent. From 1960 to 1966, he served as superintendent. In 1966, he left Vacaville to become assistant deputy director in the California Department of Mental Hygiene, and he afterward enjoyed a distinguished career in that field.

But it was a good unit, and it was a good unit because we got to start fresh. Any dual-purpose institution can have a real problem. But I think that, over all, it was handled pretty successfully.

Learning More about Inmates

And then they started pulling some of us up out of the uniformed ranks to do casework and board [Adult Authority] reports and so forth. And that's how I got to Soledad.[29] I swapped with a correctional counselor at CMF who was assistant classification and parole representative. He wanted some uniform experience, and I wanted some other experience.

It gave you a different point of view, an added point of view, something you had to be careful with so that you wouldn't fall into the ambiguity that comes in and becomes frustrating.[30] Yes, when you are doing an inmate's board reports, you get into a personal point of view whether you want to or not. If you want to get the board report done, you are going to have to get this kind of information. You are going to have a different way of getting the information than ordinarily.

Of course that did not decrease my job satisfaction. I was a lieutenant who was burning out on being a lieutenant, and I was looking for something new. I don't know how the other program lieutenants who were doing that felt about it, but it was an interesting sidelight to me. I could still continue with my regular duties, and that was where my heart was, and most of my effort. I would do the board reports if there was time. You interview the inmate. You find out about job prospects and family—the other side of what you were seeing before.

As I say, I was looking for something new to keep my brain from turning to mush, because I had done the lieutenant thing so many times that there was not that much new after I did my turn with the Intensive Treatment Center. That was about the last new thing that I did as lieutenant. So they split the thing up into programs with a program administrator, a psychiatrist, a couple of counselors, a program lieutenant, and so on. That would have covered two wings, with about two hundred inmates. Then I got off into this program thing. Dr. McNeil, the psychiatrist, wanted to start a new program: ward living, in a special group.[31] He

29. See below, chapter 5, on Soledad.

30. As John R. Hepburn, "Prison Guards as Agents of Social Control," in *The American Prison: Issues in Research and Policy,* ed. Lynne Goodstein and Doris Layton MacKenzie (New York: Plenum Press, 1989), 204, also suggests.

31. One of the reform enthusiasms of that time was the "therapeutic community." See Norman Fenton, "The Prison as a Therapeutic Community," *Federal Probation* 20 (June 1956): 26–29.

had a cop-killer in there and an ex-cop. He had a guy who abused his babies physically. And just to get this thing going, he had to have some sort of custodial presence. So I wound up being what he termed a co-therapist for this group. We used to meet every Thursday night, and they would record their group therapy sessions there in the ward during the week, and then we would play the tapes Thursday night, and McNeil and I would comment on it. That got to be kind of a strain, because you were getting close to personal situations, because I never knew that much about inmates' families and crimes as such, the cold hard details that would come out in a therapy session that would not come out of the rap sheet. So that got to be walking a tightrope.

And then McNeil was busy over at the Veterans Administration Hospital in Martinez and other places, and he did not show up on Thursday nights, and then it was all up to me. I'm telling you, I am no psychiatrist. Anyway, that particular group of inmates accepted it for the time I was there.

That was a good time for me. I was at a good age and had some juice; and I had a place to do things. It was almost like my situation at Chino and like getting back to being a real person.

I could relate and talk to the inmates. My problems were with the staff. What I learned at Chino worked fine and worked for me. The only problem I had was that people wanted to work on my watch, or my function. It got a little embarrassing after a while.

The Rapid Face of Change

I am talking about what I call the Procunier[32] era of rapid change, which began in the early 1960s. We did not have TV or radios at Chino or at

---

32. Raymond K. Procunier was one of the major figures in the field of corrections in the second half of the twentieth century. He defies classification, for he took stands that were both liberal and conservative by conventional standards of that day. At one time or another, he headed the corrections programs in five different states. He appears in this narrative chiefly in two roles. First, he was associate superintendent (that is, head of custody, Wilkinson's boss) at CMF from 1960 to 1964. Later, from 1967 to 1974, Procunier served as director of the Department of Corrections. It was this whole period to which Wilkinson was referring as the Procunier era. Procunier (born 1924) grew up in Michigan and was a Navy pilot during World War II. He began with the Department of Corrections as a correctional officer at the California Institution for Men at Chino in 1948. Procunier rose rapidly through the ranks and went to Sacramento as assistant personnel officer for the Department. He spent 1957–1958 in Utah as deputy director and then director of the state correctional system. After returning to California and serving as Departmental training officer, he was appointed associate superintendent at CMF in 1960. He left CMF in 1964 to serve as classification officer for the Department and then, in 1965–1966, became superin-

CMF until after the beginning of the Procunier era. But I have to set the stage for that. We start our period of enlightenment with this new treatment center, and we were getting into the function for which the place was designed. Then we had another change in administration. That was 1960, when Dr. Keating became superintendent at CMF. He was dynamic.[33] He wanted something done every day, good or bad. You make things happen. This kind of coincided with my time in the intensive treatment unit. Then Procunier came in as the associate warden. Both of these people had these funny IQs, out of sight, and you had to throw a rope around them to hold them down, because they would think that you could grasp things as easily as they did.

These two were matched up, and they were real go-getters. Procunier was the very first sergeant I worked for at Chino. He taught me how to run the control room. So we knew how to work with one another. The first thing we did was to change the control room procedure and put it on a good basis. We eliminated that problem. Then I thought, Boy, we are really going to make some progress here. After a period of time, I was saying, "Boy, I wish they would slow these changes down. They are going too fast." And they were. They were competing with one another, really. So we got through that period. Then the sixties hit us. There were demonstrators outside, the outside pressure groups came in. This is where Procunier tried to accommodate everyone.[34] Things just snowballed, and we almost lost control.

---

tendent of Deuel Vocational Institution before Governor Ronald Reagan called him to serve as director of corrections. He retired as DOC director in 1974 when Reagan left the governorship of California, as Procunier recalls, for he did not want to work under Reagan's successor as governor, Jerry Brown. Procunier subsequently served as chairman of the Adult Authority and in many other distinguished executive capacities in California and elsewhere. He was frequently quoted in the press and often took controversial stands. See especially William Endicott, "Prisons Chief—Man in Middle of Controversy," *Los Angeles Times*, 29 February 1972, I: 3, 22, 24; and, for example, "Why Prisons Fail; An Expert Speaks Out," *U. S. News and World Report*, 16 December 1974, 46–48; Bob Haeseler, "The Bitter Fight over Procunier," *San Francisco Chronicle*, 18 March 1976, 6. Additional information based on a telephone interview, 28 December 2003, for which we are most grateful to Mr. Procunier.

33. Procunier, telephone interview, 28 December 2003, confirmed that Keating was dynamic. Procunier recalled how he would outline for Keating all the reasons that some action or other that Keating was proposing could not work, and Keating would then tell Procunier how the action would be carried out.

34. Procunier himself concluded that his actions sometimes led to perhaps undesirable results; see, for example, "Prison Chief Takes Blame for SLA Rise," *Los Angeles Times*, 21 April 1974, I: 27, where he was quoted saying that in the state prisons, "We didn't do as good a job as we should have done over the last four or five years of controlling some of these culture groups and ethnic identification groups."

CHAPTER THREE

MY EXPERIENCE WITH EVERYDAY PROBLEMS AT CMF

Fixing Up the Kitchen

At CMF, I often got odd jobs. As when [at the beginning of the 1960s] I got into the kitchen. Of course, on that occasion I had gotten myself into some minor trouble.[1] The kitchen had always irritated me. It was deemed a punishment assignment, which I resented to begin with, because you don't get good work out of people whom you are punishing. And the kitchen—mealtime is important. How they are fed and what they are fed is important. I never could understand making the kitchen punishment. When I got into this problem, the captain said, "What the hell am I going to do with you?" I said, "Put me in the kitchen." This was before I was promoted to lieutenant. I was still a sergeant. He said, "I never heard anyone ask for the kitchen."

It was a mess, a real mess. So there again, throwing me into the briar patch worked. I wanted to get in there and see what I could do. I just could not believe it could be that bad. In the first place, the staffing was bad. They had three dining halls and only two people to run them. So I looked around and found out where I could get more help. It takes one position to relieve two and a half people. So you have a one-day position that is free. You had the tower man. He relieved two days in Tower One and two days in Tower Three, and then he would have an odd day. He was generally a utility officer or what have you. I snatched him, and put him to work in the kitchen. Then I found another one where that same thing was happening, and I put him to work in the kitchen. Then I got lucky, and we combined these positions so I had the same man all of the time. That gave me the staffing, and I gave each of the officers a dining room. Put them into competition. I got together with the food manager and had a hard time selling him on things, supplies and what have you.

1. See below in this chapter.

Sergeant Wilkinson's identification photo
Source: Viola Wilkinson.

The idea there was that you worked them until the dining rooms got so dirty that you had to have a GI [General Inspection] day to clean them up, and then you forgot about it for three weeks or what have you. My theory was that you clean it after each meal. If you keep it clean every day, then you don't have to go through that nonsense.

The silverware was always bad. This is where I was having trouble with supplies. I needed bleach and a great big tub. So on Monday, you bleach the cups. On Tuesday, you bleach the silverware. Then the next day, the trays or whatever day it was.

Scullery duty just wore the guys on that crew out. There were seven of them, and that is hot, dirty, steaming work. At three meals a day, it just wore the guys out. They could not stand it over long periods of time. So I said, fine, I want two scullery crews. You work a day on, a day off. Yea, team. So you had a lead man, and he gathered up people he could work with and formed his crew. The two crews were competitive. They did not get worn out. So then I had the proper staffing.

The convicts would come in to eat, and they would see the sparkling cups and trays and silverware and—"Jeez, you guys get new stuff? What's happening here?" They sat down at the table, and if they ran their hand underneath, they did not come up with a bunch of crap on it, because that table had been cleaned. Each officer was responsible, and they were kind of competing for the best dining room.

The captain would come over simply because it was clean. When it was all messed up, he would not come over. I got a visit from him every day after it got clean.

Then we got a new business manager, and I hit it lucky on this one. The new manager came down to see how things were—this was part of his bailiwick. He was really impressed. Best dining room he had ever been in. We talked for a little bit, and he turned out to be very friendly. It was just based on the right timing. He was new, and I guess old Henry, the food manager, begrudgingly said, "Hey, I guess it is working out. He is not as much trouble as he used to be." I got the place cleaned up, and the count situation straightened out there.

You would take them in there and sit them down, four to a table. It used to be they would count them in the corridor, 1, 2, 3, and the guy would be running back and forth frantically. So he would sit them down four at a table, count them, turn it in, and didn't have any problems. It took less than six months for it to deteriorate back to what it was before I went in there. I was there about nine months.

Another thing—the kitchen/dining room worked from five o'clock in the morning to seven o'clock at night with one supervisor. So I made arrangements with the captain to let me have a floating schedule: "I'll come in at five o'clock on some mornings and see what's happening. Then I'll go home in the middle of the day and come back for the evening feeding. Next time, I will come in at ten o'clock and work until six o'clock." Again, I got barbs from that—"Who do you know?"—and so on. But it worked because you were there with everybody, and you could put the parts together. Of course the guy who came in behind me decided, "I want a steady deal, I don't want that floating shit." So it just went down the drain.

Small Changes Are Important Changes

What I am trying to illustrate here is not "How good I was" but that all it took was a little thought, the little things. There wasn't any big hassle about doing the silverware the way we did it. There wasn't any big hassle about splitting up the two scullery crews. It was just waiting to be done. Most of the guys who worked in the dining room were school guys, and they had to really hustle to get their work done and get it cleaned up and get back to school, on the old system. With the new system, each guy knew what he had to do. Two of them would start down the wall and do the tile. Two of them would have a row of tables each to do. They found out if they did not do it, then I took note, and in the evening when I came back (I made a point to go out there after the evening meal), when they thought they were going to watch TV, they would be down in the dining room cleaning up tables they did not clean at noon. ("And you know if you are going to deal with that crazy SOB, then you might as well do it when you are supposed to. If he is nutty enough to come back here and do that, then you are not going to win the battle.") So it did not take much of that. It was not that great of a pain to them. So it was all these little things that you just do.

That was the joy of the job, figuring out those little things and what you could do. Just like combining those positions. That led to another thing. By using the same theory and combining some other positions—housing officer and relief and that kind of thing—they picked up a couple of days that were being underused with officers. They utilized the workforce. Not that the officers were not working on that odd day, but they were not working in continuity with something else that they were doing.

Let me illustrate the little things that I am talking about. One time, we had a big, bad convict, six foot seven, 245 pounds. And he needed to be escorted from one end of the building to another. So the watch sergeant was stewing about gathering up some help to escort this guy—do we iron him up? or what? One of my escort officers was retired from the Air Force, and he stood about five foot seven and weighed about 140 pounds. I said, "No you don't need all of that. You send Horn down to escort him to the clinic." The sergeant looked at me as if I was crazy. I said no, that is what you do. I said, "Do you think that big SOB, 245 pounds and six foot seven, is going to wipe that officer out in front of everybody up and down the hallway? But you send six guys down there, and he will fight you until the last ditch. So send Horn."

So here came the big guy who killed his mother, among other things. And this big inmate can hardly see Horn walking along beside him. Standard procedure. Of course I could have got Horn killed, I guess.

Those were the things that fascinated me about working with people. I asked Horn if he would mind doing it, and he said no. John would walk down there, pick the inmate up, and escort him down to the clinic, three times a week, and he would do it with other guys, too. My watch sergeant was ecstatic. He said, "Jeez, I don't need to get a bunch of people to escort these guys. It takes just one man to escort them." I told him to pay attention and find out what kind of mood the inmate is in before you do this.

But I said with the big man, if you send more than one guy down there, you are going to have a problem. Don't give him an opportunity to show off.

In the kitchen, I got to look after the small things, and I could see the benefits of that. So it was anything but punishment or a place to get rid of sergeants they could not utilize. Why did they punish me? It was plain stupidity on my part. I compromised an in-service training class. It was a mandatory class. I did not go, and the repercussions came down. Anyway, I asked for the kitchen job, and they thought they were disciplining me, so it worked out for the best for both of us. They were happy. They were off the hook. They did not have to make a decision they did not want to make, and I got to do what I wanted to do.

It was a win-win situation for me. I could have gone in and left it just as it was and not been criticized. I also could have gone in and done what I did and had fun while I was doing it. Maybe get a rose in my teeth.

What I Did as Assignment Lieutenant

Then I got promoted. It was the obvious reason to leave the kitchen. They did not have lieutenants in the kitchen. So I went to the first watch. That was where all of the new lieutenants went. That did not last very long either, for two reasons. One, there was something else happening. We had a lieutenant who was just having trouble coping with the daytime—with the corrections business, with decisions, what have you. He was also kind of a loser. No evidence of it on the job, but he would get really shaky before the day was over. So working the first watch, the stress was not as much, and he wanted to go on the first watch. Therefore they took me off and put me on the third watch. That is where you learn about brand-new stuff. It was a whole new ball game.

But meantime the job that I enjoyed most was the one I mentioned before, assignment lieutenant. You were right in the heart of things, getting that workforce going, and you sat on the main classification committee. It was a good job.

This was entirely different from the work that I did when the first inmates came, which was off the cuff. They were filling up the institution with specifics. Whether that came from Sacramento: "I need three stationary firemen, I need six cooks"—that kind of thing. They always needed janitors and people to clean up. So that was just part of my duties on whatever watch I was working.

Once the institution was well established, managing the workforce and the pay numbers and the structure in the organization was the assignment lieutenant's job. To me, the assignment lieutenant was the core of the uni-formed personnel. Because you worked both sides of the fence. You were an independent operation. You had control of the workforce, and yet you sat with the big boys on the Classification Committee, sort of working from the bottom up and then the top down.

That job had a lot of power to it. They had a thing they called the AW Files, the associate warden's files. Until they quit maintaining and using them, the AW Files were a really valuable source. One thing they had was a picture of the inmate. Another thing they had was the inmate work his-tory. Still another thing they had was the disciplinary history. These were the primary things in the file. As the assignment lieutenant, when these people would come into the institution, I would get these files. I would make my notes, eyeball the picture. As soon as the guy walked in, I would say, "You're So and So," and I would say, "Yeah, and I have got a spot for you down in the warehouse." Or as a cook in the kitchen.

We just dumbfounded them. The inmates I had working in the office said, "I don't know how you do that." And it is just you deal with five or six things, and you make your notes. So I had a small reputation. The inmates would just go out—they would not even say anything. They would just say, "Thank you." They might be back three days later and say, "I really wanted to work in the shoe shop," or something like that. But to come in and have somebody know who you are and have your assignment planned out and give you information about what you are going to be doing for the next day or week seemed to have some significance to it.

As assignment lieutenant, I met with people at the top in the Main Classification Committee. The committee met to see whether we rejected particular inmates, whether we sent them on, whether they were progress-ing. That was where everything happened. That was the ultimate for the inmate. His institutional life was determined by the MCC. I don't know really how to describe it, but it was the focal point of the whole operation.

The other aspect was that I got a lot of information, because serving on the committee were the superintendent and the two associate superintend-ents and the classification parole representative, the inside parole guy. I was the junior officer. They conversed and said what they were going to do. So I brought back a lot of information. The captain did not even get in on this kind of information. So I brought information back to him. The Classification Committee said they are going to do this or that or we are going to change this or what have you. Sometimes you could be a source of information for the associate warden, because he would not go. So that was the only feedback that they had.

Certainly none of the other staff had that kind of feedback. So they would ask me things, and I would be eager to tell sometimes—changes that were going to affect all of us, or something they were finally going to straighten out, or we were going to get money for this or that—general interest, and they were entitled to that, and there was no reason not to share it. Some of it you knew just to keep your mouth shut. There again, that depended on how long you stayed. If you did not keep your mouth shut at the right time, well, sometimes they had another one up there, and you went on to something else.

Dr. Pope was superintendent then.[2] Dr. Pope did not affect my life much. I did have to do with him on that [classification] committee, where I was the junior officer. He may have been an administrator, but he did not know about prison work.

Working on Paroles

For a while, as I have mentioned, I traded with a guy who wanted some experience in uniform. He was a CC2 (second-level counselor) in the parole department upstairs. Kenny Britt was the associate warden at the time, and he was pretty innovative.[3] So we worked up a swap where I took over the CC2's job as parole agent, and he took over my job as third-watch lieutenant. So we worked it out, and it got us a year's experience that benefited both of us. As a matter of fact, it got me another promotion. I came out on the list, and the inside parole officer was a job that I was pretty interested in. The CC2 I was not that interested in. But it paid off in the long run.

My contention was that all the ancillary personnel should go through at least six months of wearing a uniform, working the housing unit or something. It makes different people out of them. Most counselors came in at CC1, that is, the entry level. They made the same salary as the lieutenant, and they had never been in the joint before. Then they don't know how to work with the officers or inmates. That is why they should have to work in uniform for a while. Put them all over the place, work a housing unit, work the tower, before they go to their job so they can see how every-

2. Lester J. Pope, born 1910, was an internist specializing in gastroenterology. He took his M.D. at the University of Nebraska College of Medicine in 1937 and for many years served in the Navy, rising to be commanding officer of the Naval Medical School in Bethesda in 1958–1960. In 1960, he became medical director of the California Department of Corrections before serving as superintendent at CMF from 1966 to 1972.

3. Kenneth D. Britt became better known when he moved into the position of warden at San Quentin in 1973. A combat infantry veteran of the Korean War, Britt joined the Department of Corrections in 1955. See the feature story on Britt, Bill Hazlett, "Going Is Tough for Warden of San Quentin," *Los Angeles Times,* 7 October 1974, II:1, 2, 3. Britt appears further in the narrative that follows.

Wilkinson dressed in civvies to work as a counselor
Source: Viola Wilkinson.

thing works down the line, what the officer goes through, what the convict goes through.[4]

At one time, one of the institutions used to do this. They did not make
it mandatory, but one administrator made it clear that that was what he
wanted done. He paid the counselors their CC1 salary, but they had to
work in uniform first. They made sure it was voluntary, because they did
not want a lawsuit. The whole program was approached with caution. I
think only half a dozen counselors went through the program. And it did
not take those few very long to move up the ranks because they had a complete picture of what was happening. They were exposed to the whole program. They were more effective. And you did not have to do it forever, you
did not have to be a correctional officer forever. You put a correctional

4. The reader may be struck by the similarity of these comments to the recommenda-
tions for training by Ann Chih Lin, *Reform in the Making: The Implementation of Social
Policy in Prison* (Princeton, NJ: Princeton University Press, 2000).

officer up in the tower, and bring him out a month later, and all he has learned is sitting up in the tower. But you take him from the tower and put him down in the laundry as laundry officer supervising inmates and shaking them down when they come out and such things, or put him in a housing unit, where he has to feed them and put them to bed, cater to their needs and take care of them—I think this makes a good professional out of him. I liked the idea and wanted the Department to pick up on it. But there were a lot of good ideas that never got acted on as the years went on at CMF.

It was interesting doing that parole work and the paperwork and everything, especially knowing that I was not going to have to do it forever. You are the liaison. You set up the papers. You dealt with the outside parole officers. They tell you what they want, what they expect from the inmate. They will tell you when he is to report, to whom he is to report, tell him where it is. Then you prepare the inmates in the institution and send them out to the outside parole officer. My main responsibility was to get the convicts out the front gate and off the prison ground.

In the old, old days, the parole officer used to come down and meet with the convict and get everything set up and then go out and wait until he was paroled. The press of business got to be so much that they had to have someone inside to handle it. Parole officers lost too much time running back and forth.

Right at the start, I had some instructions from the parole agent about one inmate: "Tell the guy to get a haircut and report to so-and-so; he is going to work here." Then the convict comes up, and he says, "Fuck that shit. I am not going to get my hair cut. I don't give a shit what this guy says." My reply was, "Don't tell me. I am only passing along the information." So I turned him back around and said, "I'll be back out here at 11:55. You be ready to go. But you are not getting out until five minutes till twelve. Go on down to the line."

Big crocodile tears. "You gotta get me out of here! You gotta get me out of here!" I said, "What did you do—steal from somebody before you came up here to get paroled and you can't go back to the Main Line? What did you do down there? You are sure not thinking if that is what you did, and you are up here cussing me out. Didn't anyone ever tell you that you do not have to get out of this place any sooner than midnight? Your parole date is not open until midnight."

"I can't go back to the line, I can't go back down to the line."

"You go on back down to the line and you spread the word how this works to the rest of the convicts who are getting paroled. Tell them that they come up here and listen, they keep their mouths shut, they sign all the papers, and they get the hell out of here. That message is from the parole officer."

"Tell them yourself." This guy was terrified.

But I knew that if you start at the beginning, then you don't have problems down the line. I never had another guy kick loose on me coming up for parole. *Word gets around fast.* That's what I'm saying. This guy was a classic example. He was the first one I had, and it started right, and it just solved the problem. It was just a positive way of doing business. It is not what you say, it's how you say it. If they feel that you are sincere about what you are telling them, and you won't brook any nonsense, then you don't have any nonsense to put up with. Other than the prison business, as well, I found that maxim true—staff and inmates, all the way down the line.

My Style Working with Inmates and Officers

My biggest problem was, I had so many people, subordinates in particular, tell me, "I can't get a line on you. I just don't know what you are going to do next." I would say, "I understand that you like a guy you know that, 'Hey, if this happens, he is going to react this way. He is going to be the same on down the line.'" I try to be consistent, but I'm not consistent. I may have a brainstorm and say, "Hey, we are going to do it this way and see how it works." I told the officers, "You can't predict if you write a disciplinary on an inmate and send him to me, that each time I'm going to give him the same discipline or each inmate the same discipline for that same infraction. That is not going to work. That is not what disciplinaries are for. They are there to prevent other problems and straighten out problems. You are having a problem, you wrote a disciplinary, it is up to me to make it work. It may be crucifying him by giving him a whole boatload this particular time." The other guy, it may be negotiating with him and setting something up for the future: "Hey, I'm going to do it this way this time, but I'm going to put this on your back if you come back to me again. And this gives the inmate something to think about. So, again, I'm not going to be that consistent. If you are looking for that kind of consistency, you have several lieutenants around here who are that way. I suggest you get a job with them. Then you'll know exactly what is going to happen with any given situation at any given time, whether it's an appropriate action or not."

I had a couple of guys transfer because they were just too uncomfortable, and they went to another watch. Soon they were looking to come back to my watch. Some of my coworkers and lieutenants—peer group—would really get shook up because I was not predictable. One guy asked me how I knew what I was going to do next, and I said sometimes I did not even know what I was going to do until I got all of the facts and found out what the situation was. "I'll do what I think is best. It may not be consistent with the way in which I handled a particular infraction before. But I'm not going to be stereotyped. That is not the way to get along in this business." There just has to be a comfort factor for certain individuals who work in this business. They have to look at that supervisor and say, "Hey, this guy is going to do it the same way he did it the last time, and I'm going to be comfortable." If you change on them, if you point out that this situation is slightly different from the last situation, they did not want to see it that way. "You made me feel uncomfortable, so I'm going to go someplace else."

I did not look at my adaptability as an opening for the inmate to negotiate. I just looked at what the inmate told me. You know, "I did this because this happened." "I did this because I was pissed off at the guy." I always enjoyed that one. That inmate would get a better break from me than the inmate who tried to cut some corners, because in my mind he knew what he did. He was not afraid to admit what he did. So you had something to work with. You know what you did wrong, you know how you did wrong, and now let's work out a way so you don't do that again. But the inmate who is mealymouthed, or his cat died, or he just got to feeling so bad because his girl ran away from home, that is why I hit this guy in the head—no, he is just making excuses. He is not learning a thing. So the message you have to give him is that if you do bad things, you get bad things. So you lose your privileges or whatever it is.

Working as Disciplinary Officer

For a while, I was Chief Disciplinary Officer. In a way I also did that at Soledad where I handled the appeals. But this disciplinary officer position was in place at CMF before I left there. They were getting some money, and they decided to consolidate the functions and run them through one office. And you could get some continuity with the individual handling it, because he could be pretty consistent, instead of having the variation from lieutenant to lieutenant. I objected to it from the standpoint that you were taking a tool from the watch commanders. So I said I'd do this on this basis: "That they are present when I handle the disciplinary, if they want to be. It's up to them." It was unwieldy and did not work, but it was there for a while.

Not only was it hard to get everyone together, but the others were a little petulant about it. All things considered, it was not a good idea. You already had the disciplinary committee that the big boys sat on, for major things, so this was kind of superfluous. The sergeant could handle most of it as far as I was concerned. Consolidating was a different thing. I handled all of the appeals of the disciplinaries that had been handled that the inmate was not satisfied with. They would run it through the appeals process, and then I either upheld the appeal or changed the discipline. Then that went to Sacramento, and they passed final judgment on it. They had to hire an associate warden to handle that, and two guys to help the associate warden. They got off cheap with me. It was another one of those "acting" appointments.[5]

I handled anything from major complaints to a busted tape recorder to "They stepped on my lighter when they searched my cell."

Communicating with Inmates

You could not control the inmates by making their lives miserable, because of the way the law and the administrators changed things. Just as in the appeals process—thousands and thousands of dollars spent on the appeals process, instead of making a firm, hard decision, stopping trouble at a lower level. They would get their automatic review, and maybe one other, and that was sufficient. If the lieutenant handled it, and it came to me, and I handled it, then that should have ended it. That is two reviews, plus the correctional officer who had to write the disciplinary. It was serious enough to write it, so he wrote it. We just stretched it out, trying to be too good or too nice.

I did not run across any so-called inmate unions, but inmates did have organizations, and they did have recourse. For example, the inmates had recourse to talk about the inmate welfare fund and how it was being administered and what was happening to it. At some institutions, they found some discrepancies. But not at CMF, that I know of. Soledad I did not know about. It would not surprise me if Soledad wasn't one of the culprits. But I never ran into any organized prisoners' unions.

At CMF, they had an inmate council that would bring inmate grievances. That could be considered a union. The inmate council in some institutions was valuable. You heard things that you would not have heard until they were a real problem. It helped you head off things that might be going to happen. You got a feel for what the inmate body was thinking.

But it was not that hard for inmates to reach staff. You walk the hall, and this convict comes up and tells you, or two or three of them, that something is happening. "Will you look into it?" And so you would take

---

5. This theme of holding "acting" appointments and serving as a trouble shooter will come up more prominently in later chapters.

a look at it. Therefore it was not that hard to get to staff. Except at Soledad. There they just did not want to talk to you. They wanted to make you do things. They wanted to have a riot or what have you.

Of course at CMF and at Chino, if they had a problem they would grab the first officer they could find and tell him or her about it. If that did not work with that one, they would get another one. Eventually they would get somebody who would give them an answer. Or you would say, "Give me a couple of days, and I will get back to you."

From my experience, it was not that hard for either inmates or officer to talk about grievances. In other institutions, it may have been hard. Some organizations may have functioned as inmate unions. At CMF, you could talk about a kind of a union when the Latinos worked through their EMPLEO group. You had the blacks working through their Black Cultural group who brought up grievances. Some of the issues were institution-wide, but most of their issues revolved around their special interests.[6]

Mostly the grievances were individual: everything from the water does not work right in my cell all the way up to I got ripped off and raped yesterday, and anything in between. Whatever they thought their problem was. You got that every day. There was no secret about it. No one was repressed to the extent that nobody talked about it or anything else. As a matter of fact, it was the other way around. You could not walk down the hallway without getting four or five requests—"What about this?" "Can you see about this?" You were damn near abused just walking back and forth down the corridor. But that is what you were there for.

Every inmate had a problem or needed information about something. If they knew that you would listen to them, then you got conversation. I used to have a reputation: jokingly they would say, "Don't ask him, because he will take you on a trip and won't bring you back. God, that man can talk."

Some of the correctional officers did not listen as they should, and it was trouble for the supervisor. I would ask them point-blank, "Why? It's part of your job. Why don't you do it?" "I don't have to do that. I'm down there to lock them up and feed them." I would tell them, "Fine, but that is not all you do, and you heard it from me first. Okay? You don't do your job unless you answer their questions. You will find out over a period of time that you should start talking to them."

Almost to a man, there would be things happening that they did not even know about, and the inmates would bypass the officer. Nobody was willing to come to him and say that "So-and-so was doing such and such down at the end of the building and messing up our playhouse here."

---

6. This subject comes up again in the next chapter, where Wilkinson gives details of his work with special groups.

They just did not give that kind of information, and all of a sudden the officer would have a bad problem on his hands. Simply because he would not listen to the inmate.

As I figured it, it was just reluctance on the part of the officer. "If I don't listen to the convict, then I don't have to see about this." That is laziness, in my mind. Or, "Don't get me out where I can't function; don't get me in over my head. If I deal with the inmate in that sense, then I am going to have to go someplace and find out what this is all about. So I just don't listen to that, and I don't have to do anything. Or, I don't have to phone the lieutenant to see what advice he would give me on it." All the time the officer is overlooking the fact that if the inmate is there in his office, and he is asking about this particular thing, and it is something that I as lieutenant could do something about. The smart thing for the officer to do is pick up the phone and phone me. Then if we can answer the question immediately, the correctional officer's reputation with that convict is, "Hey, that is a man who takes care of business."

A lot of officers did not see that. That was an imposition on them, and they did not want to talk to the inmates or their lieutenant if they did not have to.

Some of the attitude came from resisting the manipulative inmates. That was bona fide. "If I don't deal with the guy, then I am not vulnerable." My answer to that was, "You are vulnerable the minute you stepped into the unit. More than likely as soon as you came through the front gate. So you need to learn how to handle yourself."

The Usual Prison Problems

To what extent did stereotyped problems such as drugs, sex, and gambling exist in the joint?[7] Well, the drug problem was exceptional in my experience. But that has to be qualified. In my day, at Chino and CMF, a drug bust was mace or benzedrex inhalers or illicit pills from the pharmacy. We did not have crystal meth, rock cocaine, and all those kinds of drugs back in those days. Marijuana was a rarity. Part of it in my experience is: there is a hell of a lot more drug trafficking today in institutions, compared to my time. But you have to think about what was available in my day in society in general.

You can't bring in something that does not exist. We still had officers bringing stuff in to convicts that they should not have. I maintained that it did not matter whether it was drugs or a Coca-Cola, or a drink of

7. More discussion will be found in chapter 6.

whiskey, or whatever. You were not supposed to bring anything to the con-victs, no matter what it was.

In the early days, I don't think I ran into a case of alcohol. Later on, I did. But no, I don't think it was a problem. If you want to talk about joint-made stuff, yes; but I am talking about stuff coming in from the outside. Pruno was of course a constant problem.

Pruno was hootch. They made their own. They used bread for the yeast. Or they made it out of fruit juice and sugar or whatever. There are several ways to make it. We even made it aboard ship when I was in the Navy.

But only a very small percentage of the inmates were ever involved. It mostly centered around the kitchen crew because they could make it. Transporting it was a problem. It smelled terrible. If you had any sense of smell at all, you could smell it halfway down the corridor. The supervising cook, the number two man in the kitchen, would kid me that I could not smell anything because I smoked. "Baloney. My smeller is better than your smeller, Rich." So we would have contests to see who could smell out the most booze. It used to exasperate him that I could do just as good a job as he did.

Just to give you a little sidelight about making pruno and the ability to smell it: Once at CMF we kept turning up drunks in the kitchen for a couple of weeks. We could not find the source. We took the place apart. We looked all over. We could not smell it. And yet these guys were stag-gering around, and by this time they were throwing up all over you and everything else.

It took us a couple of weeks to find it. I just happened to turn the cor-ner at the right time. In the scullery, there was a vent right over the dish-washer. They had rigged up a pulley, and they would pull their pruno up there and let it do its stuff. When they wanted a drink, they would pull it down and take some, and then they would put it back up in the vent. You could not smell it because it went up the vent. And they had two weeks of good times. We had drunks all over the place, and we were going crazy. Again, you give them a pair of pliers and a tin can, and they would make anything.

That was great. I lost a good scullery crew over that one, too. That was their game, and I did my game. We worked like dogs to find that stuff, and it was just inadvertent. They all had sheepish grins on their faces as I turned the corner when the thing was going back up in the vent. One guy even had a cup in his hand, and all he could say was, "You want some, Sarge?"

That was one of the things I liked about the job, the mental part. They were always thinking, they were always doing. And you were always thinking, you were always doing. The mental challenge, the games, appealed to me. I wish I had been a little better at it at times.

You are driving to work, and your mind already starts working: Where in the hell is that pruno? You get to work, and it is: where in the hell is that pruno? Don't get carried away with it because they may be doing something else while you are off looking for this pruno. So your mind was going just all the time in terms of trying to be, if not one step ahead, at least even. I just liked it.

The Growth of the Contraband Problem

Later on, in the 1960s, it got to the point that you could find whiskey bottles lying around. The only way it could come in was that staff had to bring it in. The visitors could not bring it in because the inmates were skin-searched after coming out of the visiting room. So, plain as the nose on your face, staff was bringing it in. It was brought in from the standpoint that it was a pretty good moneymaker.

There was a lot of money in the joint—after things loosened up, and the groups came in. There certainly was money in contraband. The officer could make money. Mostly he did it so the inmates would not bother him—not knowing that eventually the inmates would eat him alive. If you don't bring in this elephant, then we will tell your boss about all the other stuff you brought in. So the guy would get caught bringing the elephant in. Because it was just too much for that mule to be packing.

Eventually, the staff member always went down the drain, always. I lost a lot of staff myself. If it belonged to CMF, it was mine, and I lost it. I don't remember on my watches having a particular guy who was dirty, but maybe I did and just do not remember.

There were little tip-offs of what was happening. You may not have known what staff member was involved, but there were tip-offs. I do not know how to explain this, but I got a lot of free, gratis information from the inmates. I talked to everybody. There were certainly lieutenants who did not spend that much time talking to inmates, just shooting the breeze. So if an inmate came to those lieutenants and started talking, then the rest of the inmates figured that that guy was giving somebody up.

With me, we could stand there in the middle of the hallway, and I am watching the chow line, and this guy could tell me a complete story about a load of pills that came in last night, and they are in H Wing in the plumbing well down in cell 105. And we were just standing there. This was possible because I talked all the time to inmates, and they talked to me. A guy could come up and dump on me, and then when the chow line was gone and the place was empty, I would get hold of some people from the security squad and tell them what information I had and send them down there. Pretty soon they are coming back with a hangdog look on their faces but their pockets are full of pills. The inmates wanted to pull the covers off of whoever it was, but nobody could ever identify who talked to me because I talked to everybody all the time.

Changing Times Intensified the Problems

I don't know about what I saw at Soledad, but what I saw in the later times at CMF after we loosened up and had all those outside groups in: contraband had increased fifty times compared to the first ten years I worked in the Department.

It changed my job. We had people hurt, we had staff compromised, we had visitors compromised, and all that kind of thing that you did not have to deal with before all that stuff came in. Eventually you would catch a certain percentage of the people. You would find an inmate who was plowed and could not make it up and down the corridor, and he was obviously on medication, zapped out, so you would have to take care of him. Whether or not he dumps on the officer is immaterial. It is just another process, another lockup.

Sometimes he's hurt somebody or he got hurt because he was incapacitated. "This is a good opportunity to whip somebody's head—which I wouldn't do if he was sober." That is another problem. There would be fights over "That's my mule, he brought the stuff, don't be messing with him. Don't try to get him to pack for you." Then you would have a fight or a stabbing. So it changed the job a whole bunch.

It was awfully hard for the staff in general to accept the fact that this stuff had to be coming in by staff. They were always looking at ways to tighten up visiting procedures and do this and that—"Where in the hell is it coming from?" They never said, "Hey, hey, we have to do something about staff bringing this stuff in." Because you depend on that staff.

Down in the laundry at one point it was just rife with minor narcotics and mace and nutmeg[8] and stuff of that nature. The laundry supervisor was bringing it in. It finally got to the point, "Can you prove it?" "No, I can't prove it. Why don't we just shake this guy down one morning when he comes in? Then apologize if we made a mistake." We did, and nothing was found. But it cleaned the laundry up, and it never came in again. The guy was not reprimanded; he was not caught dirty. I do not know what I

---

8. These spices when soaked in water made a disagreeable drink that many people, following folklore, believed was intoxicating. The spices were easy to obtain and easy to transport, and they could be used to construct a drinking ritual.

would have done if he had been caught dirty. We would have arrested him and the whole works. I was happy it happened the way it did. He went on working, and there was no criticism—and it just quit. It was a message. "The convicts are telling on you, and I am going to shake you down, so you better quit it."

Things could be done. But no one wanted to take that step and shake down a fellow employee. I don't see that it cost me anything to do that. It did not upset me to do that. It cleared the air, and it cleared him. He was not dirty at that time. So the inmate rumors had to stop, because they were not true. They had been true in the past, but they were not true now.

And it took him off of the hook. He could quit. He could legitimately tell the inmates, "The fucking lieutenant shook me down this morning. This party is over."

Another Traditional Problem: The Snitch

The big inmate value is supposed to be "Don't snitch." But that is not as true as it used to be. Nowadays you snitch every opportunity you get to enhance your position. That change came in the late 1970s, early '80s. About the time I quit, it was changing. The old-time convict and the old-time correctional officer kept their mouths shut. You did not snitch, but that began to change. The new group of convicts that we were getting had no compunction about snitching. They would still get beat up if they got caught. That was a matter of course. The guy beating on whoever he thought the snitch was may be the snitch to you the very next day. They just took advantage of an opportunity to pound on somebody. Not that they cared about snitching. No ethics involved there, it was just an opportunity to kick the heck out of this guy, and four others to help you—why, go ahead.

In one case that we had, the officer said he was sending an inmate down to me, and I needed to talk to him. He sent this guy, and his fingers were all broken. He was a thief, and they caught him, and they busted his hands up. So he did not have any trouble telling on them. I could not prove that they did it, but it did make them prominent. I asked what kind of position it was going to put this guy in with the ones who beat him. He said "What position am I in now?"

I said, "You could get a shiv [knife] down your throat." He said, "What the hell's the difference?"

I said I would pull them up and tell them. "Hey, people, you have been identified, and watch your business, because the next time I will be able to prove what you do."

The one guy I pulled in was kind of the ringleader. He told me, "The guy is a thief, and he got off easy." I asked him, "Are you telling me you did this?" He said, "No, I'm not. I'm just telling you that it happened." I did not have any confession, so I told him what my attitude was and what was going to happen in the future and that he was my prime candidate along with two or three others. And we just left it at that. It wasn't worth it to do it. They had already broken his fingers. They had already given him his message, and there was no need to do it again. And they did not suffer for it.

You want to know why the inmates did not come to me. The inmate thinks, No. Don't do that. You deny yourself two things. You deny yourself the satisfaction of breaking the guy's fingers, and you deny yourself the opportunity to enhance your position among the inmates. So you don't come to the man and let him settle it. Until it gets completely out of hand, and then you dump it on him.

That guy's hands were a mess. Whew. It had just happened. Not a tear in his eye, either. He was not complaining about his hands hurting or anything. I said, "We can talk after I send you to the clinic. I don't know why the officer sent you directly here. Let's get you to the clinic." He said, "No, what I have to say will not take very long, and then I'll go to the clinic." You just don't know.

Accusations Were a Serious Matter

We were all subject to this kind of thing [accusations]. Any inmate could tell the story to the associate warden or me, and it would have to be followed up. I was never implicated in the sense of bringing stuff in. But we had a murder down in R Wing, and this officer immediately tried to clean up his act by saying, "I was never trained, I never saw the lieutenant, I never had any instructions from the sergeant. I just did not know what to do. They just threw me down there, and I simply did not know what to do." So that had to be investigated. He made the definite accusation that I was letting the inmates run wild down there.

It is always somebody else's fault. It was the lieutenant's fault because he did not furnish adequate security measures; he let unauthorized people come in down there. It was a bunch of nonsense. But you have to answer it; you have to go through it.

The only thing that made it difficult at the time was that we had a new administrator. He did not know this particular individual. If it had been the old administrator, he would have said, "We have been through this before." But the new administrator made much more of a deal out of it.

The old administrator would have called the guy in and said, "Hey, you're doing it again. This murder happened down there. No one is accusing you of being lax. So what are you doing here?" That would have ended it. As it was, it ended anyway because there just was not anything there.

There is always enough evidence that someplace along the line was something you have done with another inmate that would support what the guy is saying. Or at least say, "Oh, yeah, that is kind of consistent." But, again, that clears the air, too.

In that business you had to put things to bed. You could not let them linger. That is how we got into so much trouble: not facing up to the issue at the time and doing what we should have done at the time. We just let it go and go and go. We would try a stopgap, a Band-Aid here and there, and before we knew it, we had something big to deal with. My dad used to tell me: "If you take care of the little things, the big things will take care of themselves." It took me a long time to understand that. Most people to whom I quote that, nowadays, don't understand it. They use the Air Force motto, "Don't sweat the small stuff." Which is a mistake. That is why they have to deal with the big stuff.

Working on the Routine Things

Anyway, that is the way it went. Take care of daily business. You had some hard decisions to make sometimes, decisions you didn't want to make, particularly dealing with staff. But it is best you do it early, and you do it completely. It saves a lot downstream.

By the big things, I mean riots or people getting killed or officers getting compromised. All of the security things that become issues if you don't take care of them all along. It could be anywhere from bringing in a package of gum to somebody's getting his throat cut. Just take the proper precautions in terms of security. Like searching cells on a regular basis. I don't mean searching cell 107 on Thursday morning, but just search the unit on a regular basis. Otherwise you find out that some guy has cut through the bars, and he has escaped or got shot off the fence. And we did find bars that were cut. It is easy. Get a jar of Vaseline, some sand, and some twine, and you can cut through any bar if you have enough time. And they have the time. If you don't inspect the cell on a regular basis, then they will have enough time to cut the bars out.

Also you have another problem. Bars are cut, and the inmate is gone. Or the inmate is living in his cell, and you inadvertently find out that the bars are cut. So you charge him with attempted escape. He says, "No, no, no; I did not do that. The previous occupant of the cell did that." If you do not have inspection records, he is scot-free. If you take care of the little things, then it does not become a big thing.

It is a pain in the butt to do that kind of security check. So the officers have a tendency to avoid it. We found out that we needed a system for doing checks. You could not always do it while an inmate was in the cell. Sometimes you could. But it is difficult to find time to make that kind of inspection. So you had to work out a system so it can be done.

So you find out when your people are working, and you inspect the inmate's cell while he is working or at the clinic. Showtime at night was a good time to do it. Ninety percent of the population was out of the unit. There were times when you could do it on the first watch, that last hour before you go or when they are feeding. Just inspect a few cells—and then you keep track of what you have done.

But that is grunt work, and most people don't like to deal with the nuts and bolts. I like to deal with the nuts and bolts. I would make up an informal security checklist. You not only add the cell number to it, the vents, the door locks, what have you. The inmates found a way to open some locks. Let me tell you how to do it. It takes a[n old-fashioned mercury] thermometer and an electric razor. You plug up the corridor side of the lock. You break the thermometer. Then you pour the mercury in there. You put pressure on the lock and use the electric razor to vibrate it and it vibrates the mercury over to depress the pin. Then the door comes open.

How did I discover this? An inmate told me. They could not stop talking. What the hell, we established a relationship over a period of time. He would ask me why we had to do things a certain way, and I would give him an answer or change the way we did it. It was a process over a period of years, doing your job. He was going out on parole, and he said, "I've got something to tell you. The mystery of your corridor doors being open—this is how they do it." "Thank you very much, enjoy your parole. I hope I never see you in here again. I will shake your hand if I see you on the street and kick your butt if I see you in here again."

He was an old-time convict, too. I was not sure, so I had to go down and do the experiment. Convicts don't need all that stuff. They don't need radios and electric razors and thermometers (which they would get out of the clinic). An electric razor just put a strain on the wiring. So what does he need an electric razor for, what does he need civilian clothes for? The razor turned out to be a problem: "Why? Is that what you were talking about?"

It is the nature of the situation. Beating the system is what you do. We even did it in the Navy, beat the system. You had time to think about it, and it was fun. We were not killing anyone, but finding a way to get a ham sandwich at nine o'clock at night was always interesting. Or having fruit juice to drink aboard ship when only the officers got it. You could get it because they gave us linen maps of the area we were in that would fold up and fit in your flight jacket. A map was worth its weight in gold. You could buy anything on the ship with one of those.

This is true with any group of young people with time on their hands and a system to beat. It is just the extent to which they carry it out. It is also the philosophy behind it. If you do it to deliberately mess up, it is one thing. If you do it because it is a game, then that is something else.

The inmates were doing it because they had been doing it all their life. Whether they were in a group or by themselves. That is just the nature of it. It starts in grammar school: how can I snooker the teacher and not have to do this or that? Can I charm her or cause enough disruption? It just happens with some people. Eventually some become convicts, and it is reinforced. They learn more sophisticated ways to snub the system. Even I learned how to pick locks.

I learned some other things, too, that we won't talk about. I learned these things from convicts. They taught me other things—just as a guy gets sent to the joint who may not have all the burglar skills he needs, he can learn more while he is there. He can be a good burglar when he comes out. I went in as an untutored person, and I learned how to pick locks and all kinds of other things. Get any group of people together, and they will learn from each other. Sometimes it is good, sometimes it is bad. Mostly in the joint it was bad.

Of course they were trying to outtalk each other. "I know this, you don't know that. Let me teach you a few things." That is life in an institution. It definitely involved status. Not only for the inmates but also for staff.

Always Being Ready for Surprises

The guy who had worked for Disneyland and tumbled for the kids at the open house used to drive the new officers nuts. He was strong enough and athletic enough that he could wedge himself between the walls, feet on one wall, hands on the other wall of the cell on top of the ceiling so when the officer came down to count the inmates, that cell was dead empty. He could not see that guy. The officer would panic because he knew the guy was in there just an hour before when he had checked. Once that sucker dropped down right in front of that officer. The officer wrote him up. That was when I first became aware of it. I had the inmate up and told him to quit ragging that officer. He said, "I did not mean to drop down and scare him, but I am not in the shape I was, and I could not hold it any longer." I told him if he was not in good enough shape to hold it, not to get up there and be scaring that officer. It interrupted the count and everything.

It was not funny to the officer. He got the crap scared out of him. He wanted revenge. When I talked to him, he said he felt humiliated. In a sense he had been humiliated. But only he and the inmate knew about it. No one else witnessed it. But then the officer probably was not very comfortable outside the normal routine. If he had something unusual happen, then that would irritate him. Notifying me was legitimate; and it did not have to be official. But the inmate broke the rules, so you give him thirty days without privileges. He got his message across, I got mine across, and [the] officer got his across. Then you move on to other things. But it was funny. I almost chuckled in front of the officer. He waited to see my reaction when he handed the report in. I had to look up at him and keep my face straight to see what he was thinking. And he was mad. But in that business you have to expect surprises, and you have to roll with them and hope they are as innocent as that one was.

If you want to carry it to the fullest extent, listening to the inmate, he was getting paroled in six or eight months and was going back to Disneyland to do that sort of thing. So in a way he was preparing for the outside job. But I think it was a combination of things. I think the inmate was right; he just could not hold himself up there any more. If he could have stuck up there, he would have. And then as soon as the officer went to the phone, he would have been in bed snoring.

It was nice to know that guy was that agile. That is what I told the officer later. Before the incident we did not know he was that agile, that he was that clever. He could have made good use of that. So it was nice to know what he was capable of. That officer was pretty business-like, and turning the inmate in was his way of handling the situation. I think the officer's feelings really got hurt. But he was pretty distant from everyone. He eventually left my unit, and I lost track of him. He had an education, so he probably became a counselor.

Centralizing Security Not Always the Best Idea

One of the things that happened in terms of managing an institution: in the early days, watch lieutenants handled their own investigations. They found out what was going on, and who was doing what, who was a bad inmate, and so on. Then the administrators came along and developed a security squad. They put all of the investigations in one spot. Watch commanders were obligated to give them all the information we had. They were not obligated to give us anything back. It just took the guts out of being a watch commander, simply because human nature is, "I know this, and I am not going to tell you unless I have to."

The watch commander was definitely in trouble if he had information and did not relay it to the squad. But the squad was not in trouble if they did not pass along to the watch commander what they knew about his watch.

This change took place probably in the early seventies. At least at our institution; I don't know about the other institutions. It is difficult to pin it down to a particular time. I know I suggested the first security squad sergeant we had. The associate warden asked me what sergeant could we put into this new unit. I said John Vittlatchel. It was obvious to me he was the man to go in there. He got along with everybody, he had a good head, smart, and he would pick good men to work with him.

But the siren song got to him. He got just as possessive and just as tight with the information as anyone. But he was always coming to us, asking us about this and about that. It just took the guts out of it.

There was no trading of information. You have to take care of the institution. You had a situation that was going. They would not let you act on this information yourself; you had to go to the security squad. So you gave it to the security squad. Then they might come back to you and use your officers. The idea was that they might have information that you did not, and they might be able to put it together.

What it amounted to was, this kept the associate warden involved, or clued in. Before, the watch lieutenant would take care of the situation and then give the report. Now it went to the security squad, the security squad took it to the associate warden, then it came back down to you. He was clued in. That was the only purpose, to satisfy that individual. It later became Department-wide and a viable thing within itself, but at our institution it was established for that one purpose only. It just destroyed the command structure.

Originally, we handled everything, even publicity. If there was a murder on our watch, we handled it. Just as you see it on TV. The lieutenant takes the case and does his thing. When Dr. Keating[9] was there, you did your own publicity and everything else. You dealt with the newspapers and the whole ball of wax. The rest of the superintendents did not seem to have the level of confidence that Keating had in us.

The Training Programs

I will give CMF credit for our training. We had great extension courses going on all the time at CMF. I can't think of a time when we did not have extension courses from the University of California or somewhere at the

9. See the next chapter.

Program Lieutenant Wilkinson standing in front of cell
bars in CMF giving a tour to a visiting survey team (1965)
Source: Viola Wilkinson.

institution—allied with the criminal justice programs, but they also had
other programs. I still have remnants of courses I was interested in.

These were courses for the staff. This was due to Tom Murray, mostly.
He started the tradition. He was a training officer, getting ready to retire.
He started it, and it carried on through as part of the training. The peo-
ple who liked to get the money who taught these courses knew about
CMF, and so they would contact the institution and say that they had a
class or phase.

We had a guy who was a sergeant in the Modesto police department,
Dale Moore. This was at the very beginning of gangs. He was an expert
on tattoos and their meanings. Of course that has all changed now.

The best educational experience I had: I have a standard designated
teaching credential. Wen Silva gave us this class. We had 120 hours to get
in, all in one week's time. We got there on Sunday, and we worked on

Sunday and worked steadily until the following Sunday. We got in our 120 hours.

Talk about positive reinforcement: that was it. By the middle of the week we were getting pretty snotty and pretty ratty among ourselves. We would not say a word to Wen because he was up there working so hard. Our class consisted of people gathered up from all over the Department. As a matter of fact, this is how I got that COD academy,[10] because of that teaching credential. They ran the class through Hartnell College up in Salinas. Silva was a big, distinguished-looking man, and he would approach things so quietly. He would keep you going when your mind was saying "I am going to quit." But he would go right along because he was talking and teaching and doing his thing. You would look up at the end of the day and say, "Hey, you have these hours done, you have this paperwork done." I should have followed up on that.

How I Became a Notorious Male Chauvinist

As part of all of the training, I went to the lieutenants' academy at the California Highway Patrol. It was a week: "Must provide your own towels and soap. All male trainees will have meals and reside at the facility where room assignment will be arranged. . . ." That was a good academy. A really good group over there.

And there was another class I went to, down in Monterey. It was a week-long class. It was a captain's conference. Potential captains were sent down there. It was an outstanding program. But our group drew the assignment of integrating females into the Department (this was in the very early 1970s).

Anyhow, to start the meeting off, everybody was reluctant. Everybody was pussyfooting around. We had one female in the group, and she was from Central Office. We had three blacks, I think. I was a lieutenant. So, we were just fumbling around and what have you, and I said, "Okay, let me put it this way: I think women should be home in the kitchen where they belong. But our task is to find out how we are going to put them in the Department." And, man, the whole group went up. "Now I can express myself. All of us chickens peck on this chicken here."

So the blacks went immediately to the female's aid. She like to blew a gasket. The sum total of it was: it cleared the air, we got in, we did the job. The rest of the groups were floundering right up to the last minute. We were out in the swimming pool. We were through in two days' time. So we

10. See below.

had Gail, the female, give this presentation in front of the whole group, and the departmental personnel officer just went crazy. He thought that was the greatest thing he had ever seen.

Three weeks later he had us all at the Wardens' and Superintendents' conference. Gail again gives her spiel. We were all sitting up on the stage like dummies. That was the only function we had down there. All that state expense to fly us down there and do our thing, but we were celebrities. So these various groups came down and talked to us, and we found out the potential female workforce was 33 percent. We figured we could do that. It will take "x" number of months to reach this particular part, but in a year's time we will have our workforce up to 38 percent or whatever it was.

It was all laid out and ready to go. Of course none of them had a damn thing to do after that. It was just one of those things where we just had to do it. You know after you open it up, then it just worked. Every time I had to do business with Gail after that, she said, I forget just what her function was up there at Central Office, but with the information she would send, there would be a little note, "You dog, you."

We would meet at other conferences, and she would say, "I could have killed you. You loved that attention, didn't you?" So everybody was just so tickled. And Mark, the guy who was running things, he just took off. He wanted to see how the group was getting started. He said, "Goddamn, you scared the living crap out of me when you pulled that. I thought, Oh, man, this is not going to work at all." And he left. Then we got down to it, and they pounded on my head about what a chauvinist pig I was and the whole works. I said, "Well, that is okay. that I am a chauvinist pig, but, this is not getting the job done. We want to know how we are going to get women in the Department, so let's go ahead and talk about it. I will be a chauvinist pig."

Well, it took most of them to understand later on that "He doesn't really feel that way." Mark said, "I could have just kicked you. I just saw my group going down the drain, and I was just going to have a hell of a time." He checked back in a couple of days, stuck his head in, and asked how things were going. We told him, "It's going fine. We will give you a report in a day or so." We were potential captains, we were supposed to make decisions.

Sometimes it was good times. This one girl could hardly handle that. But you say what you have got to say to get things going. Then you go on with what you have to do, and you just don't deal with it any more. You deal with the task at hand. You just don't deal with the rest of it. My buddy, the other lieutenant who went down with me, he was aghast. He was a nice guy, very benign. He said, "Oh, God, what did you *do?*" I believe in getting the job done, and then you play.

The Adjustment Center

One of my last assignments at CMF was the Adjustment Center.[11] At one point they gave it a title of Lister Unit. It was one of several adjustment centers planned in 1968. We didn't build a special unit. It was an existing unit, W Wing, that we converted in 1972.

With normal inside cell construction, you have open bars and about ten or fifteen feet to the outside walls, which is a pretty good corridor. In order to make it so you could exercise people, that kind of thing, we split the corridor in half and put up a kind of metal chain-link fence, bolted down to floor and ceiling, and ran it down and sectioned it off so that you could let, say, four guys out at a time to play cards, talk to one another, do what they were going to do without having everybody loose. And with the amount of staffing we had, that was about the way we had to do it.

This screened all the cells off so that you could walk the catwalk there and observe what was going on but not have any contact. And it was too far to throw feces and whatever. So it was just a protective thing and a way of controlling the place. So it wasn't a brand-new building. It was in the Guidance Center, and it was a lockup for the Guidance Center. It was built as a lockup to begin with. So we made this conversion. And made a pretty good unit of it to handle people.

I was in charge of it. They had a lieutenant and three officers in there. I came in after the previous guy had been there a year or so, and they were changing people. When I got into this particular thing, the Adjustment Center, it was dying on the vine. As far as treatment or program goes, it was on the wane at that time. So there wasn't a hell of a lot happening. For what they had in mind to begin with, we didn't have the plant, the facilities to do that. I transferred to Soledad around then, and so I don't know what happened afterward.

We were still going to Folsom and San Quentin and interviewing inmates and telling them about the program. Seeing if they wanted to volunteer to come over and come to our unit and see if that would help any. That was the Adjustment Center.

We still had the emphasis on evaluating men for placement in the Main Line setting. To my knowledge, while I was there, no one moved to

11. The idea was to remove from the Main Line inmates "who sought to disrupt or destroy the institution" and try to get them socialized to the point that they could go back to the Main Line. Inmates in Adjustment Centers were customarily kept locked in the cells for all but one half hour each day. See especially Assembly Select Committee on Prison Reform and Rehabilitation, *Administrative Segregation in California's Prisons, Alias: The Hole, Lockup, Solitary Confinement and the Adjustment Center* (Sacramento: [The Committee], 1973), 3, 109–19, and passim.

the Main Line. Even though that was the purpose of the unit. They had been locked up so long that the Main Line was scary. You didn't have any responsibilities in the adjustment unit. In the Main Line, there was a certain amount of peer pressure that would come to bear. In the Adjustment Center, there were the guys on either side, and they could get together and do this and that. But other than that, in the Adjustment Center there wasn't any pressure.

It was an estimated eight-month period during which they moved them through the various phases and loosened up on them little by little. When I got there, it was pretty much cut and dried. One unit was held, and the other two units got to go to chow, which was one of our mistakes. They backed up on me one Thanksgiving. You've got two officers down there, and you turn seventeen or eighteen convicts loose, and they pretty much have control of the unit then.

It was Thanksgiving, and they wanted to talk. They wanted to talk about something. We got lucky. When we first got in there, you stayed inside the cages, you did not go inside the unit. Old dumb me, I couldn't talk through those screens, so I would go into the unit and talk to them.

Anyway, when this came up, I told them, "Your chow's getting cold. Go eat, and I'll come up and talk to you afterwards and we'll find out what this is all about." So they did. And we didn't have any problem at that particular time. And I did go up and talk to them. And I got my ass chewed for going down in the unit. But I couldn't figure any other way to do it to make it work.[12]

---

12. The tragic riot at Attica Prison, New York, in 1971, immediately following some tragic events at San Quentin Prison, received much media coverage and later journalistic exploration—to the extent that it remains a symbolic event. See, for example, Tom Wicker, *A Time to Die* (New York: Ballantine Books, 1976 [c. 1975]). Wilkinson adds the following aside:

> We had followed the Attica riots with normal interest. We were also interested to see if our inmates would react. Were they going to borrow from them? But the inmates did not have that much interest in it. It was just news. Like it was happening on Mars. There were some reactions from some county jails and some ex-cons on the street, but we did not have any reactions. If you did not react to the provocative statements, then there was no problem. However, if we had a convict who was running off the mouth about "kill all cops" or praising what was going on at Attica, then you had a problem. We mostly ignored it. It was in New York.
> In 1980, when there were riots in New Mexico, the staff had a lot of speculation about those events, and we talked that one up. I do not recall much comment from inmates. But the staff kept track of the New Mexico riots, among ourselves of course. I don't know if we were more interested because it was closer to home than New York was, or if it was the second time around, or just the climate of the times. We kind of kept books on that one—I don't remember what specifically, but there must have been something—how did they take over the control room? The Department may have stressed the riots, or maybe it was the change in the administration.

From that time on, the rest of the time I was in there, they were all cell-fed. We just didn't have any activity at all. I do believe the counselors were bringing them out—selected people—two or three at a time to continue on with what they were doing before. I didn't get to know all about that.

The Adjustment Centers turned out to be just dead time for the inmate and also for the staff and the Department. And there were some pretty bad situations Adjustment Center-wise. B Wing [the Adjustment Center] at San Quentin—I'm not too sure somebody shouldn't have been arrested, the way that thing was run. They simply didn't have the plant to do that. But they also couldn't keep those people on the Main Line. There was a reason for their being locked up. They were stabbing and stealing and doing the whole damned thing. So what are you going to do?

B Wing was just totally unsuited for what they were using it for. I went through it when I had to tour some young lawyers through San Quentin. That was just more than they could handle. It didn't do me any good, either. It was like a zoo. Yelling and screaming. We were there shortly after feeding time, and the inmates still had food left to try and throw. It was just bad.

Myths about the Adjustment Centers

In the early 1970s, the Adjustment Centers in the state, including the one at CMF, were the center of various charges and an investigation.[13] The charges were to the effect that Mexican and African American inmates were segregated and subjected to psychiatric experimentation and torture.[14] There was a lot of heat from the Bay Area, the Berkeley people. But this was the thing to do, to put the heat on the Department of Corrections. That was the only game in town.

But what they were talking about was the bogeyman instead of talking reality. They failed to mention that, at least when I got there, we had a whole floor of Aryan Brotherhood people. I don't know any Chicanos or blacks who were in that organization.

So there were the Black Guerrillas and one of the Mexican groups (I

13. See the Assembly Select Committee report cited above. The concept of the "adjustment center" had its origins in California in the 1950s. The 1955 ACA *Manual of Correctional Standards* makes no mention of adjustment centers, but the 1959 revision of the *Manual* indicates that "many states" were now using them (249). In theory, what made adjustment centers different from administrative or disciplinary segregation was the intensive treatment they were to provide. In practice, a number of Adjustment Centers provided neither treatment nor humane conditions. See, for example, *Jordan v. Fitzharris,* 257 F. Supp. 1365 (1966) on the Soledad adjustment center.

14. See, for example, "Covert CIA Drug Tests at State Prison Charged," *Los Angeles Times,* 2 March 1977, I:3. Wilkinson had no recollection of such experiments.

Psychotherapy group at CMF (1955–1956)
Source: State of California, Department of Corrections, *1955–56 Biennial Report.*

forget which one) and the Aryan Brotherhood, but they were all isolated on certain floors. The object was to kind of integrate the groups, maybe at the counseling sessions or such. To my knowledge that never came about. These inmates had earned their way into the Adjustment Center because of their actions on the Main Line. Probably gang-oriented, though.[15]

I was not involved in any of the behavioral therapy. Not in W Wing. They had high-powered counselors. The guy who ran that thing, the program administrator, Austin Vineyard, a nice guy and pretty heads-up, drew a pretty clear line between custody and counseling. You have your job and they have their job, and let's not mix them up. So uniformed personnel did not get involved in that in this particular unit.

I expected him to have a different attitude. I knew him before he took over the unit and before I got assigned there. He was very receptive and very helpful, but he ran it that way. In all the other units, if the program administrator was not there, the lieutenant assumed the responsibility for the unit. It was just automatic. Vineyard would appoint a counselor to have the responsibility.

To me there just is no answer if they don't want to cooperate, don't want to get along. There is no way of going except locking them up. There wasn't much happening when I got there. Not compared to what I was used to, not compared to the intensive treatment unit I had set up.

15. There is a section in the next chapter dealing with the special role of gangs at CMF, which served as a sanctuary from full gang warfare.

At W Wing they just did not have the plant to make it work.

The irony is that if you don't go to a program like this, all you are looking at is indefinite lockup in some other Adjustment Center. Are they volunteers or not? How receptive are they to the program? Catch-22, I guess. I did not see that it was successful as designed. Maybe at the beginning they had some people move on through. And then they completely blew it when they backed up on the stairwell. So that pretty much ended the unit there in terms of loosening up on them.

Just one brief comment [on the Adjustment Center]. If somebody out there has a different method of handling convicts without having adjustment centers, please let me know. The things are just self-perpetuating. You can't keep a guy that inactive and locked up that long without causing other problems. As I have said, the only way I have seen this work, and we were dealing with psych patients, was in that Intensive Treatment Unit. People did move along well there. We even got paroles out of there. It was a good move, as far as I am concerned. It took a lot of heat off of the institution, too.

It worked mostly because of the staffing and the plant.

In the Adjustment Center, the facilities were just not there. Even moving the inmates around was difficult, because you did not have what you needed to do it. You took a chance every time you did it. As in W Wing, we had an exercise period. I wasn't on the floor at the time, but the four guys we had let out in the exercise area in front of their cells—one guy stabbed another one with a toothbrush. Did a pretty good job, too, right in the neck and caught him just right. Of course all the toothbrush handles were only about an inch or two long, but he still managed to make a pretty weapon out of it and made it work.

So it could happen. As clean as you keep the building, and as tight as you are, they can still do what they are going to do. I don't know what he was pissed off about. It could have been anything, since they were in adjoining cells and could talk to one another. Pissed him off someplace along the line. Twenty-three hours a day in that cell is worrisome. That gets on your mind. You just did not have that much contact. Staff was not down there that much. The setup was such that they could not even do TV. They had a TV set down at the end, but it was hard to see because of all the screening we had in there. And only two or three people could watch it at a time, just whoever was out. The rest of them could listen to it, but in a concrete building, it was like having a dishpan over your head with somebody pounding on it. So it was pretty useless, but it was an attempt.

Maybe we needed a fish tank in there. I never got over that.

The Night I Played God

All in all, my work experience at CMF was tremendously varied and interesting. And there were some great days. One time when I was third-watch lieutenant, we were having problems getting a maintenance man to get a broken pipe fixed and that sort of thing. We were having difficulties when the lieutenants tried to get people to come in to do what they were supposed to do. So Dr. Keating said, "Put out a memo that the third- and first-watch lieutenants are in effect God." And if the lieutenants were to request something from the maintenance people, then they were to do it—and settle the problem the next morning with the chief of maintenance if they had any objections to what was done. But go ahead and do what the night lieutenants want you to do.

So there was quite a bit of kidding about: You are God from four to midnight. Then we had an incident where we had a real bad parole board report.[16] The Adult Authority had been there. Traditionally, you passed out the board reports in the daytime when you had the most help. Dr. Keating had told the inmates that he was going to pass them out that night. It was a really bad board. I had nine people to run that watch, and there were no free people to do this kind of thing. So I told the boss that I was just not comfortable with doing it: "I just can't do it."

So it finally got down to the point where I reminded him of the memo he put out about the third-watch lieutenants' having jurisdiction over their watch. So he took a deep breath and said, "Okay."

I stood my ground, but I knew I was in trouble because he was extremely angry. So I got through the night, and I told them to pass out the board reports in the morning. At five minutes to eight the next morning I get a call at home from Dr. Keating's secretary saying that he wanted me in his office at eight o'clock. And Virginia said, "Listen to me closely now. You are to be here at eight o'clock."

I was hardly out of bed. I did what I could do, shaved a little bit, and I reported. He let me sit in the office until about nine. Then he called me in. He left all the doors open. He said, "Last night, you were God. This morning I am." And he ripped me a new asshole from top to bottom. It was so good that it was difficult not to laugh. Virginia was so embarrassed she got up and left and closed the door. He kept right on talking and went over and opened the door so everybody in the foyer could hear what he was saying. I went out, and all these horrified faces were looking at me.

---

16. This was the Adult Authority described in the introduction, and it would hold a series of hearings on the inmates who had applied for parole. Those who were granted parole were very happy; those who were denied often reacted badly and behaved in a destructive way. A bad report on the results of the hearings, with many denials, thus foreboded trouble.

He really put on a show. Today I am God. He ripped me up one side and down the other.

"Hey, I don't care what kind of memo you got. You remember I am God. If you want to play God with me on the third watch again and go through this on the day watch, well you go right ahead." It was great.

CHAPTER FOUR

Trying to Hold Things Together during Change at CMF

In 1964, Procunier left CMF. In 1966, Keating went on to be a major force in the Department of Mental Hygiene. There were two tremendous egos there, as well as two tremendous intellects, and before they left, they pushed many of the changes.

Procunier and Keating Working Together

I can illustrate their style. When they first came in and were working together, the feeding program, as I have mentioned, was too slow. We were feeding the inmates in two sections, what they called the short line and the main line. It was taking too much time. We wanted to change it. (This was back when I was culinary sergeant in 1961.) Anyway, the three of us sat down one afternoon at five o'clock, and they settled among themselves how the feeding was going to go. I was astounded. I said, "Wait. You're telling me to go institute this thing at five o'clock tomorrow morning? You have got a first-watch lieutenant who is responsible for this, so in the first place he would throw me right out of the building if I tried that. And rightfully so. Number two: the inmates need to be notified. That is going to take two or three days, if not longer. All the staff has to be notified that this is going to happen. You guys come in and settle it in fifteen minutes, and tell me to put it into effect tomorrow morning at five o'clock? Get real."

They said, "Well, I guess you're right." We did advertise it for a week, and we still did not have it down pat. One sergeant came along wandering through the building on his way home. He did not have any connection with the change in the feeding. He just came along and looked at it for ten or fifteen minutes and said, "Why don't you do it this way?" And that was the key. We were all so close to it that we could not see what to do. And

Portrait of Raymond Procunier
Source: Historical Albums, California
Department of Corrections, Sacramento.

old McKinley says, "Why don't you do it this way?" and it worked like a charm. So you get lucky sometimes.

Watching Procunier and Keating operate—if your heart did not fail—was really interesting. For instance, when we built the Intensive Treatment Center. They always wasted a lot of money building and equipping mop closets, and you could not use them and what they put in there. It was not adequate. So I told Dr. Keating, "Tell them to knock that out of the contract, and we will do it out at the vocational carpenter shop, and we'll save some money." And we did. We saved about ten thousand dollars. And he took my money. I wanted it for patients who were taking thorazine and sparine.[1] You medicate them with that, and you get them out in the sun, and you are going to lose them because of the drug reaction. They can't tolerate the sun. I had an exercise area above the dining hall on the second floor. I wanted a shade up there. He took my money and spent it for something else. We had one hell of a fight about that. He was the kind who

1. Thorazine was the trade name for chlorpromazine, a standard "tranquilizer" or antipsychotic medication introduced in the mid-1950s, as noted above.

Dr. William Keating (second from left) with group dedicating CMF baseball field
Source: Historical albums, California Department of Corrections, Sacramento.

would allow you to do this. I was just a lieutenant, and he was the superintendent of the place.

But we got things done. It is a wonder we did not get compromised
along the line, but nobody got hurt as far as I know. I just plain told him,
"I expected to use that money for this shade out here." He said, "You're
right; we will have to get you money for that. We can't put them out there
where they are that exposed like that." I said, "Okay, just don't be too long
about it." And he would tolerate stuff like that. Which made it nice as far
as I was concerned. Procunier was the same way. He could take anything
from you. He expected to hear from you. A lot of guys did not understand
that and did not like him. It made him vulnerable, according to some.

Too Much of a Rush

There was too much rushing into things in the mid- to late sixties. The
crunch really did not come until the early seventies on some of the mistakes
that we had made. It ganged up on us: all the television sets, all the civilian
clothes, all the telephones, all the banquets, all the radios, all the noncen-

soring of mail. All of that began to catch up with us in the late sixties/early seventies more than anything. Then we had to start backtracking. When you start taking things away, then you have a real problem.[2]

Censoring mail was the one thing you had to do when I first started working in Chino. Sitting out there, you might have only half a dozen letters or so, or you might have several more. It was pretty mundane. You just looked for the obvious, really: "I'm going to escape, come down and get me." "Leave the stash at the third post on Edison Avenue, and I'll pick it up when I go to work"—that kind of thing. But then it would get into such things as a guy had a gambling debt, and so he had to let his people know, "Take the pink slip [title] to my car and give it to inmate Joe's wife so that they won't kill me while I'm in here," that is, paying a gambling debt. So you had [to] deal with that, and also sometimes some inmates would use the mail when they had something to say to The Man. They would just say it in a letter. That way they did not get the finger put on them: "I'm not talking to The Man, so it could not have been me that put this word out."

At that stage in the game, I did not feel confident enough to deal with any of the content, and I would just pass it on to the supervisors, people with more experience, and let them handle it. I had been there only a month or so.

Also, if there was a change in the rules, or if the Department had made new rules, then you picked up on the comments. Was anybody commenting on the change? Did they like it? Didn't like it? It could give you some ideas of what was going on, but it was mostly just family talk and personal talk. But occasionally something would come out of it.

While I did not do that job again, later one of the other lieutenants and I did make an attempt to censor Spanish mail. Other than that, I did not have anything to do with it, unless someone passed something along to me. That was one of the perks of getting a promotion: you didn't have to read that mail anymore.

The Flood of Other Changes

One of the signs of change came when the inmates started petitioning for

2. Ironically, the reaction and reversal began when Procunier was Department director, as was noted above. The shift was triggered particularly by some tragic incidents in California prisons in 1970–1971. State of California, Board of Corrections, *Report to Governor Ronald Reagan on Violence in California Prisons* ([Sacramento: The Board], 1971), esp. 21. See also a contemporary editorial in the *Sacramento Bee,* reprinted in *Correctional News Briefs,* 20 November 1974. The changes in the direction of more openness and privileges for prisoners continued through the 1970s, often at the behest of courts, even as the Department in some areas was trying to back away from some changes. The result was, and continues to be, complex and confusing, not a simple, clean-cut reversal.

these clubs, special interest and things, with the assistance of people from the outside. This was also when the administration put in telephones, radios, TVs. It was a madhouse at best. They were letting them bring in all of that. You could have six different boom box radios on six different stations, and each of them jacked up, trying to outshine the others. You had a problem in a concrete building. And then you had the TV sets. The electrical circuits could not stand it. It had to be all revamped and redone. The theft problem escalated. I can't tell you how much we paid out in damages, because when we rolled up the equipment to ship inmates out or send them to isolation or what have you, their possessions got damaged sometimes. We were paying for all of this stuff. We had to hire new staff and set up new procedures just to handle the damned equipment. All this was Department-wide.[3] So these policies all added to the problem.

When I started, the inmates lost their civil rights when they came in. There was no such thing as a phone call. It was a control factor, and it was very good because you could tell what the hell was going on. You had control, and you did not have interference from the outside.[4]

At that time, when a convict filed a complaint, the judge would just tell him that he had been convicted and to do his time, get out, and do well. Then we went through this emancipation thing, and every Podunk judge in California was establishing case law. You file from some judge from Alpine County and it becomes case law.[5] Then the whole Department has to pay attention to it. At one time, an inmate could write a sealed letter only to the director of Corrections and to the governor. One judge established that the inmate could send a sealed letter to anyone, on the grounds that the inmate could not fit any contraband into a letter. That judge completely misunderstood. So then an inmate could send a sealed letter to anyone at any place.

---

3. In fact, much of the discretion concerning what personal property was permitted was bucked down to local institutional rules. Available records do not permit exact dating of many changes. See, for example, State of California, Department of Corrections, *Rules and Regulations of the Director of Corrections* ([Sacramento: The Department, 1973]). Moreover, court decisions were often made and then in two or three years reversed. Such particularly was the case with the censoring of mail and telephone calls. See, for example, "A Claim to Simple Decency," *Los Angeles Times,* 26 February 1978, IV: 4, and Philip Hager, "Court Order for Prison Reform Upset," *Los Angeles Times,* 17 March 1981, I:1, which describe cases long in the courts with a succession of inconsistent rulings.

4. Although the complete loss of civil rights is probably overstated, most studies confirm that the period when Wilkinson began in corrections was characterized by a "hands-off" attitude by the courts. Donald H. Wallace, "Prisoners' Rights: Historical Views," in *Correctional Contexts: Contemporary and Classical Readings,* eds. Edward J. Latessa, Alexander Holsinger, James W. Marquart, and Jonathan R. Sorensen (Los Angeles: Roxbury, 2001), 229–38. The period between 1960 and the mid-1970s that Wilkinson recalls does represent the most dramatic moment in growth in inmate civil rights litigation.

5. Alpine County was notorious because, although a full, legal county in California, the population was only in the hundreds. As late as 1980, the census listed the population as 1,097.

The Department did not appeal the decision. In fact, they did away with censoring even on a 10-percent basis. Then they put telephones in so the inmate could conduct his business from inside the joint.[6] Then in 1975 the legislature restored civil rights, including the right to vote in local elections.

The Costs of Loosening Up

It was a problem just to take care of inmates' personal property. I don't know how many dollars we spent for damaged personal property. Or stolen personal property. When I first started working, you could clean out a guy and his cell, and you could put everything in a shoebox. Everything else belonged to the state. So you lock him up, and that is it. So if you broke a toothbrush or razor, it was not that bad to replace. A tube of toothpaste might be a little expensive.

That was all it amounted to, then. It did not amount to hundreds of dollars if property was being damaged, as it did later. Then there was the amount of time you spent trying to find stolen property. It was nonsense. They did not need that stuff. It became a liability. But that is what the authorities decided to do, so you adjusted accordingly. Your workload went up, and the security of the institution went down.

It also affected even the outside. Joe Blow is in there: "Hey, I lost my status because I don't have a 400-dollar boom box or TV or record player. Send me one." She is out there and can't even afford to buy diapers on her welfare check. So send him one.

Worse yet, the guy would be in debt. "Send me that 400-dollar box so I can pay off my debts and not get killed." Before, if he got in that situation, she could not send him four hundred dollars' worth of stuff. So he would have to take his thumping. They adjust to everything that is there and take advantage of everything that is there.

Dealing with Outside Groups

We are now going into the second phase of my career. First you hit them with a two-by-four if they don't conform.[7] Now, in the late 1960s, you give them everything they ask for, appease them. And then these special groups

---

6. See *Rules and Regulations*, 1974, for indications of the ending of mail censoring. After the inmates gained the use of telephones, any censoring of mail was beside the point.

7. This was a common expression referring to the folk wisdom of the story about the mule who did well after one got his attention by hitting him with a two-by-four. Wilkinson refers here simply to communicating to an inmate that he should pay attention.

started coming in. The EMPLEO, which was a Latino group. EMPLEO was based on education and being employed.[8] They had to have a staff sponsor to operate in the institution. Everybody was eager to begin with, but after that, the inmates could not handle it. The groups had people coming in from the outside. You were bringing people in from the streets to handle it. You had the Black Cultural Association, you had the Pen and Pencil Set for would-be writers, you had EMPLEO, or whatever. And somebody had to handle all of this for CMF. Guess who got the job?

So I was screening these people who were coming from the outside. Again, I wasn't the first on the job. It was one of those clean-up deals where you come in and hear, "Hey, this is how you handle it." Then you do what you can do to straighten it out. So we had to revamp the whole thing about the screening process. I looked at the paperwork, and out of 150 applications out of Sacramento that would come in for various groups, all of them had the same address on Marconi Avenue.[9] This created a real screening problem. So there were some other things wrong, and we took care of that.

I had to get a good inmate clerk. They certainly were not going to give me any free person to do it. No budget for it. You had to get an inmate who was not susceptible to bribery. There are two ways to manage getting a clerk. The first guy I had, before he got paroled, we had an association over a period of years. We learned over those years not to mess each other up. It just did not pay either one to do that. The next guy, I told him, "I'll cut your legs off right up around your neck if you screw this up." So it worked both ways. You just had to pick an individual. You do what you do to get it done.

But these outside groups were something else. They would have whole groups come in. They would have bands come in. They would have banquets. You just opened the front door and let anybody in.

On top of everything else, the outsiders took up what they called affirmative action. One guy, I do not remember his name, was in charge of the Northern California parole district. He had a secretary who was really pushing affirmative action, and she got the parole person involved. He would call and say he was Supervisor So-and-so from Parole, and it would sound official. So he would catch the watch lieutenant. At 6:00 P.M. the watch lieutenant was probably going to do what the official wanted done

---

8. Joan W. Moore et al., *Homeboys: Gangs, Drugs, and Prison in the Barrios of Los Angeles* (Philadelphia: Temple University Press, 1978), esp. 135–39, trace the origins of the EMPLEO (El Mejicano Preparado Listo Educado y Organizado) self-help group to San Quentin in 1966.

9. In this way the authorities at CMF learned that pressure groups were not all legitimate but a number with different names were being run by the same people.

and then check it out tomorrow. That was another form of pressure. The whole thing just snowballed. Everybody tried to jump on the bandwagon or be enlightened, and it got out of hand.

How the Inmates Took Advantage of Outside Groups

Even the people who were pushing the changes, it got out of hand for them. The inmate groups just ate them up—the Black Culture groups who came to tutor them. It would not be three weeks until I would have to close down a group because someone from the outside brought in marijuana or one of them got their behind patted in the back of the library. Then the inmates would apologize and say they were going to change their ways, and they would elect new officers. And the people on the outside raised all kinds of hell. They would say you cannot restrict those inmates like that. It was an isolated incident, and it did not amount to a hill of beans, and so on. Every fifteen minutes someone from Berkeley or someplace was on the phone to us. These were supposedly intelligent people pushing their agenda.

But what it was all about was the inmates' exploiting the outsiders. That is what inmates do, that is what they are. They can't resist the opportunity. It is their whole life, running this sandy candy on someone else. They are going to do what they do naturally with outsiders. That is a given. You know you are going to have that kind of trouble with outsiders coming in. So you know at some point that the privilege, be it the visiting room or whatever, is going to be compromised. So you plan on it and do the best you can. Why it used to surprise people, surprised me.

The ones who would come from the Bay Area were so naive. Most of them were educated. Still they had no idea what was going on with the inmate. You would try to explain things to them to begin with, but they would brush you off—"Here is just some scare card"—and they would want to get down to tutoring the inmate. Two weeks later the very thing that you told them would happen happened. "Didn't I tell you this would happen?" Things like bringing in a pack of cigarettes, a little bottle of booze for him, delivering a message, or what have you—dealing with the convicts or, more accurately, letting the convicts eat you up. Most of the outsiders could not see that, they could not feel that.

During orientation I would try to warn them about the convict, and they would flat-out deny it and not believe you. It was startling sometimes what they would say to you. I would tell them this is what convicts do. They would say, "No, they are not that way. You are just making that up. They are just ordinary people here." They would tell me that I did not understand the convict. These people had never been in a prison before,

Wilkinson as Activities Coordinator (word "mosque" in background) (1972–1973)
Source: Viola Wilkinson.

and they were telling me that it was obvious how I treated the convict and why they acted the way they did. It was not obvious to me. Their idea was that we should provide the inmate with a giveaway program, and my idea was we should cut their balls off if they do not perform. They were self-satisfied people who would come in and have the attitude that they were a Ph.D. and I was a dumb prison guard. Sometimes I had to react. But you pick your spots, because it got pretty hairy when they would call the director. I did not think they were doing right by letting people in the prison who had no knowledge of what was going to happen to them, who were totally ignorant about the environment and the inmate. They were vulnerable, and we did nothing to protect them.

Anything you give the inmate is something he will build upon. That is the nature of the inmate. You have to understand that that is their way.

When the groups started to come in, the inmates would scurry and warn other inmates to stay away, that this was their pigeon. They chose their sucker. But that is what they do, with various degrees of success. They do it to each other, to society, to everybody. You have to understand that and plan on it—take as many precautions as you can, and they either work, or they don't work. At least you are reasonably prepared when the wheels come off.

The outside visitors were never prepared. They never thought the inmate would do something like that to them. Especially after they were compassionate and tried their best to help. But in the inmate's mind, they were there not to help the inmate, but so that the inmate could take advantage of them. "Oh, I can't believe that." "Well, I can, because I have been watching it for a good number of years." It always worked that way, and it always will work that way. That is why they are in jail. They took short-cuts. Not out and digging and doing it as it should be done. Unlike the Ph.D. who worked his or her tail off, and who now had gotten ripped off. "Now you've hurt my feelings," one guy told me. "You're just trying to punish me." "No," I said, "I'm not trying to punish you. I am just trying to get a message across to you that you did not believe the first time I told you. You have to recognize it for what it is, when you step through that gate and start dealing with inmates."

Dealing with Outside Pressures

Then we changed somewhat. When Procunier went to Sacramento, Kenny Britt came in as associate warden.[10] It became good times again. Kenny's attitude was the same as that of the people at Chino: here is the job, do it. If you need help, come see me. But otherwise I don't want to see it, and I don't want to hear it. He came from Soledad. And he worked over at Folsom and other places. Nice guy, smart guy, but subdued. He was not flamboyant like Keating, but he had the same kind of approach. So I would shut down on these groups, and they would phone in to him, and he would say, "What did Wilkinson tell you?" They would tell him, and he would say, "Fine, then that is the way we are going to do it."

Then they really started putting the pressure on because they had people from Sacramento calling. He would tell them that there was a guy running the place, and they were not going to run it from up there. "He is doing the job I want him to do, so never mind. If it's going to be that way, it's going to be that way. You are going to have to get rid of both of us if it

10. See above and previous chapter.

isn't." So the people outside quit calling and bitching. We finally got it down to where it was functional.

Most of the opening up and loosening of restrictions came, I would say, within a five-year period. Then it tailed off. The giveaway program was still happening but not to the extent it did initially. It just snowballed and then reached its peak about the fourth or fifth year. Also the inmates got to the point where it was too hard for them to handle. They had too much freedom, so much freedom that they could get into trouble, and we were not thinking for them. This was their perspective.

The Sacrifice of Inmate Safety

What I mean by getting into trouble by having too much freedom is that they could overstep their bounds. They started to do some of the things they were complaining that we were doing, like beating somebody's head. The inmates did not have any protection. And we should be criticized for that, because we threw the safety of the inmate right out the window. Inadvertently, but right out the window.

The statistics show that the number of injuries went up, but the statistics are not official. I had an inmate keep the records, but the Department would not accept them.

I had those statistics in black and white and sent them to Sacramento. The Department did not recognize the figures because the Department had not produced them. Maybe the inmate's work was not that accurate, and the figures were more just an overview than anything. But they were an indicator and more than mere talk about the progression of violence.[11]

The point was: we did not deliberately abandon the safety of the inmate. It just came with the territory. You could not protect the inmate and run the Department as loosely as we did. If you had a guy who was after a guy down there—for sex, money, cigarettes, or whatever—in the late 1960s and early '70s, you could not go to that inmate and tell him to

11. We have been unable to find any official statistics that confirm or deny the level of violence at CMF, and so Wilkinson's testimony constitutes important evidence. One published study from 1976 did mention a special concern, but it was not relevant to violence among inmates and indeed no doubt reflected the number of very sick inmates housed at CMF: "Attacks on staff occurred most often at California Medical Facility," compared with five other California institutions, possibly because of a connection between "emotional disturbance and assaultive behavior." Lawrence A. Bennett, "The Study of Violence in California Prisons: A Review with Policy Implications," in *Prison Violence,* ed. Albert K. Cohen, George F. Cole, and Robert G. Bailey (Lexington, MA: Lexington Books, 1976), 153. There is information about reported incidents of violence in other California institutions, and the figures confirm Wilkinson's impression.

leave the guy alone, or you are going to deal with me. We used to put them in isolation. But you couldn't do that anymore.

The Attempt to Bring in Lawyers

At one brief point in time, if an inmate received a disciplinary report, he was entitled to a lawyer.[12] That did not last very long. Finally somebody got enough sand in his or her craw to say, "Hey, we're not going to do that. I don't care what the court said, we're just not going to do it." We ran it past the attorney general, and it got straightened out in a hurry. But that is how far we had gone. It was too expensive and slowed down the process. It was really stupid, too. It took about a year for that to get through the system and get rid of it. It just got out of hand.

I went up against a lawyer at one point while I was at Soledad. The attorney showed up, and we had a disciplinary meeting on an inmate accused of stealing. The lawyer recorded everything. He was real professional. At the end of the hearing, I asked the thief if he had any questions. He mumbled something. I asked if we were ready to proceed, and the lawyer and inmate said yes. So I took the 115 [disciplinary report] and ripped it in half and threw it in the trash can and said, "Thanks for coming in."

It was silly to have a lawyer there for something so minor as stealing from another inmate. So I just threw it away. Both the lawyer and the inmate were nonplussed. They did not know what to do. Finally it dawned on the inmate what had happened, and he turned to his lawyer and said, "This guy is going to get me."

I just grinned. The lawyer left, and I put the inmate back in his cell and went about my business. That inmate sweated bullets every time he saw me. But he conformed. I never had any problems out of him, and I never saw his lawyer again. That lawyer was still waiting for the other shoe to drop. He had some other clients there on other matters, so I would see him from time to time. Anyway, it was a farce and not worth even trying to handle. Later, that inmate told me the lesson he learned was, "Bringing a lawyer in here is bullshit." I told him it did not mean anything to me that particular time. All we wanted was conformity, no problems. We wanted things to run smoothly. Whatever it takes to get that, you do. That was where I used to get into trouble.

The captain we had at that time wanted to know how it turned out. I told him, and he said, "You crazy bastard, you can't do that." I said,

---

12. We have not found any records that would indicate when this rule came in or went out.

"Captain, I just did." He thought we were going to get into trouble, because the lawyer would complain because we did not follow procedure. The guy was entitled to an attorney. I figured that he had his attorney, and he could talk to him all he wanted; but the disciplinary went down the drain. I reminded him that I had the prerogative to dismiss the charges. I just did it in a different way. "Well, why didn't you dismiss the charges before the lawyer got here?" Well, because then the lawyer wouldn't see. That way I could illustrate the silliness to both the lawyer and the inmate.

To me it was the obvious thing to do. They set it all up, by God, you're going to do this and you're going to do that. They forgot that I had the option of dismissing charges. You do it in the court of law, not in the linen closet.

An Unpleasant Responsibility: Conjugal Visits

It astonishes people that inmates can have conjugal visits. They started in the early seventies, maybe a little earlier. And I eventually got the job of making reservations for them at CMF. There was a folder to manage the book work on it. And Keating wanted those units full every night.[13]

The units that Keating wanted filled were house trailers right outside the grounds. If someone canceled, it was a scramble to get the unit filled. We had a couple of people in town who moved up near the prison. There was an elderly couple, and if you had a blank spot, you could phone her, and she would be there in twenty minutes. He got all kinds of visits because she was available. She kept a bag of groceries ready so all she had to do was freshen up, grab her bag, and she was out there. She was in her late forties or early fifties. Convicts would complain about this guy having so many visits, and we would tell them why he had so many visits.

We had some problems out there, problems that were predictable and that had been voiced by some of us. People getting married in the joint— that was absolutely asinine. They would marry in prison, and then they would spend their honeymoon in the trailer.

13. "Family Visiting," as it was called euphemistically, began at Tehachapi in 1969 and by 1972 was general in the Department. California Department of Corrections, *Pattern of Change* ([Sacramento: The Department, 1972]). It is difficult to reconcile the date of Keating's tenure (he left in 1966) with the Department history. This policy was instituted directly by order of Governor Ronald Reagan: see Lou Cannon, *Governor Reagan: His Rise to Power* (New York: Public Affairs, 2003), 218–19, and William Endicott, "Prisons Chief—Man in Middle of Controversy," *Los Angeles Times*, 29 February 1972, I:22: Director Procunier instituted conjugal visiting "at the personal request of Reagan." Raymond Procunier (telephone interview, 28 December 2003) recalled that the first time Reagan requested the innovation, Procunier believed that the governor was just joking, and Procunier paid no attention until Reagan asked him about it some time later.

One of the worst cases we ever had was a couple who got married and went to the unit for their three-day visit. According to the rules, nobody checked on them, just at count time, which was a shout through the door. So they got married, and they went out to the trailer, and the guy raped her straight for seventy-two hours. Just sexually abused her. She came in, and she looked like hell. She was terrified. She wanted the SOB arrested and executed the very next day. She was a mess. He said, "Jeez, that's my wife." It made sense to him; it did not make sense to her. Out there, he'd say, "I don't get to do this often, let's go to bed." She'd say, "You've already done it six times. Let's eat." So he would beat the heck out of her.

This woman promptly got a divorce. "Convicts are terrible!" Up to that point, her friends asked her how she could do it, and she said how much she loved the guy; and he was a nice man. "He's told me everything about himself." Afterwards, she wanted him castrated. We expected to see her standing outside with a sign about how bad convicts were. But we could not arrest him for rape. It was her word against his. They were married, and "you willingly went in there with him." She was told she could pursue it, but the Department would not pursue it. She would have to take it to the police. Every now and then she would write a nasty letter to whoever the warden was to remind them how bad those convicts were. "Have you killed him yet?" I never understood it.

Then you had the cases where it was not the wife. It turned out to be a prostitute or whoever. We did not check enough. I think we had one escape from there. Of course you check things as closely as you can check them, but there was always illegal stuff coming in: drugs, booze, etc. It served no useful purpose. It does not serve to keep the family together or anything else. It was a burden on most of the families and a burden on the institution. It did not make any sense to have conjugal visiting.

I was not the very first guy to handle the conjugal visiting. I took it over from another officer. It was part of the visiting room, and then they need-ed someone to handle all of the book work. That fit in with these groups I was handling. I never understood why. The visiting staff could not do it. It had to be done by someone inside, somewhere where you could sit down and talk with the inmate and arrange the visit. I did not do that very long. I got rid of it as soon as I could.

It was easy to get rid of. I told the boss, "I don't agree with this, and I don't want to do it anymore. I'm going to screw it up before it is all over." I told him he really needed someone else to do the job. I would not delib-erately screw it up, but I might get to dreaming or whatever. Especially get-ting married in the joint, that is outlandish. It makes no sense in the prison system.

Well-Meaning Outsiders Got Victimized

There was a program, Friends Outside.[14] It was people who wanted to do things for the inmates: local preachers, do-gooders (using the term descriptively, not negatively), and what have you. They wanted to help, but they had to abandon the idea after a few years. They would meet one on one and say they were the inmate's friend on the outside and ask the inmate if there was anything he needed—anything sent to the family and so on. Just general nurturing.

I was amazed by how many people were surprised that when the convict got out, he would go to their house and expect this relationship to continue. They were not prepared for that. They did not want him that close, or dating their daughter. "I didn't take him to raise him." But of course you cannot tell them that when they are in there. "You are going to get attached to this guy, and he is going to be part of your life when he gets paroled. Just keep in mind what I told you." You cannot get them to see that the guy is going to hustle them and get to be part of their lives. They would say no, that they were helping the inmate and that was what they needed to do. I would tell them that they would be compromised in one way or another, either in the joint or afterward. Then you find them bringing contraband in. It started with chewing gum and then it escalated. There is just no dealing with inmates on a personal basis.

Of course what happened in the prisons reflected and was affected by what was happening in society in general. We used to have more police. And they were out on the street, not in patrol cars, which made a difference. The cop on the beat was a great deal. When I went downtown, there was a cop on the street by the store, and if I had a problem, he would take care of it for me. The kids wouldn't beat me up. As a five-year-old or six-year-old, I could go down to the drugstore for Mom and feel comfortable. And, again, the cop had the choice of either running a guy in or just kicking him out of the neighborhood.

Losing the Isolation Option

They had an isolation option at CMF for a while. The lieutenant had the option of putting a convict into isolation or not, and there were some

14. Friends Outside was started in connection with families of inmates of the Santa Clara County Jail in 1955. Beginning in 1969, chapters were founded all over the state of California. In later years, the focus was once again on the families of inmates. The Prison Representative Program, with a liaison at each prison, began in 1971. Information from the Web site.

other options as well. But they took the options away. Then you could not prevent anything before it started.

At one time at CMF, we had a cell for every type of inmate. We had the psych ward, post-psychotic, the hard cases. We could handle the worst in the Department. We had that system for a long time. That is what made the place run so smoothly. That and the fact that the watch commander had more opportunity. A watch commander could discipline a guy up to ten days in isolation. Just on his say-so; he didn't have to clear it with anybody.

This was good, because isolation was a huge break for us in dealing with the con men, the hustlers. They would have a thing going, all of their cigarettes, or all of this busy business, and you could interrupt all that for three or four or five days by throwing the guy in isolation. That would put a hurt on business. After ten days, that guy could lose everything. He had to start all over, because someone else had taken over his business. So, isolation was a good tool. Those guys would think, "I can't afford to go to isolation."

I think Dr. Pope was the superintendent at the time that isolation and other things ceased to be direct options for sergeants and lieutenants and instead had to go through a committee.[15] It was a culmination of the Central Office in Sacramento making that determination; it did not have anything to do with Pope. Of course in some instances, at institutions other than CMF, the option privilege had been abused.[16]

One illustration is: I got a call from an officer. Every time he was on the third floor, someone was setting the bulletin board on the second floor or first floor on fire, or somebody was getting beat up somewhere else. Or they were throwing trash cans down the stairwell at him. This was about 9:00 P.M., on the third watch. I asked him if he had any idea who was doing it. So he gave me a set of names. Then I asked the first-shift officer if he had any troublemakers, and he gave me a list of names. Some of those names coincided. Then I got hold of the second-watch officer and asked him the same thing. He gave me a list that coincided with the other lists.

So when I came in that night, I brought the inmates on the list down in groups of two or three at a time and told them that this was the information

15. Pope was superintendent 1966–1972. See the note in chapter 2. It was at some point before 1973 that the rules changed so that isolation decisions were always, at all institutions, made by the Disciplinary Committee, not the personnel on the scene, who now could not be sure that their disciplinary reports would be followed up. See *Rules and Regulations,* 1973 and 1974. Eventually the courts became involved as well; see, for example, "Judge's Ruling Hits Isolation Cell Use," *Los Angeles Times,* 10 March 1979, I:26; Philip Hager, "Court Order for Prison Reform Upset," *Los Angeles Times,* 17 March 1981, I:1.

16. See, for example, *Jordan v. Fitzharris* (25 F. Supp. 674) 1966 and *Toussaint v. Rushen* (553 F. Supp. 1365) 1983.

I had and that they were going to isolation until the trouble stopped. Then I brought down the other four or five guys and told them that I had locked up the other inmates in isolation, and if the trouble continued tonight, then I was going to lock them up the following night, because I had twelve cells over there. So it quit, and I let the guys in isolation loose, and we did not have any problem after that. Nobody got hurt. Nobody got abused. A couple of them tried to make an issue of it: "My God, I have been in isolation. Just arbitrarily." I told them it was on the books, and we could do that, and they needed to think about that.

What really happened was that the central office filled up the isolation cells. They used them for excess capacity. A very poor decision overall. It destroyed our ability to handle any type of inmate. I resented it mostly because it was a pencil pusher's decision. Not somebody who understood the institution and the fact that you had to keep a certain number of cells open in case of trouble.

We got to the point that the isolation cell was someone's permanent cell. It got to the point where I had to take the guy out of isolation in order to handle a new case. You therefore shortened the sentence of a man on isolation and just swapped cells with the new culprit. Administrators thought that population pressure was the problem.[17]

Then it really got bad when determinate sentencing came in. We could not move anybody or handle anything.

The Coming of the Determinate Sentence

They changed the parole system in the seventies. This was about the time I was doing the inside parole duty. They went from the indeterminate sentence to the determinate sentence.[18] They wanted to get tough on crime, hand out twenty-five-year sentences and heavy time. Funny thing is they compromised it, because they gave out good-time credits up front. A guy would come in and have a parole date of the year 2000. That looked big in 1970. But then they applied good-time credits ahead of time, and his

17. The state prison population in California was actually declining by 1969, but in 1972 it started climbing again and continued to climb.
18. The definitive change was set up by the legislature in 1976, but the law did not come into effect until 1 July 1977. See Jonathan D. Casper, David Brereton, and David Neal, *The Implementation of the California Determinate Sentencing Law* (Washington: U.S. Department of Justice, National Institute of Justice, Office of Research Programs, 1982), esp. 1–2, and an early report, Bill Hazlett, "Number Sentenced to Prison Increasing," *Los Angeles Times,* 16 December 1979, II:1, 3. The effect of determinate sentences was essentially to replace the power of the parole board to reward time off for good behavior, behavior as reported by prison authorities. Now the sentences were determined by judges, but under strict limits stipulated by law.

parole date came down to, for example, 1979. No incentive to earn good-time credits, and it just really messed the prison system up.

I later got right in the middle of it because I had worked under the old parole system. As I shall explain later, the warden called me from Soledad and wanted me to come down and take the position of Classification and Parole Representative, C&PR, of the institution, which I did. But everyone else had a year's training on how to handle the new system, and I did not know how to handle it. I was not doing a very good job. So I did not stay in that position too long, and I went on to other things. That [determinate sentencing] and changing the exam process were the two worst things that ever happened in the California Department of Corrections.

As soon as the determinate sentence system came in, disciplinaries went up 60 percent. Inmates just did not give a shit—"Take a few days from me, I don't care." But if you had not had those credits out in front of him, something they were not getting this month—you could see the effect. He is looking at 2004 for parole. And you don't give him the good-time credits up front, so he is looking at 2004. Well, he is going to be protective of this. He does not want it to go to 2005 because he messes up. But if you give him the whole thing and knock it down from 2004 to 1970-some odd, then he is not looking at 2004. Instead, he is looking at 1979 $^{1}/_{2}$ instead of 1979.

A Growing Awareness of Gangs in Prison

There were of course, eventually, gangs operating inside the prisons. Even Chino did eventually receive gang members as convicts; but, as I said before, not while I was there. Down in the Central Valley, Modesto, the gangs were operating then. We just did not get any at Chino. I think it was too early at the time I was there. As a teenager, I had known the Pachucos in the Southern California town of Pomona. The only reason they did not become a real force is because the war came along, and they and all the rest of us went into the service. But times were different then.

So it was after I was working at the Medical Facility that gang activity became really prominent in the prison system.[19] You always had the small

19. A contemporary account, Brian Kahn, *Prison Gangs in the Community: A Briefing Document for the Board of Corrections* ([Sacramento: California Board of Corrections], 1978), traces the origins of the gangs largely to the prisons, where they tended to serve protective purposes although soon tied into a variety of criminal activities both in the prisons and in California communities. In a 1985 summary study, George M. Camp and Camille Graham Camp, *Prison Gangs: Their Extent, Nature and Impact on Prisons* (Washington, D.C.: U.S. Government Printing Office, 1985), vii, reported that prison gangs began independently in a number of prisons and that in California prison gangs first appeared in 1957.

cliques where you could determine gangs: the East Los Angeles Homeboys, the Northern California Mexicans, the Southern California Mexicans. They would get together. But they mostly fought among one another.

Then you went to the Mexican Mafia. La Familia formed to protect themselves from the Mexican Mafia. Eventually the La Familia became dominant, and the Mexican Mafia was looking for someone to protect them from La Familia. Those were the first gangs that I knew about. Then we get into the Black Guerrilla family and the Aryan Brotherhood. This was the late 1960s and early 1970s. We had a pretty well-established gang situation on the inside by the late 1960s.

The gangs came to the surface, became more prominent, at the same time that civil rights agitation came in. The gangs had been there but they were controllable under the old system. We had pretty good resources, like the officer who did an independent research on tattoos. We had a good idea who was affiliated with whom and what we could expect—all from the tattoo study. We also had pretty good information on the various groups. I do not think that the Crips were active around this early time. Later on, they came in, with the emancipation.

Gang members knew they had someone on the outside fighting for them and that we could not do the same things that we used to be able to do. We did not have the same types of discipline we used to have, and they knew it: "They don't have any place to lock me up, no way to discipline me." So they "came out" and declared themselves gang members. The gang situation manifested itself because we changed our way of handling the institution and the inmates, and they took advantage of it. We carried affirmative action over to the minority inmate.[20] We started catering to them, which we did not have to do, and then that became a demand by the inmates. Then it became their right.

That was when it became open season on inmates who were not in gangs. That is where we were open to criticism. A lot of people got hurt

---

The gangs did not get media attention, however, until the 1970s. Joan W. Moore et al., *Homeboys: Gangs, Drugs, and Prison in the Barrios of Los Angeles* (Philadelphia: Temple University Press, 1978), provides another account, with considerable depth, of the functioning of various kinds of gangs in California prisons.

20. According to the mimeographed serial, *Characteristics of Felon Population in California State Prisons by Institution,* copy in the California State Library, in 1956 the ethnic composition of CMF inmates was white, 71.8%; Mexican, 12.4%; and black, 13.3% (as opposed to all men in state prisons, white, 59.8%; Mexican, 16.6%; and black 21.3%). In 1963, CMF was white, 74.1%; Mexican, 8.8%; and black, 15.2%. In 1970, the proportions were 68.5% white, 10.0% Mexican, and 20.1% black. When Wilkinson left in 1977, CMF inmates were 53.8% white, 12.4% Mexican, and 31.9% black (the general male prison population was 44.4% white, 20.1% Mexican, and 33.7% black). From 1956 to 1977, the average age at CMF went from 32.8 years to 29.3 years, paralleling the change in all institutions from 32.1 to 29.2.

because we did not have the resources to protect them. We could not keep the gangs down. They just ran wild with what we had to work with.[21]

We had one advantage at CMF when the gangs started forming. Every other institution was having gang trouble. It took us a while to figure out why we had so little. And you know how we figured it out? We asked the inmates. The prison gang leaders decided that they needed a place where they could decompress. CMF was that place. They could cut each other's throats at Soledad or Corcoran or wherever. But at CMF, "We don't do that. We have to have some time out." Just ask the convicts: "Hey, you have to have a place to relax, to take the pressure off." CMF seemed like a good place. And there were ways to transfer. Everybody wants to get rid of a problem. If a troublemaker from Soledad asked for a transfer to CMF, then the people at Soledad would go out of their way to transfer that inmate.

My Involvement with the Black Muslims

One of the things that came out of all of the openness to groups was the Muslim group, Black Muslims. They of course mostly preceded the gangs. But also they changed. In the early days, they were very militant towards Caucasians, or the blue-eyed devils. Very violent. They did not exist at Chino, but they were soon all over the rest of the Department. I don't think Elijah Mohammed had been paroled yet, so he had not formed the Black Muslims at the time I was at Chino.[22]

For my first experience, I saw a guy standing on a table in the mess hall preaching about the blue-eyed devils, and they were going to be slaves— all the rhetoric of the time. So we wiped him out and locked him up.[23] Over a period of time, their organization decided not to confront us. They decided to be orderly and work within the system.

They were a problem for a while before they calmed down. But at CMF,

21. In the three years, 1975–1977, 150 deaths occurred in California state prisons "as the result of prison gang violence," and the official report confirmed that the gangs were formed originally in the prisons "for physical protection against assault." "State Prison Gangs Blamed for 150 Deaths in 3 years," *Los Angeles Times,* 13 July 1978, I:3.

22. John R. Faine and Edward Bohlander Jr., "The Genesis of Disorder: Oppression, Confinement, and Prisoner Politicization," in *Contemporary Corrections: Social Control and Conflict,* ed. C. Ronald Huff (Beverly Hills: Sage, 1977), 55, put this movement into the context of political awareness. A recent treatment, in the context of prisons, is Scott Christianson, *With Liberty for Some: 500 Years of Imprisonment in America* (Boston: Northeastern University Press, 1998), 245–49.

23. When asked about this, Wilkinson explained that a few obviously surprised officers confronted the speaker and marched him out. No force was used or needed.

WORLD COMMUNITY OF ISLAM IN THE WEST
Muhammad's Mosque of CMF

February 16, 77

TO WHOM IT MAY CONCERN

    The bearer of this letter of introduction, Lt. Wilkerson
is highly regarded by the Muslim Brotherhood here at C.M.F.
for his sincereity and earnest cooperation whenever his assistance was called upon.

    We pray that the rapport that has been established be-
tween the Muslim Brotherhood of C.M.F. and Lt. Wilkerson will
be properly nurtured and allowed to blossom and produce many
more positive endeavors for the Muslim believers at Soledad.

Imam Dale Sabir (McKinney)   Secy. Aquil Nazeeh (Newson)

Rueben Saleem (Amie)
Consultant

Wilkinson's "traveling letter" from the Black Muslims (1977)
Source: Viola Wilkinson.

they were functioning under the Protestant chaplain. He deeply resented
that, because he did not consider them a religious group. I really didn't,
either, but they had a case. So he was just not giving them much attention. I did not see much difference between them and one of these other
groups. So I took them over. It was not a burden to me because the process
was already in place, and I did the same thing with them that I did with
all groups. I handled their mail the same way; I handled their Ramadan
banquets the same way. It was a perfect switch, and the Protestant chaplain thought it was great. There were only three of us who knew this was
happening: I, the Protestant Chaplain, and Britt. We did not tell anyone
else, we just did it. And our problems just ceased.

The Muslims had quite a presence in the Berkeley area. They had an excellent bakery and other interests. The men and women dressed appropriately. But in the joint, I became acquainted with them, as I have said, by picking them up and getting them off the chaplain's back. I enjoyed working with them. They were quite respectful. They had some weird ideas. They were just naive, though, about certain things. It did not have anything to do with Muslims, it was just society did not do it that way.

There were small things showing sometimes a lack of education or worldliness. Once I mentioned something about a six-figure income. Members of each temple had their own resources for funds: donations from the inmates and people from the outside. I was talking about six figures when the captain of the group at CMF showed me some money and said that they had five hundred eighty-seven dollars and some cents. So he said they had a five-figure income and pretty soon it would be six figures. They were just unsophisticated as a group.

I have a traveling letter from the Muslims. When a Muslim transferred from one institution to another, he did not go to the new institution and say, "Hey, I'm a Muslim, and I am a good Muslim." He had to have a traveling letter from the organization that he had left. When I transferred from CMF to Soledad, I got such a letter. There is another thing I will tell you later on about that. As far as I know, I am the only staff member who ever had a traveling letter from the Muslim organization.

Those guys were interesting. The captain of the group at CMF accepted me because I was doing well. I was handling their mail and their functions and any problems, their banquets, and everything. They always came with their collars buttoned and their shirts starched, which was not legal, but, anyhow, you overlooked that part. It was an easy deal. But it took a little patience to deal with their differences.

Minority Correctional Officers

Among the correctional officers, we did not have many minorities in the early days.[24] We did not even classify them at that time. It was a surprise to most of those Hispanics whom we originally hired and who had been working there at CMF for a while to find out that they were minorities. They never were a minority in Vacaville, so why should they become a minority now? When CMF began, the predominant ethnic group in

24. By 1981, when Wilkinson retired, about 31 percent of the Department of Corrections workforce, including people in supervisory positions, were identified as minority. See *Department of Corrections 1981*.

Vacaville was Hispanic. They were from Spain and Mexico because of the farmwork around the area. They were not considered a minority until they branded themselves as a minority.

They were hired as correctional officers when we first opened up and were hiring locals. You meet the guy in the grocery store, and you get to talking about getting on out at the prison, and you tell him. Next thing you know, he is taking the exams and he is out there working with you. He did not know he was a minority. Still does not know he is a minority. This all came up later because these groups jumped on the minority bandwagon. We just hired people who worked.

We also had two blacks. Otis Loggins was one officer's name, and I can't think of the other guy's.[25] They started out at CMF a little after I came. One of them was there when I got there. So we took the applicants as they came. We were not recruiting for anybody, just people in general. Most recruiting was by newspaper ads and what have you. There just were not that many blacks in there before the big push came in the sixties. Before that, we still only had three or four blacks. Bachman, the guy in the Guidance Center; Loggins; and one other guy. They were just correctional officers.

Some of the inmates made a fuss about having an African American correctional officer. The bigots did. They did not want a black guy ordering them around. I told them that they should not have committed their crime and got sent to prison. That is how to avoid that.

There was one African American officer to whom I talked a lot, Clopton. We were not particular friends as such; I just knew him as one of my officers. In the work situation, we were very comfortable with one another. So he used to tell me a lot.

Once he took a trip to North Carolina to see his folks. His car broke down out in Texas. He went to rent a car. They would not rent him a car. This was a small town, there was no motel or any place for him to live or eat. I am talking in the 1960s. So a completely strange family took care of him. That was the way black people got along in those days. Generally there was a sign to tell them where they could go.

Clopton's wife was a schoolteacher in Sacramento. They were both California-raised. They were not used to that. I would not be used to that, either, a total stranger's house. You don't even have a place to go to a public restroom.

So he had to get on the bus, the back of the bus incidentally, go to Dallas or some major city, rent the car, go back to his car. He had to leave his car with a local mechanic. So we sat for about an hour one night up in

---

25. Otis A. Loggins appears again in an important way in the next chapter.

the canteen for him to tell me this story. I asked him why he told me this story. He said he thought I needed to know this. I said I already knew, but I never knew anyone who had gone through it. "Now I am in pain; why did you tell me this?" He finally did laugh. He went to Sacramento City College as a professor. He asked me twice to come over there and get my certificate to teach. I never got around to it. I should have followed it up.

Black Officers and Pressure

We had problems with black officers. Things would come up. Unfortunately, one of the guys, the one whose name I cannot think of, got to dealing with the inmates. We fired him and even prosecuted him. But that happened with white officers as well. He was not the first. In terms of the black officers, they had more pressure on them than did the white officers. It was tough to resist that pressure. You still had that housing unit to run. Those people could make it miserable for them in subtle ways. When I say "put pressure on," I mean they would try to get the officer to bring stuff in, bend the rules.

The tip-off would be that the officer would come up and request a transfer to a different wing. Then you would get as much information out of him as you could. Sometimes he would tell you the entire story, and then you would go arrest the convict. Which put more heat on the officer, but it had to be done. Otherwise you would move him around, put him in the tower and try to get the pressure off of him. Then you deal with the inmates yourself over a period of time.

It was the black inmates who would put pressure on the black officer. That was where the pressure came from. Not the white inmates. "Hey, we are brothers, Whitey has got us locked down, he is taking advantage of us, blah, blah, blah." It was just too much for some of them to resist.

Some of them would handle it by rolling over and bringing stuff in. Others would handle it by coming to us with names and numbers, and we dealt with it as best we could. Others dealt with it by asking for a transfer. Sometimes that was the best answer. Get the officer away from that particular group and let him focus on his job. If it came up again, then you would use a different tactic.

In the meantime, you are processing these guys who put the pressure on him, and returning the favor in subtle ways. You don't let anything slide with them. You just nail them to the wall. You let them know that you were on to them, and you let the inmate know that he was dirty for trying to compromise an officer. You're mine, now, be careful what you do. It was partly a mind game, the kind that I really enjoyed. Of course you had to remember that there were more of them than there were of you, so you were going to come up short sometimes.

Until college students (or wherever it came from) started crying about racism and minorities and so on, there was not any problem with them in the prison business. If they took the exam and passed the exam, we would hire them. And that was it. They just did not apply. When we started cutting corners for minorities, then we really had an influx. Meanwhile, the original black officers who were hired under the old system, the same system I was hired under, they were working their way up the ladder and getting promotions. They did their time and paid their dues. Then all of a sudden here come these yahoos we made concessions for.

Clopton was in that original category. Loggins was in that category. They had their own opinions about the new hires. Particularly because the new hires were always asking for something, asking for you to cut more corners. You can understand that, because if you start dealing with an individual that way, then that person is going to expect that kind of treatment the rest of the way. Just like bringing a convict into the institution. What he learns first from you is what he is going to expect. Then it is your fault if you change how you handle him or change the rules—because you did not start him out right.

Assignment to Run the Academies

There was still another new group of correctional officers with whom I had a lot to do. But to get into this story, I have to go back to my service running the training academy. In 1972, they set up a training academy at the old South Facility at Soledad, and I worked that for three sessions.[26] Our primary job was to take people who normally were not acceptable to the Department—their arrest history was not pristine—and train them. This program was titled Career Opportunity Development (COD). We were getting people off of welfare rolls.[27] Both male and female. And at this time they decided to include females. As a matter of fact, I had the first eight females in the Department.[28] Moreover, nobody told me I was getting them.

26. The Career Opportunity Development Academy graduated fourteen classes between the spring of 1972 and November 1974, when federal funding ended. See "C.O.D. Academy Closes," *Correctional News Briefs*, 20 November 1974.

27. Wilkinson has the wrong impression that the program was designed to get people off welfare. In fact, the COD was a state-level work-experience training program created as part of California's Welfare Reform Action of 1971. The Department of Human Resources Development, now the Employment Development Department, administered the program. Its stated purpose was to assist socially, economically, and educationally disadvantaged Californians with work transitions.

28. Despite a statement in *50 Years,* a note in *Correctional News Briefs,* 16 October 1974, confirms that the first women came in as correctional officers in 1973, when correspondence

So at the last minute I had eight women standing there with no place to sleep, no living quarters. So I sent them to a motel for that night. It was already nine o'clock, and I had to drive them to Salinas because there was nothing around Soledad that was open. I did not want to split them up. It took two cars and two men to transport them. I had to leave the unit empty because I did not have anyone to watch it. I was mad enough to call the director at eleven o'clock at night, after I got them bedded down.

There was no notification, like they did not need any special housing or anything. So I wind up there at nine o'clock at night with eight women whom I don't know about. It took me forever to get my money for the motel. I put it on my personal credit card. Later we joked: when I pick up women, I don't just pick up one woman and house her; I pick up eight women. The next night, I made arrangements to have them in the bachelor officers' quarters.

We had some other problems to settle. The training part of it I liked. Setting up the curriculum, I liked. And you did that by canvassing the department. Getting old Joe Blow down at Chino to come up and talk about discretionary correctional law. Or you went to Folsom for a guy to come down and talk about in general how to handle convicts. Then you had some outside people come in for various things. You could kind of play fast and loose.

At the first session I had, not all of the scheduled speakers showed up. Upset me no end. I would have to fill in and talk off the top of my head. Which was okay, because I liked to talk, and they did not have any background to contradict me. And I could talk about a lot of things, what they were going to do, what was going to happen to them, and what they were going to need.

The first session was therefore kind of raggedy, but then we got it going. We got the curriculum down pretty well. I believe it was six weeks. So that had some bearing on why I eventually transferred to Soledad. While I was there, they asked me to come down and go to work after the academy. When they found out I was on the captain's list, they really asked me to come down, work as a lieutenant, and eventually do the captain thing. Everything was fine there. But the conditions under which I went down later were entirely different. I will get to that later. At that time, the South Facility at Soledad, the minimum custody area, was

---

shows that Wilkinson was active in running the COD academies. Director Raymond Procunier announced in the summer of 1973 that women would be hired as correctional officers in men's institutions, in the face of bitter opposition from the California Correctional Officers Association. By 1974, forty-four women were working. See "Prison Use of Women as Guards Hit," *Los Angeles Times*, 7 March 1973, I:23; "44 Women Serve as Guards at State Prisons; Opposition Fades," *Los Angeles Times*, 18 March 1974, II:1.

closed, and those facilities were available. We did not have any contact with the institution itself. That was a separate entity.

I had three sessions at the academy: two in a row, and one off and one on after that. A guy got sick or something at the training facility, and so I was called back. Later, in 1976, I transferred down to Soledad and retired in 1981—from Soledad.[29]

Training is always interesting, but I just did not enjoy the COD academy as much as some of the other things I did. Probably it was because I did not like the kind of people we were getting. They were not, as I have noted, pristine, and they were not the same as we used to hire, who had no arrest record, that sort of thing. I just did not think it was going to work out. I thought it would compromise the Department. Either that or I just thought, Hey, you know, you guys did not play it as close to your vest as I did. I don't know what my reluctance was, but basically that was it. We had guys in there who had been picked up for suspicion of murder and other things. But my thinking was: they were not committed to this line of work.

My Role in Integrating Women into the Department

It was in the second academy that women came into the Department.[30] We were not really prepared for them. We were not really prepared for how we were going to treat them, what our expectations were. The assertion coming down from Sacramento was, they are just as capable as a man and that kind of thing, which was not true. Of course they were intelligent enough. If you want to get into the physical part of it, however, that is a personal thing. If you are looking for help, then a 115-pound woman is not going to be advantageous compared to having a 160-pound male grabbing hold of a convict. Those situations had to be dealt with; they had to settle those problems. There were other things that I thought we had to guard against: not just unconsciously giving them preference by putting them in the towers, putting them on the front gate, putting them on the back gate, putting them in the control room.

Over a period of time, your workforce ages, develops problems—psychological problems, physical problems. A perfectly good male officer can need to depressurize, need to get away from the inmates, for a variety of reasons. One, he has had some medical problems, he feels a little vulnera-

29. See the next chapter.
30. This subject comes up again in this chapter, below, and in chapter 6.

ble. Another, he just feels he is not handling the inmates as well as he used to, and he needs to get away, and you put him on the front gate. There he deals with the public. Or you put him in the visiting room, or you put him on the back gate, letting trucks in.

The reluctance, conscious or subconscious, with the women meant you had to pay close attention, or you would wind up putting your females in those positions. It is not fair to the female, and it is not fair to the officer that you kick out. Not that they should not work there, but if you do not watch it, and you take a close look, you have the women isolated someplace.

Number two: I don't feel that they belong in a male institution for the same reason that a male does not belong in a female institution. There are certain jobs that a female should not do in a male institution. It can be done, but you just open yourself up to a bunch of problems. They cannot shake down an inmate. They cannot skin-search an inmate, which is a very important part of the business, keeping the convict clean so he does not have a weapon and so forth. If you pass that up, because she is female and he is male, so you don't skin-search at the right time at the right place, then that makes things vulnerable. So there are oddball things that they cannot do.

Also, they really cannot handle a housing unit as well as a male officer can. The privacy factor is important. She will shy away from commonplace things: as you walk down the tier, you are looking in to count a convict or whatever, and he is waving his penis at you, or he is sitting on the toilet, or he is getting dressed or undressed, or whatever. Eventually the female officer will start avoiding things. It is not her fault; that is the way she grew up, and that is the way we are. So for those reasons, and they may seem minor today, I don't think that females belonged in a male institution.

On the other hand, the people who thought they did could argue that bringing a female along was the same idea as sending the small officer to escort the giant. If you have a female officer, then you will have less trouble with the inmate. You may have less trouble of that nature, but you have more trouble of a different nature. So, what is your choice?

In my time, I think they pushed it too hard, and I don't think we paid enough attention to what we were doing, and to how fast we were doing it. A good example is what I mentioned: I wound up with eight women, unbeknownst to me. This is good planning? No. But it satisfies Central Office, saying I have eight women at the academy. Yeah, you mean I had to find a place for them to live, I had to find them this and that. We just rushed into it.

Certainly the institution was not ready. I never will forget the day when I came back to my office at CMF and found my office filled with purses. The first female correctional officers had arrived, and the watch sergeant had sent them out all over, and they left their purses all over my desk and everything else. That was one of the hardest things we had to do with the women that was special to women: to persuade them not to bring their purses in but to lock them in the trunk of the car or something. At first one or two of them were wearing skintight pants, with no pockets in the back. There was one skinny officer whose clothes looked like they were painted on. It took us a while to convince them that pants with pockets were more practical—and more appropriate.

Other Changes in Recruiting and Staffing

Then there was the minority factor. As I have suggested, we did not handle our minority hiring right. Just like the women, again, get them at any cost. We changed from hiring statewide to hiring locally.[31] Which was a big mistake. If you are hiring statewide, if the exam is given on a statewide basis, then the expectation is you are not going to work at the local facility. You are going to work at any place the opening comes up. If you don't want to do that, then take your name off the list. Or work here until you can transfer back.

To cut it down, because each place was hiring differently, they were hiring different kinds of people or in a different way, or with different expectations. There was no central standard that the Department wanted in terms of hiring somebody. You hire somebody here because he is familiar. He sacked groceries, and he is a pretty good softball player. So when he comes before the board at the local institution, "Hey, Tony is okay. We'll hire Tony." So you have a homegrown guy who plays softball, and he knows the guy who hired him.

Before, on a statewide basis, you were dealing with strangers. My first exam, for correctional officer, took place in Los Angeles. A whole bunch of strangers there. And you never saw them ever again. This was big time. At that time we had a physical exam that you had to take, too. They did away with the physical exam for a while. Later, the written exam probably amounted to thirty questions. I believe one of them was, "What is your name?" I used to proctor those, and I used to grind my teeth and just get livid. But that's the way it was.

We cut down on our workforce, lessened our workforce, and lessened the expectations of our workforce during that period. It was the grand

31. This subject comes up again in chapter 6, below.

experiment, and it did not work out. Some of the people fell by the wayside. And some of the people are now administrators, and certainly supervisors. They are not equipped to do it, or at least to the extent that I was supervised. It is not their fault; it is the Department's fault.

I think it cost us. It accounts for some of the problems that we are having—not to name names, but the warden of Corcoran State Prison, I worked with him; we were lieutenants together. He really was not adequate to the job as a lieutenant. But he wound up at Corcoran due to the expansion after I left the Department. So they had all this gladiator stuff down there. Having them fight, then shoot at them. They had like eight deaths, nine deaths down there. The whole ball of wax.[32] Simply because the man was not capable of running an institution. But due to the press, it was a brand-new institution, he had been around for twenty-five years, but he was just not up to it.

They made a program administrator out of him, which has really nothing to do with security. Then they made him warden. And he gathered up people like him. It just ran away with him.

The Department just got so big that you had to take what you could get. And this was an appointed position. The pleasure of the director. Of course one has to be recommended by somebody along the line.[33]

It startled me, because, having worked with this individual, worked closely with him, his thought process used to amaze me. His dependence on asking you, "You know, I got this situation here; how did you handle it in your unit?" Which is how things got out of hand there. People who were running those closed units were just doing what they were doing, and this guy did not have any idea. He was used to asking them what to do, or do you concur. They just figured, "Hey, I'll just do what I want to do."

That was throughout the Department. That was due mostly to size and due to the fact that back in the 1970s we hired people in a different way. We did not require certain things that we should have required. And they are now administrators and supervisors. And they do not know what to tell their people. Because they never knew.

32. Corcoran State Prison opened in 1988, and by 1996 seven inmates had been shot dead by guards, more than any other prison in the country. The 1994 killing of inmate Preston Tate led to an FBI investigation, based on evidence provided by Officer Richard Caruso and several other whistle-blowers. Although prison employees were all acquitted in subsequent criminal trials, the state of California in 1999 acknowledged that the killings had not been justified. The state subsequently authorized compensation to inmate victims and families of inmate victims. Caruso, who lost his career with the CDC as a result of his accusations, was awarded 1.7 million dollars by the state.

33. Beginning in the mid-1970s, as in other areas of society, the Department of Corrections was hit by reverse discrimination suits by correctional officers; see, for example, "Prison System Accused of Reverse Discrimination," *Los Angeles Times,* 2 January 1976, I:29.

Trying to Make a New Generation into Officers

The change in generations from the officers with whom I started was obvious. We grew up in the 1930s. We grew up with the same do right, don't lie, all the 1930s things. These kids, these people, grew up with all this madness in the late 1950s and early 1960s. No concept of meeting your commitments or doing what is right. It was a different era. We went through the war. You met your commitment, do or die for the country, however you want to put it. The 1960s people did not have that.

One of the hardest things I had to get used to with the new breed was that if they did not want to come to work, they just did not come to work. And it just irritated them when you took exception to it. You have a job where you have to post a man—it is not like working in a grocery store. But they did not get the idea. They never seemed to get the idea that this is a different type of business.

A good example is: I was down in the housing unit one time with one of the post-psychotics. The guy kicked off on me. I did not have the key to the cell; the correctional officer had the key. I was trying to hold the door shut. The correctional officer, when I finally got hold of him and questioned him, said he went to get a drink of water. It never occurred to him to help me hold that door or lock that door. When the inmate kicked off, the officer went to get a drink of water. He could not see anything wrong with that. He said, "I was thirsty." I said, "You did not see the potential for what happened down there? The guy has got to go to the clinic now because his arm is in pretty bad shape. If I had you there to help me hold him, I would not have had to put so much pressure on his arm." He said, "You had the door closed." I said, "I did not have the key to lock it. The son of a bitch was angry. He wanted out of there, and you go get a drink of water." I said, "That is bullshit. You know it is bullshit, and don't talk to me like that anymore." So I put the disciplinary thing on him, and to this day I will meet him on the street, and he is still incensed.

It was an attitude that I am getting at. They just did not seem to get the idea. In the case of the female, an incident started. If there are correctional officers around, then they go and help with the inmate. The more people you use, the less damage is going to occur to either the inmate or whoever is trying to subdue him.

So we had this female, and she just could not reach in there and grab this guy. I can still see her saying, "Ooh, ooh," like that. It just was not worth it to discipline her. She was trying her best; she just could not make it. So the inmate and I floundered around for some time and we both got pretty banged up. Which is part of the game. After it was over with, I called her in and told her, "You've got to keep this in mind: when this kind of thing starts, you have to get in and help the officer subdue the inmate. I'll tell you why you have to do that: because if this ever happens with us again, then you and I are going to fight in the parking lot. You are going to fight somebody that day. And it is best you fight the convict instead of me. So you just make up your mind that when an incident like that occurs again, you will jump in and grab him. Because if you don't do it there, then you will do it in the parking lot." Well you know what happened with that. It went right up the line. But it finally reached the point that an individual said, "Yeah, the guy's right. Why are you bucking this up to me? It is not harassment, it is not sexual harassment or anything else. It is good common sense." So they just sent it back to her and said, "Straighten out. Do what you are told."

She did not resign. Actually, she turned into a pretty good correctional officer. But she just did not understand what I was telling her. Just as the guy who went to get a drink did not understand the process. Someplace along the line they missed what they gave me, I guess. I knew that you assisted one another. I knew the potential for harm was there. I knew that I had to post a man and that if I did not go to work, it would seriously interrupt things. But these people did not seem to know that. It is not a matter of they knew it and just did not care, it is they just did not know it. So the Department is now full of people like that.

I emphasize that that period between, say, 1965 and 1975 really cost the Department. The people who were hired then and went through training in that period are the people who are running the department now. They are a different kind of person, with a different attitude, who came from a different background. It was the sign of the times. Everyone knows how it was during the 1960s.

Outside Interference in Personnel Matters

It is surprising that the minority issues and affirmative action did not cause more work and disruption than they did. Before, we would hire the people who came to us. We did not have any conversations about minorities. Then it got to be an issue. That was the thing to do. Central office went crazy. One state senator was the biggest pain in the rear the Department ever had. Always on the Department.

I found out by accident how he became a problem. One day I got a call. This was when I was running the groups who came in. The call would say I had denied some group admittance, and it was the senator's office calling. I asked the lady if she was an elected representative. She said she was not, she was the senator's assistant. I told her that I did not want to talk to her, that I wanted to talk to the senator. I wanted to know what he thought about it. It turned out that she was doing her own agenda. He covered for her, but it was her own agenda. As were others. So we got a memo from central office that said we were to be polite but to ask if it was the elected representative calling.

In the case of the woman officer, I took a hell of a chance, too. If the paperwork had not run into the right guy . . . The two before him were ready to crucify me. Because that was the thing to do at that time. But the other guy had guts and said no, this is not going to fly. So let's quit wasting our time with it. She got the message, and the rest of them got the message, and everything worked out, and she turned into a viable person. And that was all we needed to do, but we were not doing that in general.

But all of this is individual. Of the eight females I had in the COD academy, four of them were problem people in the Department. Since I was their trainer earlier on, I used to get calls at the institution. "I am down here, and this guy is doing this to me," and "I am not getting the job that I want." All that kind of stuff. The other four I never heard from. Again, it comes down to the individual. You give them the information, give them the process, and give them the idea. It works with some people, and other people it does not work with. Let me tell you this, out of the four females who called, they were the four best-looking females in the class. The four who did not call were less attractive. They were used to being denied things, but the others were used to being catered to. That is just a case of the individuals.

The same thing happened with the men. "I have never had to do anything. Why should I do it now? I didn't marry this job," one officer told me. I said, "That is great. Maybe we can get a quickie divorce here. You can go work someplace else." "What, are you trying to take my job from me?" I said, "You don't have a job. Mentally you don't have a job. It is just a place to go. You do not show up when you don't want to. You don't do a damn thing when you are here that you are supposed to do. If you did not have a job, you would have no place to go. When you get serious about the job, we will get serious about taking care of you." "Well, you know I never had to do this before. I worked when I wanted to work, I showed up when I wanted to show up." "It's not that way," I said. "Let's get personal about it. You put me in jeopardy when you don't show up. Because I am shorthanded, and I have problems when I am shorthanded. And I can go down there to straighten something out and get my butt whipped because you are not there." "Well, that is your problem." "Okay. I can take care of my problem. But your problem is going to be, you are out on the floor sometime and a couple of convicts are going to grab your ass, and someone is going to remember that you made that comment,

'That is your problem.'" His eyes got very big. "You are out there alone, buddy, with an attitude like that."

That was a tough bunch to handle. We could have handled them a lot easier and a lot better if we had insisted on the basics in our hiring process. We did not have to indulge these people to hire them, just to jack our statistics up. There were plenty of good people out there, plenty of capable people we could have hired and maintained our standard, or reasonably so. But we did not do that. The thing was, do the big emancipation thing, and we were all part of it. All of us cut corners. We could rationalize if we wanted to, but there was not much point in it. We just did not hold the line. "Maintain," as the convicts would say. We did not have to abandon ship as we did.

Celebrity Inmates

Another problem we had was celebrity inmates.[34] Juan Corona was one of them, and that was mainly the reason he was at CMF. He was the guy who killed twenty-four people—fellow farmworkers whom he befriended and then buried in the orchard. They finally caught him, and so we had him at CMF.[35] While he was there, the inmates jumped him, stabbed him several times. He lost an eye. So we put him in protective custody, but the media really jumped on it. He had been in prison for four or five years, I think. Why did the inmates jump him? The best we could come up with was that they just did not like him. CMF, as I told you, was kind of off limits to gangs and that sort of thing, but it did not work in his case. He really was not a gang member, and somehow he just wore out his welcome. It could have been something else we did not know about—canteen, sex, whatever.

One time some television reporter from San Francisco wanted to do a story on this soft-spoken man whom she thought had been railroaded because he was Hispanic. Since it was a notorious case, a reporter could make a byline with it in a moment. She came with a television crew to do an interview, and she did not want any of us around. We objected of course. But we had a room for attorney business in the sally-port area,[36] which was observable by people in the control room, but people in the room had all kinds of privacy in terms of being able to converse and so on.

34. Such as Bob Wells became in the 1950s.

35. Corona was arrested in May 1971. He was one of the first spectacular serial killers identified by the post–World War II news media, and at the time he held the record for the number of victims. He had, it turned out, a history of hospitalization for schizophrenia before he started his slaughter in the Feather River farm area near Yuba City.

36. Public entrance buffered with a security area.

So that would be where it [the interview] was held, where they would be under observation, but they could do what they wanted. But when the camera and the lights came on, this gentle man's craziness came out, and he started to rant and rave. Then the television people got on our case because we had left them alone in the room with this crazy person. And the great exposé turned into a mild few minutes on the late-night news.

We had problems with that room in the case of the famous Angela Davis.[37] She wanted to interview her clients in a closet or something. She was always raising hell as a lawyer and an activist at that time. But we had Britt there, and he said, "We have what we have, and you're handling it right, so just tell her to get out if she does not want to interview under those conditions." Of course there was a fuss, and it went to the director, and he wanted a memo on what was happening. And that was the end of it. It was just her pushing. Confrontation was her specialty.

---

37. In the 1970s, Angela Davis was famous as an aggressive, newsworthy agitator and leader dedicated to a number of radical and civil rights causes.

An outside view of Soledad Prison (1981)
Source: Historical Albums, California Department of Corrections, Sacramento.

CHAPTER FIVE

SOLEDAD, 1977–1981

At the end, I transferred to Soledad in 1977 and retired in 1981.[1] But going there was a big career mistake. As I have mentioned, I had had an offer when I had the academy there. Later, my biggest problem was the deputy superintendent, but at that time, he was in my corner: "You ought to transfer here," and so on. But it was not practical at that time. As a matter of fact, I had a pretty interesting job at CMF, and I had in Britt a pretty interesting guy to work for. I have spoken of Britt before, and I just cannot say enough about him in terms of his managerial style.[2]

The Job at Soledad

Soledad is a whole story all its own.[3] But any rate, having been asked before about transferring there, then when the time came, and I got another call, from the superintendent, Otis Loggins,[4] about going down for a promotion,

1. Those specific years covered a period of general change in California corrections. New laws, particularly, caused a crisis in overcrowding. No new prisons had been constructed since 1964, and the annual prison intake, instead of being diverted, as had happened earlier, increased from 7,500 in 1977 to 13,000 in 1981. And state prisons still were taking only about one-third of the people convicted of felonies. See *California Department of Corrections 1981* ([Sacramento: The Department, 1981]).
2. Before Britt left CMF, a new superintendent, Thomas L. Clanon, had come in. His style was not particularly forthright, and that provided an added motivation for Wilkinson to leave CMF. Clanon was born in 1929. He took his M.D. at Michigan in 1955 and trained at the Menninger School in Topeka, becoming board certified in psychiatry in 1962. He meantime served in the United States Public Health Service from 1959 to 1961 before joining the staff at CMF. He became superintendent in December 1972 and served there until 1980. In 1977, just about the time Wilkinson was leaving, CMF lost its accreditation as a psychiatric hospital—reflecting both institutional and social changes. "The State," *Los Angeles Times*, 28 January 1977, I:2.
3. A writer in "Hosanna in a Spot of Hell," *Time*, 9 January 1978, 14, described Soledad Prison as "a spot of hell in the middle of a Garden of Eden. Located on 960 acres in the verdant Salinas Valley, the penitentiary housing 2,400 inmates is a cauldron of latent racial violence."
4. This is the same Loggins who appeared earlier as a beginning correctional officer. He also appears later in this chapter. Loggins served as superintendent at Soledad from 1976 to

I thought it would be okay. But it did not turn out to be that way. So it was a pretty bad situation down there, actually working there.[5]

At Soledad, what I did varied from day to day. Originally I went down as classification and parole representative. I was not the associate superintendent's choice, and I did get my legs cut out from underneath me from time to time. The classification and parole representative handled the records and acted as liaison between the Adult Authority and the institutions. I had had some experience, as I explained. But when I was back in uniform, they changed the parole system and went from the indeterminate sentence to the determinate sentence, so that by the time that Loggins pulled me up down there, I was behind times in terms of training. They spent a year training all the classification people in the new system, so I was deficient in that. Then I had the additional problem of dealing with the disappointment of the staff who had already had somebody for that job. Unbeknownst to them, Loggins decided to put me in, and it was quite a shock. "Now what do we do?"

Let me give an example. It was my job to set up the parole papers and get them to my secretary to do the time situation, the log situation on them. Then she was to give them to the typist, and then we were to parole the inmate that afternoon. She was in that job because of the deputy superintendent. So there came this day to parole a guy, and she deliberately held those papers. Then she gave them to the typist to type up at ten minutes to four. And this guy was supposed to be paroled at four. So the upshot of that was that "We are going to have to put you out there in the dark, there is nobody to pick you up, so what do you want to do? Wait

<hr>

1980. Loggins (1930–2003) grew up in Muskogee, Oklahoma; served in the Air Force; and attended Langston University, Vallejo Junior College, and California State University, Sacramento. In 1968, after he had encountered Wilkinson but while he was still at CMF, Loggins became the first African American correctional captain in the Department of Corrections. He rose through the ranks to become training officer for the Department and ultimately served as superintendent at Soledad and at a new prison at Avenal, and he also served with distinction in high-level administrative and staff capacities in the Department. After he retired in 1989, he was a counselor for Friends Outside. Information and documents generously supplied by Mary Loggins.

5. Opened in the 1950s and designed as a model reform institution, Soledad comprised three different institutions, all under the same superintendent, with a deputy or associate superintendent or warden to run each of the three units (as described below). Wilkinson noted that he "worked in each and all of the units at one time or another" between 1977 and 1981. In 1977, Central had 39.1% white inmates, 26.5% Mexican American, and 33.0% black; North had 34.3% white, 23.2% Mexican American, and 40.4% black; South was 40.2% white, 25.0% Mexican American, and 32.7% black. The proportions had not changed much by the time that Wilkinson left in 1981: Central had 32.8% white, 34.3% Mexican American, and 31.2% black; North was 31.7% white, 27.8% Mexican American, and 39.1% black, while South was 38.1% white, 24.4% Mexican American, and 35.9% black. The facilities were designed to hold 2,981 inmates but in 1981 housed 3,670 (*California Department of Corrections 1981*).

and get out early in the morning and catch the bus that goes by?" And he says, "Yeah, that's fine with me." So I went on home, and I get a call from the deputy superintendent, who should have known that, from his job, he would not know if I was paroling the guy or not. So someone had to tell him. This was about eight o'clock at night. He was saying, "Get your butt over there, and get the guy paroled, and get him out on the street." I told him what the inmate and I discussed, and he said, "I don't care, just get him out on the street." So this poor guy ends up about nine o'clock at night standing at a very lonely bus station in front of the institution with no resources at all. That is a classic example of the lengths people would go to at Soledad. I promptly dismissed my secretary, which caused another brouhaha: "You can't do that," etc. My only answer to that was, "I just did it. I am not going to have that individual working for me."

That is the kind of thing that slowed me down in my work at Soledad.

Then I went from classification and parole to acting associate warden in charge of the appeals. In the disciplinary process, you filed a disciplinary to be adjudicated by the lieutenant and either approved or disapproved by the associate warden. It just went up the line. But then the central office put in an appeals process. So then the inmate could appeal it, and you had to go through the process of rehearing it. They gave that job to an associate warden. I covered that job in an acting capacity.

The associate warden would review the case, reinterview the inmate, and make his decision and send it to Sacramento. Nine times out of ten they would say okay, it was taken care of, and that was the end of it.

At Soledad, being short of staff, the guy who had the job before me got behind, and I must have had a wheelbarrow full of those appeals when I took over the job. Many times I would have to go to other institutions to interview the inmates. If you were lucky and knew people, you could send it to the person down there and have them interview the inmate and render a decision. So I did that job for two or three years.

The appeals job was a pain in the neck, but it was an interesting job. You learn some good things. I can remember one that was kind of the reverse. The guy was complaining about his mattress. He had just transferred down from someplace, and he was complaining about the condition of his mattress. It was an old appeal, so the mattress had disappeared. But I went down [to] the warehouse people, and they had no way of exchanging mattresses or keeping up on the sanitary aspects, such as "We'll do six mattresses a day in the sanitizer." They just had not set up anything, because it is a chore to go over there and clean out six mattresses a day and put six new ones in. Sometimes those mattresses were in those cells forever. People coming from other institutions get in there, and that is all the guy has got. So if you get an appeal like that, you could do something with it and make a difference.

Through that inmate appeal, I established something. Of course the warehouse people complained, but Sacramento told them, "That's what the appeals process is for. Whatever he says on there is what you are going to do, so get used to it." So one could make changes that way, but whether they lasted or not was something else again.

Then I took over one of the programs—again in an acting capacity as acting program administrator. That gets into the part where I tore things up and moved my office down there. In the unit, there were a certain number of convicts, and they were supposed to have a program. And I was the program administrator. At Soledad, I never could see the program—just keep them from hurting one another. That was about it.

The Challenge of Program Administrator

There were three hundred inmates. (At CMF, the program units were not that large—about two hundred.) I had done the same thing at CMF as program lieutenant, but at Soledad, as I say, there wasn't any program to administer—just keep them quiet, keep them from hurting themselves, and cut down on the disciplinaries. This was right up my alley; I understood this better than the other program.

They had two officers in the unit, and they had 150 inmates on either side. Only one officer could be down into the unit at a time, so it would have to be either the left side or the right one. So he's down there, and supervisory staff never showed up. There was no office in the unit. But we made an office.

There was a program lieutenant, the second in command, but there was no captain. The program officer was in direct command. The lieutenant was supposed to handle the disciplinaries and the day-to-day routine. But his office was up on the Patio. Below him were the sergeant and the correctional officers.

Everybody operated from the Patio by remote control or something that I never did understand. The normal thing to do would have been to put the program lieutenant down in the unit and have him operate from there, doing the disciplinaries and so on. There was a reason not to. Sometimes you could get into a disciplinary in which you would need an immediate lockup, and you had that kind of cell on the Patio—if an inmate got real hot and that sort of thing. You did not have that option down in the unit.

But I just plain wanted to be there. I would rather have spent my time on the unit than I would on the Patio. It was a personal thing. Nobody understood that, and I did not want to rub it in too hard that "I would just rather be down there with the convicts than be up here with you."

Outside athletic activities at the prison during Wilkinson's tenure (guard tower in background)
Source: Historical Albums, California Department of Corrections, Sacramento.

The point was, staff just never showed up down on the unit unless they just had to, for some particular function or other. The way I learned it was, you spent your time down in your unit, assisting the officers, listening to convicts, and so on. If you were up on the Patio in the administration building, then no one could talk to you. You were leaving two officers down there who would just have to function on their own. So you move your troops down into the building, and your problems just drop off dramatically. You could get something settled in five minutes instead of festering. And the officers knew, "I'll handle what I can handle, and there is a guy sitting right over there who will handle what I can't handle. I don't have to wonder if he's going to show up today or tomorrow or the next day. He's right there."

So the purpose of moving the office down on the unit was to give contact with the officers every day, with the inmates every day, and you just cut your workload down by being down there. I also told them, "I am changing the structure. I am not going to have all the regular people off on weekends." All the administrators were off on the weekend, and I couldn't see that. I euchred the superintendent into letting me take Sunday and Monday off, and have the other program administrator take Friday and Saturday off. Whoever set up North Facility scheduled the regular people off on Saturday and Sunday, including the administrators. I got my unit and said this is nonsense. I am taking Sunday and Monday off, and you will have an administrator here on the weekend. The lieutenant would have the tools, if he needs to use them. I never heard of a lieutenant calling an administrator at home. A lieutenant could do anything that needed to be done in the Department, and there was a piece of paper to back him up.

And that was quite a chore. Once you get used to it, it's hard to change. But the inmates were running wild. The administrators were gone on Saturday and Sunday. They did not know what went on. Hence a Monday meeting was necessary to catch up. And the correctional officers were bitching: "I don't have any good days off, because you made me work Saturday because you took Saturday and Sunday off."

So every Monday morning, there was a big meeting about what happened over the weekend. And the warden said, "What are you going to do about the Monday meeting?" Well, I would miss it. It worked pretty well. It worked pretty well for me. The correctional officers knew there was an administrator there to help out. They had to pay attention, and they had to do right on the weekends.

Again, trouble just dropped off dramatically. We had a nice easy move. It did not take the officers long to understand that this was the way we did things, and that we did it on Sundays as well as during the week. It gave continuity, and it settled down after a while. But it still did not prevent our having a riot.

The Riot

The riot was an entirely different thing, and it had nothing to do with the unit as such. It just happened that the canteen was over on that side of the compound, which affected my unit.

We had many occasions where we had a lockdown, for a month or two.[6] But with the one big lockdown that we had, we wound up completely changing the inmate population. And there were six hundred inmates there. We just started shipping them out by the busload and getting a busload in from somewhere else. And the whole North Facility remained locked down for a year.

6. The riot described here took place on 13 June 1979, but it was not noticed in major California newspapers. Newspaper reports did appear concerning another riot, which was very serious, in December 1979 ("2 Prisoners at Soledad Killed in Riot, 17 Hurt," *Los Angeles Times,* 7 December 1979, I: 28; Wilkinson believes that this December riot took place in the South Facility). Clearly such incidents did not all make the news at the time; in fact, surprisingly few did. Vernon Fox, *Violence behind Bars: An Explosive Report on Prison Riots in the United States* (New York: Vantage Press, 1956), also comments on how few "incidents" were reported in the news media.

The whole facility was out of business. The schoolteachers were washing dishes and packing lunches. We cell-fed the inmates for a year. In a way, it was kind of nice. In another way, we sure weren't getting much done.

We always had many confrontations where we had to herd inmates around with tear gas or fire off weapons to get them to go back to their cells. Things were not very well controlled. In addition to the six hundred convicts in the North Facility, over in Central, there was a typical old-fashioned prison built in the 1950s. And then there was South Facility, which was a kind of minimum-custody outfit for inmates getting ready for parole, inmates who did the yard work, inmates who worked in the fields. It was probably 400 population then.[7] The total for the whole complex was about 3,500 when I was there. It was big, but not by today's standards—out at Solano, they have six thousand inmates now.

At Soledad, we could get help from other units if there was an incident. Normally each unit would respond. Generally the units could take care of it themselves. If they needed extra help, they would put out the call, and you would take off and go to the unit that was having the problem. I can remember doing it on one occasion. The alarm went off, and I just happened to be on the Patio, and so I went with the rest of them down to see what the problem was. It was an inmate fight, and they had one of the officers hemmed in down in the corner of the building. So we took care of that. It was not necessarily a big deal.

When the riot happened in my unit, we stayed on the ground until people from Central came over and provided the weapons.

Normally you tried to have someone on the ground, get as much staff in there without leaving the other units down. Sometimes what happened was you had an incident going in one unit, and you pull your staff out, and then the trouble goes into the unit you pulled your staff from. Normally if you were having a problem in Central, then you would try to pull your people from North Facility, because the inmates in North Facility, due to the distance, were not aware that anything was going on, and it didn't excite them or get them up in arms. Vice versa, if you had something going on in North Facility, you didn't pull from the other unit in North Facility, you pulled from either South Facility or Central for added help. That way it didn't spread.

About the big riot—I was standing right there when it happened. There

---

7. As described in the introduction, Soledad started out as a model reform institution, and the different parts, although sharing centralized services, could operate relatively independently, permitting "the development of smaller and more specialized prison communities," as it was expressed by Blake McKelvey, *American Prisons: A History of Good Intentions* (Montclair, NJ: Patterson Smith, 1977), 336–37.

were bleachers and a ball field out there, and I was talking to one of the counselors, and all of a sudden all hell broke loose. Guys started getting up on top of the bleachers and shouting such things as "Let's take over now!" It caught us flat-footed for the moment, and communications were not very good. I had no way of communicating with the administration building. I had no way of communicating with my unit. I was just out in the middle of the ball field.

So I unobtrusively and quietly made my way down to the unit to see what was going on with the correctional officers and make sure that they were aware and knew what was going on. They by this time understood that it was a riot. But that put me to a phone, so I contacted the administration building and the control room, and they were just beginning to get the idea that something was going on. So I explained what I knew about it and that I was going to lock my unit down and go from there.

But they needed to tell me if they were going to force the inmates in with tear gas and that kind of thing. I did not want the doors locked so they could not get in. In the meantime, the rioters tore up the canteen—just out of spite, I guess. And then we decided, "Let's make an announcement that all you guys who want to go back to your cells, go." Man, there was a mad dash to get in the building. So we popped the outside door, and they went in. But then they decided that they did not want to get back in their cells.

By this time, they had passed us guns down the gun well to our cage, where the officers stayed. It was barred and looked just like a jail cell. So we had access to firearms because there was a tunnel or a stairwell behind each officers' station through which you could bring these guns over the roof and down inside and control it inside. All of the shotguns were loaded with bird shot so that you would not really maim somebody, but you could get their attention.

So they passed the guns through, and I put two officers up on the second and third tiers, and we fired the weapons up into the ceiling. That just encouraged the inmates to go in so we could lock up.

The aftermath of that was that by shooting at the ceiling, we blew out all of the lights up there, which were quite difficult to replace, because the building was so tall.

So that was about all there was to the riot except for the aftermath, the lockdown and the cell feeding and so on. But after a while, the unit really did begin to stink. We finally worked out a program to get extra staff to take the inmates out two at a time to shower and put them back in, working their way down the line. But it takes a long time to process three hundred people that way. We had to do it that way because they were locked down for a year.

Wilkinson's claim for clothing damaged in a riot (1979)
Source: Viola Wilkinson.

The lockdown continued because we wanted to change the population, and it takes that long to transfer that many people. We had no way of disciplining anyone for the riot. There was not really any way to sit down on somebody—"Joe was out there talking trash and getting people excited," but he was just running off at the mouth. Did he cause a riot or not? There wasn't any way to tell. So the only thing to do was just to dump everybody and spread them out through the Department. And it just took that long. That decision was probably made by the central office. Whether or not our superintendent had a hand in it—I rather think that he might have. Loggins was gone by this time, so I didn't have the access that I used to have.

At Soledad, it seemed to me that we were on riot status all of the time.[8] I didn't feel that we had any control down there, and any time they wanted to take off on us, they could. As a matter of fact, they did it in small, subtle ways. Not answering the ducats, calls, and passes.[9] You would page for a guy or tell the officer to send him up, and the SOB doesn't show until the next week. That kind of thing was constant at Soledad. You did not have any kind of control. At CMF, if you sent them a ducat, they showed up on time. If they didn't, you had a place you could find them, and you had a place for them—the whole works. But at Soledad you just did not have the staff or the facilities. The inmates were in control, in my way of thinking and in my experience at other institutions. I wasn't used to that. It made a hard time for me.

An inmate took a swing at one of my correctional officers, and I called him into my office and said, "The way we used to do this in the old days was: you take a poke at an officer, and we drag you into a corner and we beat the shit out of you. And maybe even break your legs. If you ever raise your fist to one of my correctional officers again, I will go back to the old way of doing business and probably break your legs. Now get the hell out of here."

Well, this got right back to the deputy warden, and he asked, "Did you threaten to break an inmate's legs?"

I said, "That is out of context. You tell me the rest of the story, the rest of the conversation, and I will answer."

"Well, it has been reported to me that you threatened to break an inmate's legs."

"Well, you go back to your source and have them repeat the whole conversation, and then we will talk about it."

And that was the last I ever heard of it. So the inmate apologized and the whole works: "I sure hope I don't get into trouble. I was frustrated at the time." It was a female officer he took a swing at. She was the one who passed the conversation along. I said what I said to that inmate in front of her and a couple of other officers.

---

8. Doug Foster, "Prison Chief Talks about 'Pressure Cooker,'" *Salinas Californian,* 5 January 1980, shows that Superintendent Loggins, foreseeing trouble, had for more than a year tried to get authorities in Sacramento to allow him to set up some preventive security measures. In this instance, some intelligent administration was frustrated by bureaucratic delay in a context of budgetary cutbacks—another factor contributing to institutional malfunctioning. Loggins also held the long-term change in inmate types responsible—the change from property offenders to convicts who had committed violent crimes, and the prison was not designed for such a population, an opinion that Wilkinson also held.

9. That is, failing to appear when stipulated by one written order or another.

The Administration at Soledad

It has always been my contention that when you build an institution and staff it, whatever mistakes you have in it will be in that institution fifty years later. You never get rid of them. You have that flavor, and it permeates. It is a virus. Staff does not all transfer at once, and they don't all retire at once. There is always something there to perpetuate the virus. And it is the same way with what we did with these exams. We put a virus in our computer and it is still eating us up. And they can't quite get rid of it. They will never get rid of it without a major upheaval, and I don't think we can afford that.

CMF was not perfect, nor was Chino, but some places were better than others. They showed a better understanding. Some places had better training. And some places had better administration. Oh, boy, did they ever!

All of this is one man's opinion, but some of it has some support. There is a book called *The Melancholy History of Soledad.*[10] It covers the period before my time there. It is a background tool in terms of my information on the administrators who were there then. I was in the Department during the time the author is talking about in the book. He was there when the case law came down about getting water to the inmates, and putting plumbing in the cells.[11]

Before I went to Soledad, I thought the author was crying in his beer and making too much of things. When I got there, I had a different attitude. But he still overdramatized things. I think he was a counselor. His main point was not danger to the staff, but how miserably the inmates were treated. There was a basis for that, but not to the extent he has in the book.

When I got to Soledad, I could not help contrasting the difference between Britt at CMF—"Here's your job. Do it. If you need help, ask me"—and the deputy superintendent at Soledad—"I'm going to put the fear of God in you and drive you." Then I came, and he did not have the scare card, for he encountered someone whom he could not scare, and he did not know what to do. He had no resources; he could not make it work. He could not do anything. He just did not know what to do with me. I had nothing to be afraid of for a couple of reasons: one, my work wasn't that bad, and, number two, I could have retired any time I wanted to retire.

10. Min S. Yee, *The Melancholy History of Soledad Prison, in Which a Utopian Scheme Turns Bedlam* (New York: Harper's Magazine Press, 1973). The author uses a tone and rhetoric from that time that is very strong; chapter 2, for example, is entitled, "Conditions of a Shocking and Debased Nature."

11. See below in this chapter.

The deputy superintendent was one of the guys who had asked me to come down there four or five years earlier. But when I finally got there, he could not stand me, because the warden had brought me there, and, as I commented, the deputy superintendent had somebody else slated for the job. That blew everything out of the water for him. But Loggins, the superintendent, called me there, and put me in the job of classification and parole representative. So I did not have a chance. I have mentioned my lack of knowledge and the training the other people had under the new parole system. But in addition, I was cut off at every corner by the deputy superintendent and his cohorts. I did not press it, because I was not going to be there forever, and they were.

At CMF in the early days, prisoners were used to control prisoners, as I told you. But when the old people went out, and new administrators came in, it happened less and less. But at Soledad, it was the norm. Soledad had at the time what they termed "The Catalyst Program," which was just another term for the "con boss" setup, but they dressed it up with fancy words. They had an inmate who had the administration's ear, so he had something to deal with, with the convicts. "You get in my basket, and I can take care of you," or "We can get this," or "We can do that—I have the boss's ear."[12]

Loggins

Loggins, the superintendent, was a sergeant out at CMF in the early days. He was one of our two blacks whom I mentioned as the only two black people we had in the institution for a while. Loggins was assigned to me, and I put him in a relief position. He relieved the watch sergeant and another sergeant two days a week. Then he worked outside. So this is the training routine. Anybody knows that when you want a new watch sergeant, and you want him trained, you put him into relief so he knows the job and everything. So okay, I lost my watch sergeant, my regular one whom I had had for about eight months. So why not put Loggins in? He was black!

I get a call from the boss, "Can we do this?" Will the convicts take it?

12. John R. Hepburn, "Prison Guards as Agents of Social Control," in *The American Prison: Issues in Research and Policy,* ed. Lynne Goodstein and Doris Layton MacKenzie (New York: Plenum Press, 1989), 199: "The use of prisoners to control prisoners is a widespread practice." George H. Gregory, *Alcatraz Screw: My Years as a Guard in America's Most Notorious Prison* (Columbia: University of Missouri Press, 2002), describes from a correctional officer's point of view what happened in one institution when inmates were permitted to run the prison.

Otis Loggins as warden of CTF, Soledad
Source: Mary Loggins.

"What did you do, did you hire him as relief sergeant? Or did you hire him as a sergeant?" "Well, I hired him as a sergeant." I said, "Why is it a surprise to you? I told you when I put him in as relief sergeant, I was going to do that. To me it was plain as day that I told you I was going to make him watch sergeant when the time comes. So why are you surprised now?" And that was the end of that.

Loggins had one hell of a time because the black convicts demanded too much of him. He had one hell of a time. As far as staff went, a sergeant is a sergeant, and you do what you do, and that was it. So there were no problems there.

Anyway, he became watch sergeant, and he stayed for about four months, I think. Then they made him a training sergeant, a recruiting-type thing. Then he got promoted to lieutenant and went to Central Office. He continued to advance, and we were in contact from time to time over the years. Then I went to the orals board, and he was on the orals board for captain. So the other two people on the board were not looking for me. That was pretty obvious. Loggins was trying to be supportive. And before

I left, he said, "This guy was doing affirmative action before there was affirmative action." And we said good-bye. I came out twenty-fifth on the list, the last guy on the list, but on the list. And it was strictly because Loggins had insisted, "Put him on the list. I get to put somebody on there. You get to put somebody on there. Put him on the list."[13] It caused quite a stir, particularly with my peers out at CMF.

I had some really bad experiences. Even Clanon, the superintendent at the time, was surprised that I made the list. He said, "I would not have ranked you that high." I said, "Well, you are a psychiatrist, and it does not surprise me. Because you don't know much about penal institutions"—a really brilliant statement, but if he was blunt enough to tell me he would not have done that, I didn't see why I couldn't be blunt enough to tell him what I thought. But that is not the way he took it.

Career Barriers

That was part of my problem all through the whole thing. It started in Chino. I really should have been more subdued, more observant, with less talk. But that is my style, and you have to take what you can get. I had just a middling career. I could have done quite well with it. The pattern was just like what happened in the academies. I did that three times. They asked me back twice after the first one. Then somebody asked the training guy in Sacramento how I did, and he said, "He did fine, but I would not hire him again." No explanation, no reason, but he hired me three times.

I suffered on those oral exams from the old CMF captain because of thirdhand information. When asked, the captain would tell the board that he supervised me and, "Hey, this guy is a pain in the ass." So unless you were really outstanding, they treated you like a pain in the ass. I never did too well with orals anyway. I always talked too much or said too much. That was my weak point. But mostly the attitude was: "Hey, the guy does good work, but he is a pain in the ass." I was there to do good work. I don't remember actively being a pain, but I guess you can do that and not know you are doing it.

Regardless, things were never all that bad. For example, it never occurred to me that I could ever actually lose my job. In my mind, they had no basis for firing me because my work was solid. They would have had to have some trumped-up charge that didn't have anything to do with work. I knew I was okay.

That is what they couldn't understand at Soledad. "You know this guy

13. Being on the list permitted Wilkinson's pay to rise while he was in an "acting" capacity.

is not threatened by losing his job and moving on to something else or doing this or that." Why would I feel threatened? I had a big old house on the grounds. I had everything else going for me. It really didn't matter to me where I worked. I went back to uniform for a while. Then they pulled me back to do the appeals, and I had to go back into civvies. To them, going back into uniform was a demotion, but it wasn't. Again, the briar patch, I guess. I just did not think like the rest of the people.

Problems with Administration

Soledad was the most poorly administered place I have ever seen. Not only in the prison business, but any other kind of business. It was horrendous. Those people were so tender, so horrified, and so afraid for their positions that they would constantly try to cut each other's throats and operated in little cliques. Soledad was big enough that you had a superintendent and two deputy superintendents. You had the main facility, north facility, and south facility, each an area competing with the others. So that created problems.

So there was a lot of dirty work going on. Deliberate destruction, by the staff. One administrative officer and the deputy superintendent were great buddies. Both of them should have been disciplined as far as I was concerned. Once this administrative officer and I were discussing an incident that had occurred. The correctional officer was trying to tell us how he felt about it, and what he felt ought to be done, and I went to his aid to help him explain what he was doing. Later, the administrative officer says, "Hey, we gotta stick together." I said I thought that was what we were doing, and he said, "No, administrators gotta stick together." I said, "No, no, no. Staff has to stick together, which includes correctional officers, staff." I said, "Do you think you could do your job without that correctional officer? Who would do his job if you castrated him?" He said, "Well, I don't care about that. We just have to stick together." I said, "You and I don't have to stick together. I don't like the way you keep your business."

I did other things to upset the old-timers at Soledad. When Loggins was there, he was lonesome. He was living down in that big superintendent's house without his wife and family, because they did not want to move. Both of us liked to play chess. Plus we had a prior association from working at CMF. So we spent a lot of time off the job that way. So you're bound to get your viewpoint across every now and then. Which also caused resentment, particularly with other administrators. Really all it was to me was—I knew the guy, and I didn't know anybody else. And besides that, I could beat him at chess every once in a while. It broke up his week, and he really did not have anybody, he was on his own. He did not want to come over and visit us. He knew Viola, but we lived on the grounds, and that would have made too much of it for those people. If I had lived in town, he might have come in for cup of coffee or something. But not on the grounds.

The Baneful Influence of Soledad

Soledad was a mess that spread to other institutions when Soledad people were promoted. The old Soledad thing carried over and screwed up other institutions. Soledad was responsible for more case law than all the other institutions in the Department of Corrections combined. They changed how we treated inmates.

There was a lock-up unit at Soledad that did not have plumbing. So the officer had to carry water to the convicts. So they played games with that by saying they were not going to give the inmate the water. So then a complaint was filed, and "You will put plumbing in those cells."

At CMF on S Wing, we had clean cells. There was no plumbing, just Chinese toilets. Nothing they could hurt themselves on. It was great for psychotics and really hard cases. A few days in there, and they wanted out, they did not want to go back there. But because of Soledad, we had to tear the cells up and put plumbing in all of them. It ruined the perfectly good lock-up cells.

Another problem was firearms, shooting people. It happened at inappropriate times in inappropriate ways. This carried over to Pelican Bay, where they had a good setup, a hard lockup.[14] But they overdid it.

Inmates at Soledad

We had different kinds of convicts. We had the burglars, the repeat offenders who were in their forties, the burnouts. And at that time we were still handling check writers and embezzlers—white-collar stuff—as well as the hard-core stuff.

Down at Soledad, we had an inmate steal from the canteen. Everybody was in a quandary about how to discipline him. He did not have any money to pay back to the canteen. I think the draw was a twenty-dollar

14. Pelican Bay State Prison opened in 1989 as the state's first "super-max" facility. The term referred to a Security Housing Unit, intended by Corrections for difficult management cases, prison gang members, and violent maximum custody inmates.

or thirty-dollar draw, something like that. So when he came before me, I told him that, "You can go ahead and draw canteen. But if you draw fifteen dollars' worth of canteen, then you have to pay the canteen fifteen dollars. That means you spend thirty dollars that month. And you keep doing that until you get the canteen paid back. Because if you don't have canteen, if you don't have cigarettes, candy bars, or whatever, you will be out stealing it, and that is another problem. So if you spend fifteen bucks at the canteen, that's what you pay back. If your folks can afford to send you thirty bucks a month, then you spend your own thirty bucks and the other thirty that your folks sent you goes to paying your debt." Those guys from the parole board from Sacramento thought that was hot stuff. "Wisdom of Solomon," one guy said. It made sense, but it had never been done before. I was not even sure it was legal, but that was somebody else's task.

They would have taken the conventional action—you lose your privileges from now on or a few days' "good time"—but, no, you have to realize that a man has to function. He is going to function one way or another, so he might as well be functioning your way. Actually, he kind of wrinkled his nose, he knew what kind of break it was, but he still wanted to negotiate. He said, "Could, you raise that so I could draw twenty?" I said, "You've got those other debts out there, don't you?" He looked at me and almost got out of the chair. What was bothering him was that he had borrowed cigarettes and stuff, and he had personal debts out there. That was why he was stealing from the canteen to begin with. And he did not clean them up. So what he was going to have to do with this thirty bucks was: he was going to have to spend fifteen of it on the canteen, which he would promptly give to the guy he owed, plus he had to give fifteen in restitution to the canteen. He needed that other five bucks for his candy bars and cigarettes for himself. I told him that was too complicated for me. He never did admit that he had other debts, but his eyes sure got big when I mentioned it.

The Black Muslims at Soledad

I arrived at Soledad with that traveling letter that I mentioned. Everybody there was apprehensive about the Black Muslims. The staff did not deal with the Muslims; they did not nod to them or acknowledge them or anything else. Three of them were standing out in the Patio waiting to go back to their housing unit. You could recognize them by the way they were dressed. I went over to them and told them who I was and told them I had worked with a group of Muslims in Vacaville and asked them how things were going along. They did not know what to do.

I told them to meet me the following day; I had something I wanted to show them. You could tell that they wanted me the hell away from them. But they came up the next day in my office, which was right across the Patio. I took that traveling letter the Muslims had given me. I told them I was showing the letter to them for one reason: if they had any problems, I had helped the group out in Vacaville, and if they had any problems there at Soledad, I would see that they got what was coming to them. I said I did not have any interest in the organization, one way or the other, but I would treat them fairly. I told them the story of how I helped the other inmates. A few weeks went by, and the staff wanted to know why on earth was I dealing with the Muslims, because they did not acknowledge them. "We don't mess with them." After a couple of weeks went by, and nothing happened, I figured they were not interested. Then they came to see me about some property that had been mishandled. And they were right, it had been mishandled. It was easy to correct, but they could not take care of it on their own.

They had the local imam (priest) come in on a regular basis. My reaction was that I wanted to punch that guy in the mouth. He had a snotty, miserable attitude, and he wanted nothing to do with me or any other staff member. There was really deep resentment there. While the inmates made it a point to introduce me, he was not going to have any part of me, in any way, shape, or form. He was from the outside, and he ran the local temple. He saw me as interfering with his territory and usurping his authority—I don't know how else you could take it. His counterpart in Vacaville had thought what I did was great. I was taking care of things he would not have to.

Of course all of the Muslims had a demeanor about them. If you were at all tender, they would get to you. They had that blank look and stare, and they would not give an inch. So you had to learn how to deal with that.

But at Soledad, this demeanor had had an effect on the staff's attitude towards the Muslims. It was petty. I could understand that the imam from the outside might resent my dealing with them. But I could not understand the staff's negative attitude toward me because I worked with the Muslims. "Are you going to use these guys to gang up on us?" That was the attitude I got from them. I used to tease the staff pretty heavily. I would tell them I was "connected."

Some of them about halfway believed me. They had a correctional counselor in there who was a native Mexican. In a way, he was way over his status in life. He was a nice guy, he did his job and everything. But he understood how gangs stuck together, and so he got apprehensive that I had my own gang. You can't resist those opportunities sometime to work with their minds a little bit.

The Muslims did not have a problem with me. They accepted things and realized that there was something in it for them, more than they had before. I took care of the day-to-day things with the Muslims. They did not ask for much. They knew if they had a problem, they had a staff member who would listen.

I would be down in the housing unit, and one of the Muslims would walk by. We would nod and say "Hi," and the officer who was with me would be shocked. "That was a Muslim." "Yeah, that was why I said hi." "You talk to Muslims?" It was just crazy. I don't know how it got that way. The staff had completely lost sight of what their function was. I would tell them the Muslims were convicts, and we were supposed to deal with convicts. We were supposed to manage them, to take care of them. That was why we were there. Still they asked me why I was dealing with the Muslims. "Why don't you ask me why I am dealing with the clerk in my office? It's because I need him, and he needs me."

This was in the last half of the 1970s, and in the joint, the Muslims were probably on the way down. Out of sight is a better way to put it. They were probably just as active as they ever were, inside and out, but just nonconfrontational and subdued and not a problem.

Promotion and Transfer Problems at Soledad

Going to Soledad, I knew there was not going to be much out there for me. But I went to Soledad with the thought that that promotion was going to lead to other things. Soledad had so many unfilled positions. And at that point, I did not care whether or not I was paid for doing a particular job. So if I was acting associate warden, then that satisfied me. Just knowing I could do the job satisfied my ego. I would much rather have had the title and the money at that time. But for me, the important thing was to find out whether or not I could do the job. It would just prove to me that all those people who thought I was not promotable material were wrong, because there I was, doing that job. That was a big boost for my ego and settled a lot of problems for me.

I never got so far along that I lost contact with the correctional officers out on the line. One time when I was offered a promotion, I was tired of being a correctional officer. I was a correctional officer a year longer than I wanted to be, or than I should have been, in my mind. So I could relate to that when I was dealing with someone who was a three- or four- or five-year correctional officer. Even though later I was stuck as a lieutenant, I knew right when I became a sergeant how lucky I was not to be a correctional officer anymore. Not that it was a bad job. I had simply worn the job out. It did not satisfy me any longer.

So as the penologists suggest, if you stayed too long in one position, you would burn out as the convicts burned out. Crime is just too damned much trouble. That same kind of burnout is what you get if you don't promote, or at least get something new. And that was what I liked at CMF. There were so many things going on there that I could do. I could do the program lieutenant job, I could do the board reports if there wasn't anything else available in my line. And I did watch lieutenant I cannot tell you how many times.

The same condition affected correctional officers as well as lieutenants. Just strictly watching the convicts and putting them to bed and so on—that gets old after a while. Nothing is happening. There is nothing proactive about it. "It's ten o'clock, so go to bed. It's six o'clock, and you've eaten your dinner, so don't get into any trouble until it's time to go to bed, and then we'll put you to bed." Doing this over and over and over again gets to be old hat, whether a person is educated or not.

So you had to seek something new or pick up and transfer someplace else. And you might not get something new if you transferred someplace else—except a whole new staff you had to get acquainted with, and a whole new plant that you have to understand.

Getting to Know a New Plant

I think people overlook how important it is to know your building, your plant. That is a tremendous comfort. I noticed that more and more as I was at Soledad. It took me a long time just to learn how to get around—not knowing where stuff was, not knowing what key fit what. At CMF, I knew where all the nuts and bolts were. Some I had the opportunity to tighten up before the inmates even got there. I had seen the blueprints. I knew about the boiler house. I knew about the pipe tunnel. I knew about the eccentricities of the elevators and getting in and out of the visiting room. All of those things I did not have at Soledad.

At CMF, in one of the pipe tunnels we had a guy who tried to squeeze under the grill cage and got his head caught. He had a lot of grief and a lot of screaming and yelling to get his head out of there. There was about a six-inch space so water could drain out of there, and he decided that maybe he could crawl under that and get out. But he did not even get his head out of it, and he got trapped there. I do not know how long he was there, yelling and screaming before somebody found him. I don't know how anybody found him down in the bowels of the institution, unless someone was just going by to make a check on something.

You could go all over the institution through the pipe tunnels. You could go from the boiler house to a stairwell and up into a building and that sort of thing. So knowing those things was a help—just getting around in case you had a riot up on the second floor. You did not necessarily have to move your troops through the main corridor; you could move them through the pipe tunnel and come up behind the inmates and shut them off.

So when I got to Soledad, I would have to stop and ask somebody— hopefully not an inmate!—how did you get from here to there?

The Problem of Location

The plant at North Facility was built originally for vocational training, school, and things along that line. Then the inmate population changed, and you no longer had people there who were susceptible to such things as vocational training. Then it became a warehouse, and so it became a problem, and that was not necessarily the fault of the staff. That was just what happened.

Soledad was bad, but one has to take into consideration not only the plant but the location. To be fair, Soledad Prison was isolated. It was down in the Salinas Valley, thirty miles from Salinas. The closest town was Soledad, which was perhaps ten miles away. Soledad had a small population, one or two thousand, to begin with, something of that nature.[15] And then the next town of any importance was King City, which was another sixty miles down the road from Salinas. Soledad was an isolated place for staff, and so you did not get many requests to transfer to Soledad. You did not always get people promotionally: "Oh, no, I think I'll pass on Soledad and wait for CMF or the Men's Colony or some other place to call me. Because living conditions are not that ideal down there."

Then you get into the minority people, and they really had a problem. In the Valley, there was no housing for them, and they just felt uncomfortable. When I had the COD academy there, the administrator at that time was a black man, and he needed gas for his car, and it was ten o'clock at night. He asked me to follow him into town and sit in the car while he got gassed up. That was how uncomfortable he was down there. So the minority people would have to live in the Monterey Bay area, another fifty-mile drive through the canyons. It was not very conducive for the minorities.

If they had a choice, the best people would go somewhere else. That was one of the reasons that they were always short twenty-five correctional officer positions and other positions—people just wore out down there. Even

15. The 1960 census reported a population of 2,837; in 1970, it was 6,843.

Wilkinson at an office party during his work at Soledad
Source: Viola Wilkinson.

the superintendent wore out. He was there, and it was "Man, get me back
to Central Office!" Not only Loggins, but a couple of others you could
attribute that to, also. We had a guy named Al Stagner [acting superintendent in 1981] who I thought was a top-notch man, and he told me
frankly, "I am just getting out of here as soon as I can get out, because the
living conditions are just awful"—compared to what it would be in
Sacramento or over in San Francisco or some place such as that.

So that was a bad start for Soledad. A guy really had to be desperate for
a promotion if he transferred there promotionally. So you did not get the
people who were real enthusiastic.

Living on the Grounds

Now if you lived on the grounds as I did—I couldn't ask for any more: I had a house that was 65 feet long and 40 feet wide, two bathrooms and the whole ball of wax—plus a kitchen you could slaughter a steer in. There again, the reason it was that way was that it used to be an old stable, and the chief of plant maintenance said that he would take that old thing over, and he would do some work on it using state materials, but he would do all the work himself and make it into a residence. "And when I retire, someone else can have it." Well, I don't know what happened, but he just went whole hog, and that place had amenities that would make you blink your eyes. Ironically enough, he retired early—I think with a little bit of help, because he just went too far with it and spent a lot of money on it. But it was a nice place.

So I didn't have that kind of problem, and most of the people who lived on the grounds didn't, either. But if you had to live off the grounds, you had a problem—like the minorities who lived over in Monterey, simply because they were uncomfortable in Salinas as well as Soledad.

Viola and I were having fun down there. She really liked it at Soledad, the folks she met in town, the things she got involved in. And this was new country to us, so on my days off we went all up and down the Coast—Carmel-by-the-Sea and so on. And the money was good.

Leaving the Department

When I retired, I was on a captain's list but, except for acting time, not on a captain's salary. I did not get any additional salary for being program officer, just my step up to CPS III from CPS II. But being program officer was what I was doing when I just got up one morning and decided that I did not want to do that anymore. So I told them I was turning in my papers for the first of July. I think it took until the fourth or fifth. I did not even have my retirement papers in. I had to support myself for three months until my retirement stuff caught up with me.

But I was not any more irritated or upset that I had been down there. I just got up one morning and thought, I think I just won't do this anymore.[16] I thought I had to give them some notice. I don't think I needed to, really; they had someone to plug in there in a minute.

Mostly it was scattered, pretty undefinable, the five years at Soledad. I

16. In addition to the personal feelings expressed here, it is intriguing to notice a study that suggested that "levels of job satisfaction may have declined among officers over the past decade," using data from the 1970s and early 1980s and surmising that changes in rules and workforce composition played in to a declining level of satisfaction; Francis T. Cullen et al., "How Satisfying Is Prison Work? A Comparative Occupational Approach," *Journal of Offender Counseling, Services and Rehabilitation* 14 (1989): 89–108, esp. 91, 105.

was everything and nothing. Again, keeping busy, something new. Like that appeals job that gave me a title of acting associate warden, but it was a really lousy, pain-in-the-ass job. They had to get the other guy out of there because he let it pile up on him and darned near ruined him. So if it was going to be a problem, it was okay to put someone in there about whom you really did not care. Get the guy you care about out of there. They couldn't take anything away from me. I already had all I was going to get. I did not really care what their opinion was on a personal basis. It really was not that disturbing. I enjoyed cleaning the thing up. The thing that did kind of upset me was that they had a woman who had been super-intendent at the women's institution, but she displeased the director, and since she served at the director's pleasure, she lost her job. So they slated her into this job that I was holding down. She was an all right person, working with what she had, but they did not give her very much. She was a product of affirmative action and did not have any background or groundwork to back her up. She was moved along through the Department until they made her superintendent at the women's prison. It was a mistake. They should not have done that to her.

I had to clean up this job, which was okay, because if I had not been working at that, I would have been working at something else. And I did enjoy getting around and talking to all the inmates and sometimes leaving the institution to go to another institution. It was okay with me.

But she was slated to come into the job as a permanent position. So I got it straightened up, and I almost completed the backlog. It was night-and-day work. You would work on the backlog in the daytime when you work on the inmates, and you work on the new stuff that comes in at night. So this former superintendent came in to take over the position. I was not sure where I was going after that. That was when I ended up as program officer. But she did not know how to do this job.

I was doing my job and teaching her how to do her job. And she was not above saying, "You know, I don't have time to go over to Central to interview this inmate. Would you go over and interview him?" But that was how it was at the end. I was on my way out. I really did not care. If I had had my career ahead of me, I might have handled it differently.

My very last day? I said that when the riot started, I was talking to a counselor on the ball field. It happened to be a female, an Oriental, Okugu. When it came time for me to retire, no one was interested, other than a couple of people I had met, a couple of sergeants whom I thought were pretty good people. They came by and said good-bye and so on. But Okugu brought me a cake! And that was it for retirement. (I am not much into that, anyway. I was relieved.)

I have been continuously told that I could not work in the business today. And I do not dispute that. But by the time I was finished at Soledad, I had seen an awful lot of changes.

It was a crazy career for me. I never did seem to get my feet on the ground. I always seemed to be dealing with the oddball things, like the Muslims and those damned groups. Those were kind of iffy situations, and so you don't assign somebody to them whom you are particularly interested in.

Mostly it turned out pretty well.

CHAPTER SIX

REFLECTING ON BEING AN EMPLOYEE IN THE PRISON SYSTEM

So working in the Department, I had to think about my own circumstances. But I also had to think about the people with whom I was working. And the whole institutional system.[1]

Employee Organizations

Employees in the prison system did try to protect themselves by organizing. The original organization, which existed when I started out, was the California State Employees Association, CSEA. That was all you had. That took care of the entire state and all state employees. It was not exclusively Corrections or Cal Trans or any other state department. You had to be a member in order to have some of the benefits, particularly insurance. At that time, we did not have a credit union for us. But the local one in Sacramento allowed CSEA state employees to participate for twenty dollars.

Subsequently, the prison people, correctional officers, started the CCOA, the California Correctional Officers Association. Then this turned into the California Peace Officers Association (CCPOA).[2] It became a really militant union. This organization was just for correctional officers. To heck with the rest of the world.

---

1. Wilkinson comments: "When I was working, I read a lot about corrections, and I heard a lot about what professional penologists thought. No doubt all of these ideas affected the way I viewed my job. Sometimes I agreed with the experts, and sometimes I did not. And often they did not agree with each other."

2. According to the CCPOA Web site, the California Correctional Officers Association was organized formally in 1957. By 1978, the group had 2,500 members and opened a Sacramento office. In 1982, after state employees were granted bargaining rights, the CCOA won the right to bargain for correctional officers and was renamed the California Correctional Peace Officers Association.

They made heavy campaign contributions. They could really sway an election. It was a very militant group compared to what it has been over the last years. It included all uniformed personnel—except that you lose it once you hit the middle-management level. You can join, but you have other obligations, because, when you strike, management fills the places.

In order for one to keep his or her head above water, you have to join the organization. They now make it very plain. I can't speak from personal experience, but only from talking to others and reading the newspapers. They even sponsor television programs like "Save Our Streets" and "We Walk the Toughest Beat in the World."

They are really impressed with their own importance. "The toughest beat in the world"—something that they cannot even compare to an earlier time. Then there were different facilities and everything. These officers have radio control, they have alarms they can push, and they have got the whole ball of wax. As a correctional officer in my day, you went down there, and you did not have anything except the telephone. If you couldn't get to the telephone, then you had a problem.

But nowadays, they have a button you can push that they carry right with them, and fifteen people will run down to see what kind of trouble they have. We did not have walkie-talkies. The only thing we had was radio patrol cars at Chino because we had 2,600 acres to patrol. Finally, just before I left CMF, we got in the personal, handheld alarms for the correctional officers. Since I have been out, they are like SWAT teams. They have the radios and other devices. So they have immediate response and backup. They don't have to depend on the things that we had to depend on. What we did and how we did it depended more on relationships.

I kept the CSEA membership until I retired. I never joined the peace officers group. You could join and pay your dues as long as you were in uniform; it did not matter what rank you were. But if you were management, and a lieutenant was middle management, it was not for you. They had benefits, too—insurance and what have you.

The union never affected my work. Of course on an individual basis you would have a union officer trying to use the union for leverage. For example, "Hey, don't mess with me. I am the shop steward," or, "The union says we are going to do it this way." "Okay, fine; we will do it that way when the state says we are going to do it that way." Then you would cool them down and let them know that was not an avenue for them. So they would go back to what they should be doing. Nothing so big as sit-downs or strikes. But it is a club, and it is a threat.

We had meetings at San Quentin and other institutions when we were first forming CCOA, the California Correctional Officers Association. We were exploring the possibilities of forming a union for uniformed personnel.

At that time I don't think we at CMF had too many people in CCOA because originally, when we had a meeting at San Quentin, one of the subjects that came up was that the MTAs [medical technical assistants] were in uniform. Some of us from CMF were holding out for the MTAs to be part of CCOA. They wore uniforms. But the people at that time just wanted correctional officers, custody people, in CCOA.

There was a difference between the CCOA and the CCPOA. They were competing. CCPOA is the organization that is still going now. The first one, the California Correctional Officers Association, was beginning to steal membership from CSEA. In 1979, somebody in CSEA surprised everybody by getting a little mosey by saying "Let's have a sickout." To my knowledge, it did not affect CMF. [3]

CMF was pretty easy. It was just a different place. With a little talking, you could control things, you could shut things like this off pretty well, much more so than at other institutions. We had a little better rapport with our people than most institutions had, and we could sit around over a cup of coffee and discourage some people or say there was a better way to do it. So I kind of think that is what happened. We finally just did not have too many "sick" people. "What is the purpose? What are you going to gain? You are going to need that sick pay some day when you break your leg." That kind of thing. Letting them know that it didn't make sense. There wasn't any threat there, or anything. Although we had a pretty tight follow-up on sick leave.

You had people who didn't understand about sick leave. They thought that that was an entitlement. A sick day a month was an entitlement. So they would use that sick day and keep about five days on the books. But they would take their sick day per month. We tried to discourage that for several reasons. The main one was, if you're not sick, don't take sick leave! In the early days, the captain and the associate warden were pretty tough on sick-leave time. So they did have a policy where they would send a supervisor out to check on a guy. I never particularly cared for that. I know I would have had a fit if they had sent somebody to my house. But I would not have taken a day a month.

Then it kind of shifted. CCOA kind of petered out. It became a benign thing, like CSEA now. It still existed. Just about the time I was quitting, they started to call it California Correctional Peace Officers Association. That was when they started emphasizing "We walk the toughest beat" and all that macho stuff. That was just about the time that I gave it up—the early 1980s, maybe the very late 1970s.

3. Both the California State Employees Association and the California Correctional Officers Association, for example, made statements and tried to mediate or lead when some correctional officers started a sick-out and threatened to strike in 1979; see *Los Angeles Times*, 21 March 1979, I:21, and 10 April 1979, I:3.

So it was there, but it did not affect me—for two reasons. One, I did not pay any attention to it. I was neither for it nor against it. Actually, if you pinned me down, I would have to say I was against it. But I did not have an alternative to suggest to replace it, so I just kept my mouth shut.

Compensation and Hours

Compensation did become an issue in my day, because we ran a long time without raises. They would give us a raise of 5 percent, but it would be 2.5 percent now and the other half later. Then we never saw the other 2.5 percent. One time we got into where there was a 10 percent raise, and they gave us 2.5 percent now, and we never saw the rest. That became an issue. But it did not go through the union. It was straightened out through CSEA and other means because it affected all state employees.

Sometimes pay for correctional officers was low even in California.

At the beginning, I was getting $255 a month. They even had a raise right before I applied. Before that, it was even lower, maybe $140–$180 a month. My dad made $140 a month in the late thirties. So that was not a bad salary. California was able to raise salaries, when they decided to do it after the war. There was so much money there, after 1953, tidelands oil money, as I mentioned, and they were not constructing a lot of prisons, because they did not need that many. They had three under construction. After the construction costs, there was a whole bunch of money left over that went into salaries.

Later, increases came when the Department was not hiring enough people to staff the institutions. Before that, you did not need that many people, you did not have that much competition. But now you had to pay a comparable wage to the guy who was going to run a computer or what have you. So the wages went out of sight. As I mentioned, a four-year correctional officer will make as much if not more than I did after thirty years, which is not too surprising, because times change, and there is inflation. It is not unusual, working a few overtime days, to have a correctional officer make $50,000–$55,000 a year now.

When I was working at Chino and CMF, there was no overtime pay. It was not until I went to Soledad that they started paying overtime. Before that, the time was all compensated time off. So from a supervisor's standpoint, it made it difficult to get a relief in there when someone was sick or out. Some supervisors ordered men in, and the officer would have to deal with that. In my case, when I was working the first watch, there were not that many people to deal with, and it was easier for me to handle as I described it, to convince twelve people that, "Hey, we have to do this as a group, and it will be painless for all of us."

The Guard Subculture

I am not sure what the experts mean when they say guard subculture.[4] Perhaps not so much for me, but in the old San Quentin, Folsom philosophy, yes, definitely. As a group, the guard force stuck together, and there was a difference between them and administrators.[5] The guard force was the thing: "Them dummies up there don't know what the hell they are doing, they cannot operate without us. So we stick together and we don't get into trouble with that kind of people."

That was the old philosophy. There continued to be a certain amount of it, but that was due to the administration. At Soledad, there was a chasm between officers and the administrators, and that was the administrators' fault, as I said with the story about the guy who told me we all had to stick together. It was not the officers' fault. They would have been perfectly happy to be part of the organization.

It was true that the officers socialized together, as I have said, at both Chino and CMF. Very definitely. In my day, a sergeant would be right in the middle of it, along with the officers if you stopped for a beer. Maybe on occasion a lieutenant; it was not that structured. Mostly the correctional officers stuck together. They had things in common. I hate to use the term, but "upper staff" did not lend themselves to socializing because they felt that there would be favoritism. But it was not unusual to get invited on a fishing trip or a gold-panning trip a guy was planning up in Placerville. In my time. But before that, officers only associated with officers, sergeants with sergeants, not exclusively but primarily, almost exclusively.

4. Susan Philliber, "Thy Brother's Keeper: A Review of the Literature on Correctional Officers," in *Incarcerating Criminals: Prisons and Jails in Social and Organizational Context,* ed. Timothy J. Flanagan, James W. Marquart, and Kenneth G. Adams (New York: Oxford University Press, 1998), 131: "Part of the difficulty of learning whether or not a guard subculture exists lies in knowing how to measure such a subculture."

5. Philiber, "Thy Brother's Keeper," 130–31: "Whether or not a guard subculture actually exists, some guards' statements make it clear that they think it should exist, especially if it implies solidarity. As one officer pleads: 'Practice comradeship. It is important that a corrections officer be able to trust and depend on fellow officers. A show of uniformed and unified force is important, not only for your sake, but is essential to your credibility as a guard force, both to the inmates and to the administration.' Another CO inserts that the uniform worn by guards is an important symbol as being united as 'the solidarity brotherhood of the wearers of the uniform.'" Wilkinson comments: "Most of that I agree with up to a point. To wear the uniform to signify brotherhood, no. To signify that you were an official of the department so the inmate can recognize that, and your fellow officers can recognize that, yes. That statement is pretty dramatic, brotherhood and solidarity to the extent they are saying. But you did have to have an understanding amongst staff, that no matter how much I dislike you, we are both wearing the same uniform, we both have the same responsibilities. If you get into trouble I will support you as you will support me if I get into trouble. As I have suggested, that should have come with the job. The uniform was just a distinguishing thing so the inmates would know whom they are dealing with."

How much people socialized together depended on the institution. And I say the institution only because of the locale. At Folsom, a good percentage of the officers lived on the grounds. At Soledad, a good percentage of the officers lived on the grounds. As I mentioned, the nearest town of any size was Salinas, thirty miles away. In Vacaville, no. You were into Little League, into church, your neighbors. We had our functions, our dances, but mostly we were pretty well integrated into the town after the first year—and that was only because the townspeople were unsure of us the first year.

Officers set their own goals within the parameters they are given, yes. I will run this housing unit this way. Mahaffy, the way he ran his thing was like a Swiss watch. If you did not belong in his unit, don't even approach the front door. Jones down the street was, "Hey, you can come in and see your buddy, but don't cause any trouble." As far as decision making, they participated in decision making. At least they did on my watch, because I needed their input, and they needed mine. [6]

To follow up on that, since it has come up, when I went to Soledad, the first week I was there I was administrative officer of the day. I could not even find my way around the building. So I get a call at ten o'clock at night that there was an incident over in Central. So I questioned the lieutenant, "Hey, what do you think?"

He said, "I am not going to do your goddamned job for you!"

I said, "Hang on a minute. I will be right over there." So I took off and the first thing I said was, "What in the hell is the matter with you? You are a lieutenant. I expect that information from you. Now you have a problem. I don't know what kind of a problem you have got, what you have done, and what your expectations are. Don't give me that bullshit about me doing my job. You are a lieutenant. You can do any job in here, and you have a piece of paper to back you up. If you don't want to take on that responsibility, then that is what the AOD [Administrative Officer of the Day] is for. Call me, and we will take care of it. Don't give me that crap. You are perfectly capable of taking care of anything that happens around here."

That ticked him off. It took weeks, months, you know. Then the word spread, "Jesus, be careful when you call that SOB. He will expect you to do something."

---

6. Philliber, "Thy Brother's Keeper," 131: "[Lombardo] argues that [the guard subculture] does not [exist] for the following reasons: COs are not recruited to the job for task-related purposes, they do not set their own goals; they are not interdependent; they do not have democratic organization or participation in decision making; they work in a competitive atmosphere of distrust; and they have poor communication." Wilkinson comments: "The last two items, poor communication and distrust, I will buy. The rest does not fit with my experience."

At CMF, we did not even have administrative officers. If something happened on your watch, you took care of it. You wrote your reports, and you presented them to the man the next day. Down there in Soledad, everything went by the Administrative Officer of the Day. And so you did not have to do anything. That lieutenant took exception to the fact that I did not think he was earning his money, that he was not living up to his responsibilities as a lieutenant. I told him I had been a lieutenant longer than he had been in the Department. "So don't tell me about the position. Listen to me, and I'll tell you how to be a lieutenant."

Subordinates may not have made the final decision, but they had a lot of input. I consider that we were part of the decision-making process. Just as I was part of the decision-making process for the associate warden or the captain.

One of the old, old things in the prison business is: when you get a rule that does not make sense to the correctional officer or make sense with what you are trying to do or with safety, you enforce that bad rule to the hilt. Do not pass up any opportunity to use that rule. Then they will do away with it, because it will cause so much trouble. It is pretty effective in our business because: there, again, if you want to talk subculture, we would get together and say this thing is eating us up. Let's see what we can do about it.

The change in the feeding in the kitchen that I have mentioned was this type of thing. It was causing too many disciplinaries, it was causing too much hassle, and due to these procedures, we were not getting the inmates fed properly. So we just started enforcing them and putting the pressure on, saying, "We have to change this, we have to change this. Here is what happened yesterday; here is what is going to happen tomorrow."

Correctional Officers Who Were Conflicted

I have seen officers stop at the front gate and psych themselves out to come to work. They would go over the salary benefits and then psych themselves out that maybe they can get by today. Before they walked into the institution, they would just come to a dead standstill at the front gate. A lot of them were females. But a lot were males, too. They were just not suited for that kind of work, but they could not let the salary go. The salary was particularly dominant with females. You take a single mother or a woman who has been on welfare and such and is broke, and you start paying her a better-than-average salary with benefits, she is doing well. If they were feeling vulnerable, then they were really in a bad spot.

A lot of the women got into corrections work for the salary and had no interest in the business and really were not equipped to do it. It was strictly for the salary. A lot of men came in for the salary as well. But being a male in a male institution, they were able to overcome a lot of things that females could not, as I have suggested. So just being female was not the problem; being female with all the baggage that they had to carry was the problem.

Male or female, you had people who were absolutely just not suited for the business, under any circumstances. You had to do what you could with them, and they had to do what they could to make it work for them, and eventually they would disappear. Get a job at Radio Shack or something.

So what made them a mismatch? They did not have the psychology of it, the mental attitude. No confidence in themselves, or overwhelmed by what they thought was a dangerous situation. It is hard to say. With the females, they would work for about a year to eighteen months and then go on disability—psychological, or my back hurts, or something. It was quite common.

For a while it was really unusual to see a woman last over eighteen months. They would function normally without any problems, and then they would start to say they could make more money on disability and not have to put up with this nonsense. We had males who did that, too, but not to the same extent. They usually did it after ten or fifteen years. But with the females, they were just in the wrong place. In my time, as I have explained, we had people who always worked the gates, always worked the tower, always worked the control room. "Don't put me where the inmates are," was their concern. Then their time on sick leave went up; all kinds of problems would arise.

Then you had older people who had back trouble, but what they really had was problems being uncomfortable around inmates. I have a habit of touching people on the shoulder, on the side, what have you. I would be talking to a guy and reach over and put my hand on his side, and he has got a corset on—not because he has a backache or anything, but so when an inmate tries to stab him, he does not kill him. We had some people working there who went to that extent. We used to have one officer who would stuff magazines around his waist. I never understood that. I would ask them why they worked there, and they would say they needed a job. "Hey, man, you're going to be crazy before you get out of here. Unless you change." Just like the guy who had to psych himself up out at the front gate just to come in—I don't understand why he even bothered to come in. Go get something that you can handle and be comfortable with.

Fear

Fear was a concern for us.[7] We were concerned that this guy is not doing his job. Or the administration is not giving us this tool. But you and I are okay, and we'll take care of one another. However, it was not prevalent in our daily routine. It was an unspoken thing that we would cover each other. As I said, at one time, we had fourteen lieutenants, and there was not a dime's bit of difference among them. We were competitive, and we were individuals; but our age and background and qualifications were the same. We instinctively reacted as one. That was the way we were trained, raised, and naturally reacted. There is an advantage in that.

Sometimes correctional officers are alone. And, yeah, there was fear. At Soledad, all the way up to the guy who was isolated in the front office and never saw a convict. Other institutions were probably similar. We just never talked about it, and we knew we were together enough to take care of what happened. So we relaxed.

At CMF, on only one occasion did we use outside resources like the police or the militia. We did have to alert people from time to time—police departments, highway patrol. The only time we had outside help was when the Black Panthers were going to pay us a visit, a demonstration. We were just taking precautions so we would be able to handle crowd control and things like that. We notified the state highway patrol that they were coming, and they took their appropriate steps.

We reacted seriously to the Black Panthers because a couple or three years before that, they had armed themselves and walked right into the State Assembly when it was in session. That demonstrated to us that they could bring arms and be pretty serious. We had gunmen on the roof and cleared the parking lot and the works. When the word got back to them, they called off the demonstration. They decided not to come up and face the possibility of getting shot.

Fear never lets up over the years. So it's nothing new or old. You have your apprehensions. The young fellow, his experience is the movies he has seen or television programs. The old guy, "Hey anything can happen at

---

7. Kelsey Kauffman, *Prison Officers and Their World* (Cambridge, MA: Harvard University Press, 1988), 215: "Fear was not the exclusive province of young, inexperienced officers. Even those deemed most capable by their peers—officers with years of experience—were afraid at least part of the time if they were still in contact with inmates." In 1966, a California prison official, John P. Conrad, "Violence in Prison," *Annals of the American Academy of Political and Social Science* 364 (1966): 113–19, pointed out that the incidence of violence "is small and the numbers committing it are smaller. . . . In California in 1964, there were exactly 146 fights and stabbings reported in our prisons. The rate per hundred prisoners was 0.62." Given the population involved, this was a very low rate. He believed that competent staff could keep the rate down.

any time. And I've spent twenty years at this, and I'm getting tired of it, being on the alert for that number of years." And then it begins to weigh on your mind, and then they begin to look for a job on the front entrance or in the tower. Eventually the officer will wear out if he doesn't get promoted or get different jobs. But it is very true that there is that apprehension, at least part of the time. Different people in different ways. Some people are actually afraid. Other people are just apprehensive. You get tired of being on the edge all the time.

One recent writer who used to be a correctional officer writes that officers have been beaten, killed, and raped on the job.[8] That is true. My first experience with that was in the Guidance Center at Chino. They had a Youth Authority wing, and it was running wild. The inmates finally took it over one Sunday. They took the officer up and bound his hands and put him in a cell and molested him—not really too badly, but they did molest him.

So guess who they put in the unit to replace him? But I wasn't there very long. They just needed someone to take the officer's spot. I was probably there a month, maybe. That made up my mind, at that point, that I would never work in the Youth Authority if I could avoid it. They were just kids. We made a mistake by putting them all together. What we did after that was to spread them out among the A numbers, the old numbers, the people who had been incarcerated in the thirties and forties—old-timers. And they would not put up with that nonsense. After we got them spread out through the institution, we didn't have any more trouble with them. The old inmates would put knots on their heads in a minute. But you put them all together, and you have all kinds of trouble.

Working with Officers

Sometimes what the correctional officer did made it hard to deal with an inmate. Sometimes an officer would confiscate some small thing that was not strictly allowed, such as a cap or a picture. They took it just because they could take it. That used to incense me.

Of course you had to back the officer up when the inmate complained. If the officer was clearly within the rules and regulations, that was what you conveyed to the inmate. Pay attention next time. Stay away from the officer.

Then you get the officer in. However are you going to talk to him? Some of them you are legitimate with, some of them you just blast. "Don't put me through this again. Get realistic when you deal with the inmates. You are taking advantage of the convict. If you are going to use your

8. See Gary L. Riddle, "The Forgotten Cops," [Vacaville] *Reporter,* 24 March 2002.

authority to take advantage of the convict, then it is okay for me to use my authority to take advantage of you. Does that work for you?" That was the first time some of them ever thought of it, that they were taking advantage of their position.

The officers came to prison work with an extremely wide variety of background and experience. Some of them I termed mamma's boys, silver-spoon people. It came to be that many or most of them were just people who never had anything themselves, never had status. So they got their status when they put the uniform on. Typically they had just floated through high school. Dad worked occasionally. Low economic background, just living from day to day. Some of them, fifteen minutes at a time. They get a job by answering twenty-five questions. Next thing they are hired. That is what I am talking about as one of the things that hurt the Department. The COD academy was taking people who had hinky rap sheets that the director would review and say that's not so bad, let's put them through the academy and get them off the welfare rolls

Generational Change among Officers

Young officers were another problem, as I have said. That is where staff got a double dose. They got it from the young, nonthinking convict, and they got it from the young, nonthinking correctional officer who appeared out of nowhere: "Who raised this SOB that I have to supervise?" So in a sense it was harder on staff.

The young officers were not thinking too well. If they wanted to do something, they did it. If they did not want to come to work that day, they didn't come to work. If they wanted to tell you that you are full of shit, they would do it. They might ask you for a favor right after they tell you that you are full of shit and not worth a damn. How about putting me in that good job down there in S Wing? They saw no difference. They have been taught to express themselves, and they do. Very inappropriately. They cannot see the difference. It is perfectly all right to curse out your supervisor and tell him how dumb he is and then in the next breath ask him for a favor. They couldn't understand why you reacted to that.

But that was the sign of the times. That was no different than the young inmate. They were not housebroken.

In my experience, the younger officers would have more favorable attitudes toward inmates.[9] When I was working, the average age of the inmate

9. Philliber, "Thy Brother's Keeper," 130, points out that there is conflicting evidence from different studies. Two of them report "no relationship between age and punitiveness."

was thirty years. That is for the entire Department. I imagine it is younger now, with all of the growth. It must be around twenty-six years. The younger correctional officer was clued into the music, the morals, and society in general. He more easily understood the inmate and where he was coming from.

I found that I would have to reeducate myself from time to time—when the new music came out or whatever it was the kids were doing, I would have to have a speaking acquaintance or an overview of it. Rock and roll I had a difficult time with. I had to listen and know what songs were current. As I got older, and they got younger, then it got to be more and more of a chore.

You were also distanced from the emotional picture, too. I was not down there on the line with them as I was when I was young. But I still had to understand the convict culture. You had to understand what was happening with society. It was just like a little city, but a city in which the population got younger, not older.

One sociologist concluded that "Although most [guards] are not particularly punitive towards the inmates, they believe that most of their fellow guards are punitive."[10] In my own case, with my peer group, I would have to subscribe to it—handling disciplinaries as a lieutenant, as opposed to another lieutenant over here. I would try to be adaptable and make it more than a cut-and-dried situation, whereas my buddy lieutenant over here was right down the line, doing it by the book. So it was true in my case. That was my perception. That probably came from Chino.

I got boxed into a situation where in the beginning I was too rigid. That was the way we were taught. Then I was too lenient: we are all here, we have to get the job done. Then when I transferred to CMF, I was too tough. The staffing was thin. The inmates were not conforming, they were not going to work on time. Then I don't know what the hell I was at Soledad. But times changed, and I learned my business a certain way, and I did not change as quickly as times changed and the climate in the institution.

At Chino, I was probably a little more lenient because the inmates were guys my age, or they were first offenders, and I could relate to them. You had to know where they were, you had to meet all those commitments. Then I went to Vacaville, and as long as the inmates were inside the fence, and you didn't see them do anything, everything was okay. I would get into trouble trying to stop this or going down the line that way, that is, taking action before something got out of hand. When I first went to Vacaville,

---

Another one reports "a positive relationship between age and favorable attitudes towards inmates."

10. Ibid., 131.

the attitude was, "Don't do anything unless you have to do it." Then it changed again to: "Give them all the breaks you can give them."

My philosophy when I went to Soledad was to scare those people down there. I think I mentioned something about an inmate taking a swing at one of my officers. I told him how we used to do it in the old days. Now I was succumbing to the Soledad thing.

And you know what? Not one person mentioned that to me. Not the officer, not the supervisors, not one mentioned it to me. How come there wasn't a beef on this guy? It just sailed right on up. In one case, the supervisor was going to make something of the threat to break the guy's legs. It seems to me that at some point someone should have said, "Wilkinson, what's the matter with your head? You're supposed to have a disciplinary on this guy, and he's still out there running around."

Women Correctional Officers: A Special Problem

The women highlighted some of the things that were going on. Often they were dependent upon a male. And they had kids. I think of the original eight, out of which we had problems with four adjusting. They expected too much. In the end, I think we lost only two of those women, and all the rest stayed with the Department. That is great. But understand that the first eight were probably pretty well looked at.

I can remember one woman . . . I felt so sorry for her. I took them out to the range, and she turned black and blue from that shotgun. She could not get it to fit in right. It kicked up. It blacked her eye. It blacked her arm. Most of them had bruises. She hung right in there. No complaints. No nothing. From what I heard, later on she became a really good asset to the Department. I think she went to Sierra, one of the camp centers. She had the right attitude. She knew what she had to do. She was tired of the welfare roles and sucking on the hind teat.

Most of them had that attitude to a certain extent. Two or three did not. They were there because they were forced into it, and they really did not want to be there. But then they got looking at the wages and decided to give it a try.

It did not always work that way with females. They just don't belong in a male institution. To get full value from them. It has nothing to do with intelligence or physical ability. It is just a misfit for them. The things I am talking about are basic, even beyond the privacy factor for the inmate.[11] I can't quote

---

11. The courts in *Bowling v. Enomoto*, 514 F. Supp. 201 (1981) ruled that inmates (initially, male) had the right to be free from supervision by correctional officers of the opposite sex. This ruling was later reversed on the basis that prisoners had no reasonable expectation of privacy in their cells; see *Grummett v. Rushen*, 779 F.2d 491 (9th Cir., 1985).

the statistics, but it is startling the number of female correctional officers who fell in love with inmates.[12] Some of them were smart enough to wait until they were paroled and then marry them. Most of the rest of them got their jobs compromised because they fell in love with the inmate. It was not what you might think. A male officer could do the same thing—what I call "social bribery," so he can get along with the convicts.

The failure rate on the females, as I have noted, was pretty high. It was not their fault. It was just the whole thing. There were just too many things that did not mesh. Perhaps we should have or could have paid attention to some of those things. The attitude was, hire females; they can do the same things that male officers can do; aren't we great for recognizing it?—instead of realizing that we are going to have a problem or two here, and we are going to have to make an adjustment here or there. We did not do any real planning.

When the visiting breaks up at the end of the day, all the inmates coming back in have to be skin-searched. So you have two female officers in a position where the officers usually skin-search the inmates. You have to take the two female officers down to a housing unit and bring back two male officers to do the procedure. That is not doing the job; that is causing a problem. It is not the females' fault; it is not the males' fault. None of those guys wants a female looking up his rear end at the end of the visit.

Common sense tells you that a female cannot fill this position as a male can. So if you are going to hire women, you have to make a setup for this. We did not. On the first day, the watch lieutenant did not even think of this; he never planned that far ahead. It came time to skin-search, and he was going to send two officers over to the visiting room as he normally did. The two officers happened to be female, and they went over there. The visiting room sergeant said, "Oh, no."

So the sergeant called up the lieutenant and said, "If you want these two gals to do a skin-search on a male, I'll send them over, and you drop your pants." The lieutenant said, "Oh, Christ, I forgot about those females!"

A little thinking and a little planning ahead could have avoided that problem. But there was a lot of the "throw them in the water and let them swim" thinking. If they don't make it, they don't make it.

---

12. Both Lynn E. Zimmer, *Women Guarding Men* (Chicago: University of Chicago Press, 1986), and Dana M. Britton, *At Work in the Iron Cage: The Prison as Gendered Organization* (New York: NYU Press, 2003), report hearing many stories about women correctional officers' involvements with male inmates. Neither author is persuaded that these stories amount to much more than prison folklore. While we have not found any useful records to indicate the extent of the phenomenon, Wilkinson remembers two specific cases, and he heard about others in the system. But he comments that the reason the instances were so startling was that, though the cases were few, they were far more than were expected at the time. No one was prepared for this when women first came in, and he thinks the problem may have diminished as officers received more training.

You had that attitude, and you had the other attitude: Let's make this thing work. We will start you out here until you adjust, then we will move you over here later on. Or we will put it in the procedures that you will stay out of the visiting room during that part of the day. We will have an officer come down from J Wing or the officer from H Wing will come down when they get the call. You will be sent to those units.

But we did not do any of that. Some of it we just overlooked, some of it someone just plain said, "Piss on it. I want a correctional officer, and I want a full-fledged correctional officer, and I am going to show those guys they did not send me one." It just varied with the person.[13]

In hiring the minorities and the females, the change, I would like to underline, was in the hiring practices. The thinking was: this is the altruistic thing to do. Nobody was thinking about the details. I am not saying it would not have worked, but the details had to be settled before they could get an even break. That was the purpose in hiring them, to give everybody an opportunity. So why give them a clouded opportunity? Why set them up for failure? All the enlightenment did not bother me that much, but let's have some proper thinking and planning along with it.

Central office was just thinking numbers. Eight women; what do you mean you have to house them and they are a problem? On the books, we have eight women. The deputy warden at Soledad at the time normally would let us tour groups through the institution, but he did not accept the women. I could take males through the housing unit, but I could not take the women through the housing unit. Nobody from Sacramento told him that these were bona fide trained people and they were to take the tour as part of the training. He said we could not bring them through. I said they were going to be working here in a few weeks. He did not give a darn. He told me I could not bring them through.

That was the second COD class [1972]. By the third class, we had most things straightened out. I knew what to anticipate. Of course some attitudes did not change. The deputy warden's wife was my secretary. So I did not get to test him out as I wanted to. He was a macho man; you knew that by just listening to his wife talk about him.

But he was the man who said yea or nay. The trainee was the loser.

---

13. By 1981, in a pattern familiar elsewhere in American society, female correctional officers were sometimes reporting sexual harassment not just from inmates but particularly from fellow correctional officers. Larry Stammer, "Female Guards at Prisons Charge Sexual Harassment," *Los Angeles Times,* 4 June 1981, I:3. Britton, *At Work in the Iron Cage,* confirms that sexually harassing behavior from male inmates toward female correctional officers remains commonplace, while sexual harassment from fellow officers and supervisors may be somewhat less prevalent.

Dropouts, Transfers, Promotions

The tours were important to show these people what they were going to be facing in the housing units. Our first trip through the housing units, we would lose one or two. They would just quit. No way were they going to work in those conditions: "Do you think you are going to throw me down into that madhouse?" They would take off, head out on the highway, hitchhiking their way home.

It was always noisy on the third watch during the inmates' time. They were always out in the corridor, talking, playing cards, whatever. It is noisy in a concrete building. You take a stranger down there who has never seen anything like this before, and if he is tender to begin with, then twenty minutes later he has his satchel on his shoulder and is out on the highway looking for a ride. If that was what they had to put up with when they became correctional officers, they did not want to do it. So we would always lose one or two.

We would lose some people who had some family problems and needed to take care of those things before committing to that life. Unfortunately we had some people who thought they would go home and relax and then come back later and pick it up. They were always dumbfounded when you explained to them that this was their opportunity: either take advantage now, or don't come back.

Then not everybody would want to try for a promotion or take a promotion. They would have to move, and they would have to start at the bottom of the seniority ladder again.[14]

Sometimes a good supervisor could overcome these reservations just by daily contact, if only by going down there to say hello. But it was true that as officer seniority grew, they did have options for particular jobs or days off, and if they made sergeant, they would start at the bottom of the pile, and it did disrupt their personal life.

That's one of the reasons I didn't transfer until the kids were out of school. I made the first move because I had to make it to get the process started. But the kids were young enough that it did not throw them off stride. You do lose all your status when you become a sergeant, and some officers just could not give that up. A sergeant is a supervisor, and he goes down and talks to somebody who's on the list. And somebody asks him to transfer. "I am a living example. I transferred, I made sergeant, and it's not that bad." But this is a major factor in any system.

Some people will move any place any time. They are ambitious, to be

14. This point is also made by Lucian X. Lombardo, *Guards Imprisoned: Correctional Officers at Work,* 2nd ed. (Cincinnati, OH: Anderson Publishing Co., 1989), 185.

warden tomorrow or director in a week, so they will move any time. I've had many tell me, "I've been here three years, and it is time for me to transfer." Those people get promoted, but their heart is not in the institution.

Some guys just stayed in one place. They knew the operation, they knew the plant. They had no interruption of their lives in moving from one place to the other. There is something to be said for that, I guess.

If such a guy had gone on to make deputy director or something like that, I don't think he would have had the experience that somebody else would who had moved around. But, heck, they make deputy directors out of people who walk in off the street, out of the personnel department or something like that.

It used to be, when I went into the Department, that the administrators had all worked as correctional officers, sergeants, lieutenants, right up the line. So they knew what you were doing, what was going on with the uniformed personnel. But as time went on, you got people who were promoted who did not have that background. They were promoted out of the counseling series or whatever. CC-1's were on a par with lieutenants, but CC-1's did not have any supervisory duties. Lieutenants did, of course. Strictly watch commanders, that kind of thing. But the Department would take counselors who had gone through the series, and the next thing you would know, they are program administrators. They had no concept of what the people in the uniform had to learn and had to do. That hurt the Department. Not that the counselors or whatever were bad people. Some of them were quite good, but they just did not have the experience. They could not even say, "I remember when somebody stole my lunch when I first went to work." That was a good lesson. Some of those people should have had their lunch stolen and realized they were not all that good. They just did not have the inmate contact, and they did not understand what the problems were.[15]

But investment in the institution was a big thing for us. And California made an attempt to offset this by hiring locally, by institution. Unfortunately, it had very little success. It made it worse, because you were hiring locally, and you get the guy who is sacking groceries in the grocery store or the guy whose dad owns a filling station where he has been working, and you are not going to move that guy. You can offer him whatever you want to offer him, but he has nothing to lose. So this was a short-lived policy for us. If you were hired locally, you did not have to think about going someplace to get a job as a correctional officer, and you did not have to transfer, and you could just stay there. In fact, I had a very close friend at Soledad who did that. He wasn't confused about Soledad because he had never seen any other institution. He made it all the way through to captain and then retired, and so he was quite happy with it.

---

15. This point is made also in another context in a previous chapter.

Interior view of the Central Wing at Soledad (1981)
Source: *CTF: Correctional Training Facility* (Sacramento: California Department of
Corrections, n.d.).

So they tried that, and it didn't work, and they went back to hiring
statewide.[16] That was about the time they changed the testing process for
promotion and went from 60 percent written, 40 percent oral, straight to
the oral exam, and a lot of people dropped out there, including yours truly.
I needed that written examination to keep in competition. I just couldn't
do it strictly on an oral, so my promotion was stopped there completely for
a while. I think probably the change in testing did some damage throughout the Department. When they went to each institution for the oral interviews, they did not have the same people asking the same questions. So the
people down at Podunk City might hire this type of person, and the people up around San Francisco might hire that kind of person, and you did
not have any consistency. The written did give you consistency. And they
had a traveling oral board that went throughout the state. And each institution did not do it independently. But the new way spoiled the testing

16. Carlos M. Sanches, "Attracting and Selecting a Top-Notch Staff: The California
Experience," *Corrections Today*, December 1989, 58, 72, 166, believed that the Department
finally found the right approach.

process and did not do the Department any good. But I am sure that they got some good people out of it anyway.

Coping with Convicts

Many writers on prisons have emphasized colorful and sensational subjects. For example, we did sometimes use prison slang or argot. We might say that someone pulled his covers or pulled his blanket—someone snitched on him. And while we did try to avoid the inmate terms, we did use such common expressions. Everybody understood.

I have on occasion, and other people have, too, in order to get information out of a guy when you are interviewing him, said something like, "What would happen if somebody planted a knife in your cell?" They got very talkative then, but you had to be very careful with it, and you certainly couldn't be serious about it. But then what the inmate did not know was how serious you were or were not. If you got one from San Quentin or Soledad, he would believe every word of it. Somebody who was from Chino or the Men's Colony or CMF—"That's bullshit, they don't do that." You had to pick your spot, and it depended on what you were after. So for what it's worth, that sort of thing did happen, and it did get talked about.

And about sexual behavior in prison that is supposed to be so notorious, well, I was upset from the standpoint of one inmate taking advantage of another. At Chino, we were death on it because of the dormitory situation, and also because of the climate of the times, just coming out of the forties. We really didn't have it at Chino. I do not recall that I ever had an incident at Chino. But one time I was standing out front by the chapel with my work crew. We were laying a brick wall. All of a sudden, two inmates came flying out of the chapel. Father Cooney was throwing them out of there. He caught them back in the chapel doing their thing. Cooney was a big Irishman. They literally came flying out of there, bodily. Then they became mine. I took them over to the office. They were immediately transferred out of there. That was it for them. You did not get a second chance for homosexuality. Part of that attitude came from the type of program Scudder was trying to run. Part of it, as I suggested, was the carryover from the general social attitudes of that time.

When I got to CMF, homosexuals were a way of life. That was partly why the place was built, to house homosexuals. They were problems at other institutions. They were problems for us. That is why we kept them locked up at first. That is why we moved them en masse for the first couple of years. I guess Keating and Procunier kind of busted that up, but we were ready to agree that this segregated population was a pain in the butt from the very beginning. No one, however, had the courage to make the decision that, while some of them were going to have to be locked up, most of them we could let out in the general population, and we could deal with any behavior on an individual basis.

So integration came in that age of enlightenment, and the world did not come to an end. We did have a whole bunch of problems with it. But my attitude about it was that our main worry should be that we had some big burly bully or a whole group of people preying on a weak individual. That really upset me. As far as sexual orientation, that did not make much difference to me. That was their problem, not mine.

We still did not tolerate public behavior. Just as they were free to play cards. But if you caught them in a poker game, gambling, they were arrested. They were free to associate with one another in the housing unit, but if you caught them having sexual relations, then they got arrested.

My problem was with rape. It did not have to do with sex; it had to do with the violence, in my mind. One individual or a group of individuals preying on another. You were supposed to protect the inmate. If you had rape going on, then you could not protect them.[17]

We had some big-time problems when we spread the homosexuals out in the general population. We had some who refused to go into the general population. They wanted to stay locked up. Over a period of time, we just kind of put it to them, "Why, you have had enough time to wean yourself. It is time you got out." By this time the institution had settled down and accepted that we were no longer housing the homosexuals separately.

One of our biggest problems was the "straight" inmate harassing the homosexuals. A couple of individuals—homosexuals—helped us take care of that. One young man, who weighed probably 140 pounds, probably five-six or five-seven, stepped out of the mess hall to go back to his housing unit, and this big inmate dude—it happened to be Bob Wells—says, "Hey, honey what are you . . . ," and this kid decked him. Big time, right in the middle of the corridor. In front of all of his friends, the kid decked him. When the big man got up complaining, I said, "I am sorry, Bob, I was looking the other way. I really did not see anything. What happened?"[18] So that incident helped the situation, made them think that some of those guys fight back: "Maybe I had better be careful what I say and what I do." Golly, that was funny. And I just lied like a dog, because I did see exactly what happened.

17. Wilkinson's account of prisoner rape highlights a problem few administrators were willing to acknowledge openly. Human Rights Watch, *No Escape: Male Rape in U.S. Prisons* (New York: Human Rights Watch, 2001), surveys the contemporary prevalence and consequences of prison rape.
18. See chapter 2, where Bob Wells was introduced.

That kid was quick. He hauled off and popped him and knocked him flat. There was probably a foot difference in height and forty or fifty pounds' difference in weight. Talk about getting surprised, Bob Wells got surprised.

But the integration evened itself out. We had a lot of trouble with it, we bitched about it. Some of us bitched a whole lot, especially a couple of my peers. But my attitude was, it was something I did not want to deal with, but it was there, and it had to be settled. The boss said it was okay to do it this way. So then you go ahead and do it. That did not mean I liked it, and it did not mean I wanted to work that hard. It was easier to do the job before, when you moved them en masse. Over a period of time, and I am talking about a short period of time, six to eight months, certainly a year, people could not believe that you ever locked them up and moved them en masse and herded them around.

I cannot put a date on this. It was probably 1957–1963, in that time frame. There were good practical reasons for the change, too. We had reached our saturation point under the old system. We had only 135 people in a unit. Once that unit got filled, we were going to have to part-time fill another unit if we were going to keep the homosexuals segregated. So being practical, they said don't treat them that way.

Homosexuals continued to come to CMF from other institutions. Then over a period of time, it got so they were not a problem at other institutions. I mean over a considerable period of time. In some institutions, that did not happen until the late seventies. There again, that was strictly due to bed pressure. CMF did not have any empty cells. CMF was primarily for therapy patients and psychotics, so you did not waste a cell on a homosexual. So you learned to keep him in your own organization. Practicality or lack of money settles all of these things. You can talk therapy and all that kind of good stuff all you want to; but these things are done because they have to be done.

In a sense the behavior was constant with a certain group of people. I mentioned Bob Wells. He always had to have a "sissy"—even when he could not get it up anymore. That was his status symbol. There were a lot of other inmates who were not as flamboyant as he was. Yet it was constant with them. The homosexual went to him for protection. If the price of that was doing him every now and then or walking down the hall with him like his wife or girlfriend, well, then, that was the price an inmate paid for protection. So, within that group, yes, it was constant.

Given the population as a whole—1,800 convicts—no, it was not flamboyant. There wasn't an orgy every day, or whatever. The act itself was not public. They would get off in a broom closet or someplace, a cell or something. There was no way you could keep them under surveillance all of the time. They had plenty of time to get off in a cell someplace, or in a ward or in a shower if the officer was busy somewhere else. If they were really desperate to do their thing and not get caught, then they arranged for the officer to be preoccupied with something else. They had a point man out there in case the officer came back before they were through. It was not hard for them to get together. They would seek each other out. But that was minor stuff, very minimal. Homosexuality has always been prevalent in all-male institutions.

Nor did it increase in the late 1960s and 1970s. There were just more opportunities. Before, we had them all confined. If they did it, they did it with one another. There was not any big hassle in the homosexual unit. But when we spread them out among the population, it became more noticeable and became more of a problem. We had some people pretty badly hurt. It was either two guys saying no, that punk is mine, not yours. Sometimes it was the other way around. It would be two homosexuals taking the attitude, "Don't muscle in on my business."

Quite frankly, most of the homosexuals were joint homosexuals. They were not homosexuals on the outside. Inside, they did it mostly for protection, for canteen items, what have you. That was their way of getting along. But I did not notice any real increase. I noticed we had more to do after they were spread out in the general population. I had to spend more time watching for this kind of stuff. As far as an increase, no, I don't think so. You did not have any more homosexuals, but you did have some people out in the Main Line participating who would not have participated before. Some people liked to experiment. Some people were closet homosexuals in the Main Line, and we did not know about it, and this was their golden opportunity. That surfaced, and we probably would not have had to deal with it if they were all locked up. But as far as more homosexual activity, no, it was just more observable. The same amount of screwing went on in the closed unit as went on in the general population when we let them loose. That is a personal opinion.

The inmates often complained about the homosexual activity. A lot of them were scared to death that they would succumb. I had a few who expressed the idea that "Now that it is available, how can I resist it? Why are you putting this pressure on me?" I had the other reaction, too: "I don't like those people, and I am going to mash them in the head every time I see them. Get them off the Main Line." So all we could say was, "You have to learn to live with it."

Occasionally they would bash one in the head. Occasionally one of them would get a miscue and start flirting with a guy. The next thing you know, he is decked and lying on the floor. It was a combination of making the change and making the process work. We did have more to deal with, but there was not more homosexuality.

You could get some irate inmate complaining, as one did who went to get some laundry soap out of the janitor's closet and found two of them in the laundry room doing their thing. "Goddamn assholes, get them out of there!" He was just incensed that he had stumbled in on that. He said it was disgusting! Well, yes, it is disgusting. Of course he was probably the guy who ripped off some kid on the streets. But he won't talk about his crime; he would talk only about these guys he had to live with.

By the time I got to Soledad, times had changed, and inmate attitudes had changed as well.

Generational Change in the Inmates

Just about the time I left the Department, prisons were suddenly not very interesting any more. Most all of the case law had been developed, and, most of all, the horror stories about abusing the inmates did not have widespread validity.[19]

Because of the drive-by shootings, the senseless murders, this kind of thing, the mood is different. Back in the 1960s and '70s: those poor bastards in prison, the guards are mistreating them and the system is mistreating them, and all that. Then you save their souls and get them out of the joint, and now they are shooting everybody up. So it is not fashionable anymore to deal with this thing.

There used to be a stigma on an inmate. But for many years there was not a stigma. Used to be, you go to prison, and you had to live with it. It was reflected in whether or not you got a job, what kind of job you got, or how you were treated.

Then during the sixties, it used to be an enhancement to go to prison. If you were an ex-con, you had it made in the early seventies. A good example of that is country music. You couldn't sing country music unless you had been to jail. It was carried so far that Johnny Cash said he had been in jail when he had not.[20]

Inmates are forever. Every generation will have them. At Chino, you could see that older convicts had status. I did not see it at California Medical Facility that much. There were young people—the Pepsi generation—showing disrespect.[21] They would show disrespect to everybody. It

---

19. See the introduction for some discussion of context.

20. Cash had been arrested at the U.S. border for drug possession in 1965 and given a suspended sentence. His live albums, *Johnny Cash at Folsom Prison* (1968) and *Johnny Cash at San Quentin* (1969), were among his most famous recordings; his songs highlighted a sense of solidarity with the inmate audience.

21. Geoffrey Hunt et al., "Changes in Prison Culture: Prison Gangs and the Case of the

did not matter if it was an older convict or a warden or what. They were just sassy kids who did not understand where they were and what could happen to them.

In certain cases, when they got on the inside, they were taught respect. In certain cases they learned on their own, that if I don't straighten up, I am going to have a problem here. But you still had that small bunch who wore their pants down around their ass and ran off at the mouth.

They did get knocked on their ass because they were inadvertently running off at the mouth to a guy who had had a belly full of it. He was generally an older inmate, and he would bust the kid in the chops and say, "I don't want to hear that shit," and then go on about his business.

You might get a complaint from the inmate who got bopped about how he got mistreated. You would have to tell him, "You had better straighten up your mouth, or it is going to happen again." Then of course you are an asshole. He may call you that. After you take care of that problem, he probably won't call you that again. That is, I would discipline him in terms of writing a 115, sending it to one of my fellow lieutenants suggesting a way of handling it if he agreed. Then the inmate would learn, "I don't talk to that convict like that because he will punch me in the nose. I don't mouth off at the lieutenant because he will take my privileges away from me or lock me up in isolation or whatever if I do." So he learns, but among his own group his pants are still hanging below his ass, and he still has the "Lancaster walk." Then the institution tolerates it. The older convict does not have to put up with it, the staff does not have to put up with it, they are just doing it among their own group and satisfying themselves and not really bothering anybody else. This is a source of amusement at this point.[22]

'Pepsi Generation,'" in *Incarcerating Criminals,* ed. Flanagan, Marquart, and Adams, 118–27, esp. 122–23: "The prisons were full of younger prisoners who were described disparagingly . . . as 'boys trying to become men,' and the 'Pepsi Generation,' defined as 'the young shuck and jive energized generation.' . . . According to our respondents, the 'Pepsi Generation' went around wearing 'their pants down below their ass' and showing little or no respect for the older inmates, many of whom had long histories of prison life which normally would have provided them with a high degree of status." Generational change at CMF was the subject of substantial comment in Morrie Camhi, *The Prison Experience* (Rutland, VT: Charles E. Tuttle Company, 1989).

22. Geoffrey Hunt et al., "Changes in Prison Culture," 123, quote a thirty-eight-year-old "familia" member who described the young inmates in the following way: "They are actors. Put it this way, they are gangsters until their fucking wheels fall off. . . . I'm a gangster too. But there is a limitation to everything. See I can be a gangster with class and style and finesse and respect. [Give] respect and get it back. That's my motto, my principle in life. Do unto another as you would like [to] have done to you. These kids don't have respect for the old timers. They disrespect the old men now." Wilkinson comments: "We are talking about a different convict. You are talking about a gang member; you are talking about a Latino. The philosophy and the thinking is entirely different than it is for an old-time convict and a sassy white kid. There is a whole other thing going on here with the Latino that is equated to the

But the older cons complained bitterly about the way the kids were messing up the prison. Isn't it poignant, isn't it terrible? Poor guy can't even commit a crime and do good time when he gets into the joint, because of those damn kids. Poor bastard. And you can expand that to old-time correctional officers, old-time staff. They can echo the same sentiments. It is not comfortable to run a prison, as it used to be. There is a lack of respect. The kids are spontaneous and screw things up and bring the heat down. Staff just use different words. The kids screwed everything up. Damn snot-nosed kids.[23]

The Worst Aspects of Handling Inmates

Everybody has a vulnerable point. Mine was anybody spitting on me. When I was playing football in high school, a guy across the line from me spit on my hand. So I beat him with my helmet, and I got kicked out of the game. I could not play in the line anymore. When you get tackled, and six guys are on you and one spits in your face, you can do anything. It always has been a personal struggle of mine. Then you add an inmate who has active TB, and he spits in your face, it makes you sick. Those with TB would do it deliberately. It was their only defense—most of them were pretty weak. Or they were unhappy because they had TB. Then they start giving the officer a hard way to go, so I would go down to settle the problem with the guy, and you didn't have too many tools to work with anyway. So you are talking to him and he ups and spits a big hawker between your eyes. Then I would wonder if I had TB. You can't haul off and bust the inmate as you would want to. It was just terrible. I hated going to the TB ward.

I busted a guy once defending myself, but never for spitting in my face. I can't think what happened. Sometimes sudden moves make people do funny things. But the inmate always had to make the first move. And then you're okay. When it came to the physical stuff, you had to give the inmate a way out. You had to talk to the guy, let him know his options. Let him know that there were enough officers present to subdue him, and it would

---

old Mafia, the Don. I have respect coming. Ask this thirty-eight-year-old guy what he was doing when he was the age of this kid he was talking about. He was just as sassy and disrespectful as anybody else was. But now he has earned his thing: 'I am tired of being a banger and a ganger. I just want to relax and get this heat off. Why don't they respect me and I don't have to deal with it, and I still have status without having to work for it.'"

23. As indicated elsewhere, the inmates much more often had a background of violence rather than offenses against property, and the general public implicitly and explicitly recognized such changes in the prison population; see, for example, Bill Hazlett, "Prison Violence Grows with New Breed of Inmate," *Los Angeles Times,* 9 February 1972, I:1, 22.

be better if he took a walk down the hall with you rather than start something. That was the way out. You gave him a chance to cool off. You still reported the incident; you just did not escalate it.

One guy, Sheik Thompson, was a boxer at one point in life. On the outside, he was "Tiger," and he was pretty prominent in boxing, fought some good people. He got into the joint—and pain did not mean a thing to him. Pain activated him. One time at Folsom the officers were taking him up the back stairwell to lock him up. Thompson was fighting them the whole way so they just picked him up and threw Thompson down a whole flight of stairs. A normal inmate or person would have been stunned. Thompson hit it like a rubber ball, got right up and cleaned up on two officers before the rest could get down to him. The pain turned him on. When we used to move him we made sure he was not near his locker, because Thompson would strip his clothes off and get a jar of Vaseline and rub that stuff all over his body. Then you would ruin fifty dollars' worth of clothes trying to catch a greased pig. He was famous for that.

Then we had another guy named Maxie who would take his pants off and defecate in his hand before he let you move him somewhere. Then you had some real problems trying to catch that sucker. But you just played it by ear; you had a job to do, when it comes down to it. That is why you try to give the guy a way out. You still have to take care of the problem. It does not mean you are going to let the problem go by.

The subtle part of it was you had to convince the guy that he was not going to face humiliation going down the hall while being subdued, but he was still going to suffer the discipline. This was not a pass. It was a delicate balance between getting the knife or whatever and convincing the guy that you didn't want to fight but that he was still going to be disciplined. That is a catwalk that takes a lot of treading. Most times it worked, particularly in the old days. But not with the Pepsi generation. The earlier guys were doing it out of frustration; they just couldn't solve it any other way. Sometimes they were looking for some attention; sometimes they really meant to cut some guy's throat for their own personal reasons. The Pepsi generation was just showing off. It was as stupid as it could be.

Injuries and Death

The worst thing I ever saw was in the hospital unit. The MTA called me to come down. He said they had a mess down there. Somebody had taken this inmate into the cell and butchered him. Wherever there was flesh, it was gone. He cut his buttocks off, his arms off, he cut his throat, and his feet were hog-tied. He literally cut him to pieces just as in a butcher shop.

We found the culprit later. But I never saw anything that messy and that sickening before or since.

It turned out that the killing was over a homosexual relationship. These two guys had been sneaking off in cells and doing their thing for some time. Then the assailant decided to see how this would make him feel. It was done during sex, we found out later. The guy's hands were tied and the assailant reached around and cut his throat, and then he butchered him. It was a hospital unit, and therefore it was not manned with security like a regular housing unit. The MTA wore a uniform, but he was really charged with two responsibilities: custody and the medical end. When the MTA would administer pills, then the people would have a chance to go into a cell and hide or do their thing or whatever. The officer could not be faulted; rather, the staffing pattern was at fault. This incident straightened out the staffing pattern in a hurry. We got what we had asked for. Also, it got the MTAs out of uniform. They wanted out of uniform, and we wanted them out of uniform. I used to grade them on their performance. All I could grade them on was security. But they were not hired to handle security. And this incident helped straighten things out. The inmate's death was tragic, but it probably saved other people downstream.

It is not a pleasant thing to see. People see it on TV and don't realize this. On TV, a guy gets stabbed and you don't see any blood. People cannot believe the amount of blood that comes out of someone who has his throat cut. It is under pressure, too. You stab a guy in the back, even six or seven times, and it is not going to kill him. Although you can die later of a stab wound.

Another thing you never forget is this awful whack!—I cannot make the sound—of someone getting hit with a baseball bat. God, what a sound. It is like dropping a watermelon on concrete, only worse.

However, because of the type of institutions where I was employed and also because of my promotions, I did not see a lot of violence and bloodshed. I did some first aid at Chino, but not much. The guy has a bad cut on the arm and is bleeding, and you apply compression, and that sort of thing. At CMF, it did not take but five minutes to get a medically trained person on the scene. We stopped the bleeding and did immediate first aid. If someone was hit in the head, then you would keep him down to try to prevent further head injury.

On a couple of occasions, with inmates who were always making suicide gestures, the doctor sewed them up without anesthesia. This particular doctor was tired of the nonsense. So he said, "I'm not going to give you a shot, I am going to sew you up cold turkey." And he did. And that slowed them down. One guy had his scrotum torn to pieces. We could put that guy in a clean cell after completely shaking him down, and then walk by later and he would be whittling on his scrotum or his penis. This is the same guy who killed that kid in the hospital. He would make a small incision and then he would run a shoelace or something underneath his skin all the way back. He put bits of razor blades under his toenails, and you would miss the blades when you skin-searched him. It was almost impossible to keep him from getting something with which to cut himself. So, he learned what the world was all about. This doctor worked on his penis without anesthesia. Of course the guy loved the pain, but the word spread, and the doctor was not above spreading it himself. It changed some minds, and it changed the situation. But the guy who loved pain had a smile on his face and thought everybody ought to have that experience.

Depending on the unit, suicide could be a major or a minor problem.[24] Inmates who were labeled suicidal had special treatment, or certain things had to be done for the inmate. The officer had to do suicide watch or pay close attention. That could be a problem, because the officer could be criticized if the inmate committed suicide on his watch. But if it was a normal housing unit, and an inmate committed suicide, that was on the inmate. It would not affect the correctional officer other than the mess he had to clean up and the reports he had to write. It might affect some sensitive people if they find a guy hanging or something.

The first one I personally found had done something that couldn't be done. That inmate hanged himself sitting down. He took his tee shirt and rolled it up, tied it around the window bars, which came to his waist, and he sat down. When I found him he was up against the wall, just sitting there, all purple with his eyes bulging out. He must have been serious because he did not flop around; he was just sitting as if someone had placed him there.

Then you have a problem with the locking devices. In this particular case, the deadlock was not on. In some locking devices you had the lock on the door. Some doors had two locks. Other doors had a bar that was on deadlock. So you are locked down, making your tour, a guy commits suicide. You want to get to him as soon as you can. If it is a deadlocking device by the bar, then you have to run all the way back down and take the bar off and hope no other cells are unlocked. Then you have to run back down and unlock the cell, get into the cell, and get the device from around the inmate's throat as soon as you can. Hopefully the guy will start breathing again. We were not too big on CPR back then. I don't think we even knew about it. Then you run back down to the office and get on the

24. A useful survey of the prisoner suicide literature is Alison Liebling, "Prison Suicide and Prisoner Coping," in *Prisons,* ed. Michael Tonry and Joan Petersilia (Chicago: University of Chicago Press, 1999), 283–360.

phone, and hopefully by the time you get back down to the cell, the guy is beginning to breathe.

In a dorm situation, it was easier to get to the guy. Sometimes the body was too high up, and you could not reach to cut the rope, even if you had something to cut it with. You can't hold him up with one hand and try to take it off with the other hand. And so you had to get help, an inmate or someone else. Most inmates were real sympathetic and helpful when it came to suicides. Some of them were not: "I didn't like the sonofabitch anyway." But the empathy was there in most cases.

There were so many little bits and pieces. It just plain exasperates you when you try to make things better, and the convicts do not care, or they just deliberately mess it up for themselves. They were often definitely self-defeating. Here you take all of this time, energy, and trouble to make things better, and the inmate does not care enough about himself to take care of himself.

A Last Word on Administration

Mostly, I am glad I did it the way I did. I just wish I could have made it to a position where I had some real influence. People who were not capable to make such decisions made a lot of the decisions at Central Office. It should have been staffed out. In a big place like Central Office, it is easy to lose track of people and of what is going on. It got to the point that where if an order came from Central Office, the institution followed it. No one thought about the decision or if the guy who made the decision was qualified, or did it fit that particular institution. .

In the Central Office in Procunier's day, his philosophy was: If you have a bad administrator, I will take him or her to Central Office, and you don't have to mess with them. I will send you a good person. Which he did. But then he got the Central Office so loaded that it could not function. He was doing it out of the kindness of his heart. He was that kind of a guy. He had a tremendous mind that could handle anything. Nothing was a chore to him. He had perfect confidence because he had always been right.

Central Office got to where it was stagnant. They either made a wrong decision or did not make a decision at all. They could not get it right. They had the tools; they were just not using them properly, if at all. And we could not get to those tools. It was more stagnation than anything else. There were few good ideas that came from Central Office. One guy at Central came from Chino. He never had a good idea, but it did not matter. He was never going to retire. He was around forever. And why would he quit with the job

Portrait of Kenyon Scudder
Source: Portrait in the possession of
the California Institution for Men,
Chino.

that he had? Once I got a phone call asking me if we had seen this individual at our institution in the last few days. Someone tried to cover for him
saying, "I think he's gone to Susanville" or someplace. Turned out he got
busy at home doing a project and just did not show up for work. It took
them a while to find out he wasn't there. He had things to do with records
and statistics, and going to other institutions was legitimate. With Procunier,
it was not that big a thing: "We just have to watch him more closely." What
they should have done was fire the sorry SOB.

I hate to say this, but anything after Chino was an anticlimax as far as
feeling useful. I did not know at the time that Chino was too good to be
true. I thought it would last forever. I had no idea it would not. I had no
plans to transfer. But I enjoyed it so much down there I thought that was
the way they did it everywhere. If I had been smart I would have checked
around. Just my first visit to San Quentin should have told me that it was
not like that everywhere. My attitude was that I worked for the
Department, and that took precedence. But that was not the case in other
institutions. Elsewhere you worked for an individual, and that took precedence. That was where my big mistake was.

At Chino you did not work for an individual. You worked to satisfy
somebody like Scudder or Procunier, but you did not work for anybody.

You worked for the Department. That stuck in my mind, and that was what I used to tell people. I don't give a damn what you think of me or how you are doing it. My job is to satisfy the Department, you are just another individual here.

I just never gave up on that idea.

How This Memoir
Was Produced

In May 1999, William Richard Wilkinson agreed to permit John C. Burnham to record what Mr. Wilkinson could remember of his career with the California Department of Corrections. Although the conversations between the two were informal, Mr. Wilkinson's sense of how events proceeded shaped the overall narrative. The interviewer assisted occasionally with questions of two kinds: questions to prompt continuation of the narrative, and questions to prompt recall of material and comment relevant to the scant sociological material then available concerning correctional officers (most of which is cited in notes to this book). Mr. Wilkinson responded as he could and as he wished.

No question or subject was considered out of bounds at any stage, as is obvious from the many sensitive issues covered, but relevant memories often did not exist.

The conversations were then transcribed.[1] Mr. Wilkinson has the notable capacity to tell stories, in a style that shows clearly in the preceding chapters. Indeed, the transcribers found that he tends to talk in paragraphs, and so the job of transcribing was relatively easy.

The transcriptions were edited in two ways. First, where necessary, they were rearranged by chronology and subject matter, a task that after a preliminary draft also involved the second editor, Joseph F. Spillane. Second, the conversational language was modified for clarity when necessary, and facts were checked. Some further brief conversations took place for the purpose of filling in a few gaps and clarifying points that were unclear. These further conversations soon became unproductive.

At that point, the manuscript was returned to Mr. Wilkinson for review. He was not inclined to change much except to request that in several places the names of some people be deleted and a more general identity be used instead. After further revision by both editors, including much shortening, Mr. Wilkinson was given the manuscript to review again.

The introduction was drafted primarily by Joseph F. Spillane, with contributions and revisions offered by John C. Burnham, but all of the editing was very much a collaborative effort.

---

1. We thank Steven McGann, who did most of the original transcription.

INDEX

Scudder, Kenyon, xii–xiii, xviii, 1–2,
    12–13, 16, 17, 20, 24, 28, 29–30,
    32, 189. *See also* Chino, program
security. *See* prison security
security checks. *See* Control Room
seniority, employee, 7, 175, 176
sentencing, determinate, xvi, 114–15,
    136; indeterminate, xii, xv–xvi,
    114–15, 136
service experience, correctional offi-
    cers, 3, 14–15, 84–85; inmates, 11
shifts and scheduling, 3, 4, 7, 43–44,
    47, 66, 139–40
sick leave, 47, 162, 163, 167
sick-outs, xix, 162
Sixties changes, 28, 55–56, 62–63,
    80–81, 98, 100, 129, 171–72,
    182; and American society, 112,
    128; pace, 100–101, 105, 108. *See
    also* contraband; discipline; genera-
    tions; inmate rights; outside groups
sleeping on the job, 5–6
snitching, 81–82, 178
social context of prisons, xviii–xix,
    xxii–xxiii, 28, 77–78, 80–81,
    100–101, 112, 170–71, 178, 182.
    See also generations; Sixties changes
social control, xx–xxi
Social Security, 51
sociology of prisons, ix–x, xvii, xx–xxi,
    154, 160, 164–66, 171–72, 178. *See
    also* correctional officers, study of
Soledad (California State Prison at
    Soledad), xiii–xiv, xviii, 74, 76,
    115, 117, 122, 124, 172, 178;
    administrative deficiencies,
    145–46, 148–49, 150; Black
    Muslims, 151–53; conditions in
    1977, 135–36; geographic loca-
    tion, 155–56; inappropriate use of
    firearms, 150; influence spread to
    rest of CDC, 150; inmates, 150;
    lack of control, 144; lack of pro-
    gram, xxii, 138; supervisor-officers
    relations, 165
Soledad Brothers, xiv
Stagner, Al, 156

suicide, 186–88
Sykes, Gresham, xx

television in prison, 62–63, 95, 100,
    102–3. *See also* inmate personal
    property
Terminal Island, 59
theft by inmates, 72–73, 81–82,
    102–3, 109, 150–51
therapeutic function of corrections,
    x–xiv, xv–xvi, xx, xxii, 91–95. *See
    also* Chino, programs; correctional
    officer organizations; psychothera-
    py
Thompson, Sheik, 185
Tidelands oil money, 16, 163
training. *See* recruiting and training
tranquilizers. *See* anti-psychotic med-
    ication
transferring institutions in CDC, 17,
    175–76
tubercular inmates, 184
Tucker's Farm, 7–8

uniforms, 16, 17, 48
unions. *See* employee organizations
utility officer position, 6

violence, xiv, xxii, 80–82, 95, 185–86;
    against correctional officers, 144,
    169, 172, 184–85; and contra-
    band, 60, 80; controlling violent
    inmates, 11, 128–29, 184–85; cor-
    rectional officers' changing
    resources against, 161; correctional
    officers' fears, 167–69; and gangs,
    116–17; generations, 182–83, 185;
    integrating homosexuals, 55;
    increase with Sixties changes, 103,
    108–9. *See also* riots
visiting, Chino, 18, 26–27; CMF,
    52–53, 173. *See also* conjugal visit-
    ing; outside organizations

Warren, Earl, xi
Wells, Wesley Robert ("Bob"), 49,
    179, 180

HISTORY OF CRIME AND CRIMINAL JUSTICE
David R. Johnson and Jeffrey S. Adler, Series Editors

The series explores the history of crime and criminality, violence, criminal justice, and legal systems without restrictions as to chronological scope, geographical focus, or methodological approach.